Postcolonial
and Queer Theories

**Recent Titles in
Contributions to the Study of World Literature**

The Tales We Tell: Perspectives on the Short Story
Barbara Lounsberry, Susan Lohafer, Mary Rohrberger, Stephen Pett, and R. C. Feddersen, editors

Robin Hood: The Shaping of the Legend
Jeffrey L. Singman

The Myth of Medea and the Murder of Children
Lillian Corti

African-British Writings in the Eighteenth Century: The Politics of Race and Reason
Helena Woodard

Styles of Ruin: Joseph Brodsky and the Postmodernist Elegy
David Rigsbee

The Image of Manhood in Early Modern Literature: Viewing the Male
Andrew P. Williams, editor

The Worlding of Jean Rhys
Sue Thomas

Ulysses, Capitalism, and Colonialism
M. Keith Booker

Imperial Knowledge: Russian Literature and Colonialism
Ewa M. Thompson

Demythologizing the Romance of Conquest
Jeanne Armstrong

Camelot in the Nineteenth Century: Arthurian Characters in the Poems of Tennyson, Arnold, Morris, and Swinburne
Laura Cooner Lambdin and Robert Thomas Lambdin

Writing the Body in D. H. Lawrence: Essays on Language, Representation, and Sexuality
Paul Poplawski, editor

Postcolonial and Queer Theories

Intersections and Essays

Edited by **John C. Hawley**

Contributions to the Study of World Literature, Number 101
Emmanuel S. Nelson, Series Adviser

GREENWOOD PRESS
Westport, Connecticut • London

Library of Congress Cataloging-in-Publication Data

Postcolonial and queer theories : intersections and essays / edited by John C. Hawley.
    p. cm.—(Contributions to the study of world literature, ISSN 0738–9345 ; no. 101)
    Includes bibliographical references and index.
    ISBN 0–313–31591–4 (alk. paper)
    1. Homosexuality in literature. 2. Homosexuality and literature. 3. Homosexuality in
motion pictures. 4. Homosexuality. I. Hawley, John C. (John Charles), 1947– II. Series.
PN56.H57P67   2001
809′.93353—dc21   00–057660

British Library Cataloguing in Publication Data is available.

Library of Congress Catalog Card Number: 00–057660
ISBN: 0–313–31591–4
ISSN: 0738–9345

First published in 2001

Greenwood Press, 88 Post Road West, Westport, CT 06881
An imprint of Greenwood Publishing Group, Inc.
www.greenwood.com

Printed in the United States of America

The paper used in this book complies with the
Permanent Paper Standard issued by the National
Information Standards Organization (Z39.48–1984).

10 9 8 7 6 5 4 3 2 1

Copyright Acknowledgments

The editor and publisher gratefully acknowledge permission for use of the following material:

Chapter One is from Dennis Altman, "Global Gaze/Global Gays," *GLQ* 3:4 (1997), pp. 417–36.
Copyright 1997. All rights reserved. Reprinted by permission of Duke University Press.

Chapter Two is from Tom Boellstorff, "The Perfect Path: Gay Men, Marriage, Indonesia," *GLQ* 5:4
(1999), pp. 475–509. Copyright 1999. All rights reserved. Reprinted by permission of Duke University Press.

for John V. Craig

Contents

Preface

Enter any bookstore in the western world and you will surely be able to find paperback travel handbooks such as the *Spartacus International Gay Guide*. Now in its twenty-eighth edition, this most popular and detailed "Baedeker" offers over 25,000 addresses of accommodations and places of entertainment throughout the world, with accompanying descriptions, evaluations, warnings, and enticements. Among the encomia included in its promotional material are such outré descriptions of the book as "the gay Bible," suggesting the devotion with which readers turn to its pages in preparation for world travel. The globalization of gay culture that this also demonstrates further suggests the topic that we hope to address in the chapters that follow: the growing need for postcolonial theory to engage with gender theory (and, more specifically, queer theory) to enrich its ongoing consideration of race and class.

This collection considers the wide variety of sexual expression and self-description throughout the "emerging" world among men who love men and women who love women. In the following pages writers address the interchange between, on the one hand, western notions of "gay" and "lesbian" that ground popular travel guides and, on the other hand, those less starkly outlined (and often, therefore, less politically potent) local designations for similar sexual expression among men and women. Our topic is significant and timely because it is arguably only in the most recent years that issues clearly related to "gay" and "lesbian" rights (and among these, the first would perhaps be self-definition) have surfaced throughout the "non-western" world. Sometimes advocates for a more aggressive public discussion of such issues discover in western models of homosexuality the only globally recognizable characteristics, frequently homogenized in the western political arena as *the* gay "sub-"culture or, worse, "lifestyle." The debate among the chapters in this book therefore relates to the implied imposition or willing embrace of the heavily capitalistic, white, yuppified, and (most vociferously, at least) male model demonstrated by *Spartacus*.

On the other hand, this book will demonstrate that local discussions of same-sex love present themselves, at least to western eyes, as remarkably fluid. In fact, the writers here—who themselves hail from many parts of the globe—consider the implications of the designation "queer" as an alternative term that may remain less hegemonic, less weighted down with colonial baggage. In the process of negotiating terminology, the chapter authors explicitly examine the theoretical underpinnings of postcolonialism that speak to local sexual rights and to the possibilities for transnational commonalities that may (or may not) transcend a new imperialism.

We have tried to be clear about the subject position from which each of us writes, and to avoid orientalization that exoticizes and "others" the non-westerner, or that blandly translates the "other" and obliterates all difference. The western commodification of gender identity politics can be powerfully suasive, expressed in such recent books as Lucy Bledsoe's otherwise fascinating *Gay Travels: A Literary Companion* (1998). Here the American reader is offered "close calls, perfect moments, unusual and erotic encounters, personal discovery, cultural exchange (and collision), and disastrous trips"—all in dubious service to "the essence of travel for gay men." In these few words the marketing department manages to be essentialist, voyeuristic, sexist, and consumerist. The tone is quite different in an observation like the following from Frank Browning: "As an American, as a white man, as a creature of the late twentieth century, as a male who grew up when the *New York Times, Time, Life, Newsweek,* and all of television and radio regarded homosexuality as either criminal or diseased, I am incapable of experiencing my desires with the touch, smell, and sight of a young Neapolitan in Italy or a Sambia tribesman in New Guinea—two places where homosexuality has a rich and ancient history that few make much effort to disguise" (3). Even here there is a sense of the interloper, but a clear recognition of difference, and of valorization of what one can never fully understand or possess.

The extent to which a postcolonial world may help interrogate—or delineate— a "post-gay" world is, therefore, central to the present book, and the chapters that follow, fascinating in their diversity, will attempt to suggest what *that* term might imply in an increasingly globalized world.

WORKS CITED

Bledsoe, Lucy Jane, ed. *Gay Travels: A Literary Companion.* New York: Whereabouts Press, 1998.

Browning, Frank. *A Queer Geography: Journeys toward a Sexual Self,* rev. ed. New York: Noonday, 1998.

Postcolonial
and Queer Theories

Chapter 1

Global Gaze/Global Gays

Dennis Altman

> What was fundamentally invisible is suddenly offered to the brightness
> of the gaze, in a movement of appearance so simple, so immediate that
> it seems to be the natural consequence of a more highly developed
> experience.
>
> —Michael Foucault, *The Birth of the Clinic*

Over the past few years I have been involved in several debates about how best to understand the emergence of a western-style politicized homosexuality in Asia, and about the usefulness of the concepts of "gay" and "Asia" in these debates. At the 1992 Asia/Pacific AIDS Conference in Delhi there were real tensions within the gay caucus—which met, symbolically enough, in a park opposite the conference hotel in which organizers once claimed no meeting rooms were available— between those who defined it in terms of ethnicity. In the end it was an ethnic Indian from New Zealand who insisted that the white gay men from Australasia should be regarded as legitimate members of the region.

It is easy to point to the artifice of "Asia," to say that any concept that includes Uzbekis and Koreans and Bangladeshis might as well find room for Australians. But this argument ignores the historical and racial ties of settler Australia to the western world, ties that make our claim for inclusion in "Asia" sound ignorant of history and look like a new form of colonialism. My own involvement in these debates has been a part of an evolving research interest in the growth of self-conscious "gay" communities and identities in Asia, and the problems of such terms are reflected in much of my research. Some readers of the first draft of this chapter complained that the term "Asian" was too broad to be of value, yet it is frequently invoked by the groups themselves to stress certain commonalities in their histories and experiences.

I come to this research as a privileged, white, Australian gay intellectual, with access to considerable resources (intellectual, economic, political). But I am also very dependent on those people I am researching who have far greater cultural and linguistic knowledge than I possess, and whose explanations of phenomena reflect as much as mine a particular set of emotional and intellectual positions. In this situation I see myself as co-researcher, ultimately dependent on both the goodwill and self-interest of my informants.

The anthropologist can usually assume her "otherness" from the subject of his study. In my interactions with Asian gay men this assumption fails to hold up. My research builds on social interactions with people in a variety of settings ranging from sitting on the beach in Bali to meetings in air-conditioned halls at AIDS conferences in Berlin and Yokohama, and is predicated on my sharing a certain common ground—sexual, social, political—with those of whom I speak. I would argue that the best understandings of the gay worlds have come out of this way of working—see, for example, Edmund White's account of pre-AIDS gay America, *States of Desire*—but both academically and ethically this sort of "participant observation" poses dilemmas.

In researching the development of "Asian" (specifically archipelagic southeast Asian) gay worlds I am both outsider and insider: indeed, I have had the experience of meeting Asian men, engaged in gay political work, who have been influenced by my own writings. Thus I am engaging with men where there is a complex power dynamic at work: I represent the power, prestige, and wealth of the west, but because we are meeting on a terrain of shared sexuality where mutual desire is an acknowledged possibility, and where I depend on their goodwill, the power dynamics are not simply unidimensional. My relations with Asian lesbians reflect a greater distance, and so far I have not been able to make more than very superficial contacts (not least because of the ways in which international AIDS politics have opened up space for homosexual men but not women). I constantly have to balance what I *seem* to be seeing against an awareness that my "informants" are telling stories for which I am the intended audience and that often fit their desires to see themselves as part of a "modern" gay world.

These relationships are further complicated by two contradictory trends. On the one hand, Asian gay men, by stressing a universal gay identity, underline a similarity with westerners. Against this, on the other hand, the desire to assert an "Asian" identity, not unlike the rhetoric of the "Asian way" adopted by authoritarian regimes such as those of China, Indonesia, and Malaysia, may undermine this assumed solidarity. Moreover, the ubiquity of western rhetoric means that many informants use the language of the west to describe a rather different reality. For example, the *Gay Men's Exchange*, a four-page photocopied "zine" produced in Manila, includes a two-page "Gay Man's Guide to Coming out," reproduced from a popular American publication (Muchmore and Hanson). The language of this and other western publications helps determine not only the language used in groups but also who might feel comfortable in discussions and how they may explain their own feelings to themselves. Last year in Manila I watched the film *Victor/Victoria* on local television. Although it is ostensibly set in Paris in the 1930s its characters speak of "coming out" as "gay." Such "politically correct" historical anachronisms presumably send messages to the larger audience who may have seen the film on prime-time television.

Gradually, western lesbian/gay theorists and activists are beginning to perceive the problems of claiming a universality for an identity that developed out of certain historical specificities. In his introduction to a recent book of "queer theory," Michael Warner writes:

In the middle ground between the localism of "discourse" and the generality of the subject is the problem of international—or otherwise translocal—sexual politics. As gay activists from non-western contexts become more and more involved in setting agendas, and as the rights discourse of internationalism is extended to more and more cultural contexts, Anglo-American queer theorists will have more cultural contexts. Anglo-American queer theorists will have to be more alert to the globalizing—and localizing—tendencies of our theoretical languages. (xii)

None of the contributors to this particular book take up this challenge—despite its title, *Fear of a Queer Planet*, American "queer theory" remains as relentlessly Atlantic-centric in its view of the world as the mainstream culture it critiques. Equally intriguing is the apparent lack of interest in "queer theory" in most of the non-western world, and the continued usage by emerging movements of the terminology "lesbian" and "gay."

SEX/GENDER/SEXUALITY IN "GAY" "ASIA"

In late June 1994 there was a large demonstration in New York City to commemorate the twenty-fifth anniversary of Stonewall, the riots at the New York bar of the same name, which is, as a result, claimed as the birthplace of the contemporary gay/lesbian movement. The organizers went to some trouble to invite groups from the rest of the world—including the "developing" world—to participate, obviously believing that the events being celebrated were of universal relevance. In ways that would shock many anthropologists, a claim to the universality of "gay" and "lesbian" identities is emerging in the rhetoric groups such as (to speak only of Asia) Bombay Dost, OCCUR (not an acronym, but referring to the sense of "something happening") in Japan, Ten Percent in Hong Kong, Pink Triangle in Malaysia, the Library Foundation in the Philippines, and the lesbian group Anjaree in Thailand ("Anjaree—").

It could be objected that these groups represent only a very small part of the homosexual populations in these countries, and that their use of language and symbols derived from overseas means they will be unable to mobilize significant numbers within their own societies. But twenty years ago the gay movements of North America, Australasia, and western Europe similarly spoke for very few, and their growth was unpredictably rapid. Of course this happened where the largely American symbols could be made relevant to local conditions (as with Sydney's Gay and Lesbian Mardi Gras, which has become a uniquely Australian version of what elsewhere are "gay pride parades"). But in a world where more and more cultural styles are imported and assimilated there seems no reason why a western-style gayness should not prove as attractive as other western identities.

The question is how to balance the impact of universalizing rhetoric and styles with the continuing existence of cultural and social traditions. Let me cite an encounter with a young Filipino in a bar in Quezon City, Metro Manila, early last year. Ricardo had just come from a meeting of his university's gay group, and was full of excitement at the prospect of an upcoming campus gay event. He spoke with enthusiasm of a march the group was organizing in the neighborhood, and of a play that had recently been presented in the bar where we were sitting.

The bar itself requires description: Cinecafé combines elements of a cafe, a bar, a porn video showroom, and a back room for sex. All this is contained in a small, three-story building on a back street far removed from the tourist hotels of Makati and Ermita, with a clientele that is almost entirely Filipino. At the same time there are certain aspects of Cinecafé that very clearly link it to a larger global gay world: the posters, the magazines, the films themselves (extensively French and American) are the same that one might find in similar establishments in Zurich, Montreal, or Sydney. In many ways, Cinecafé is a third-world version of the male sex-on-premises venues found in Los Angeles, Melbourne, or elsewhere, though it is much smaller and less well appointed.

Ricardo himself (like so many middle-class Filipinos, as fluent in English as in Tagalog) sounded remarkably like the young men I had known in the early 1970s in America, Australia, and western Europe, and spoke indeed of gay liberation in phrases that were very familiar. This encounter raised a whole set of questions about the meaning of terms like "gay" and "gay liberation" in very different cultural contexts, for the streets outside were the streets of an undeniably third-world country, and the men in Cinecafé, while in many ways shaped by western influence, were themselves part of Filipino society, seeking each other out in ways similar to the ways homosexuals seek each other out in the west: they were not at this establishment to meet westerners or other foreign tourists (as some theories of the globalization of sexuality would have it).

There are equivalents to Cinecafé in other parts of Asia. The past decade has seen the growth of a commercial gay world—beyond its few existing bastions, such as Bangkok and Tokyo—which now extends to most of the countries of Asia where there is sufficient economic and political space. Both affluence and political liberalism are required for a commercial gay world to appear: that it appears to be bigger in Manila than in Singapore is due to a number of factors, of which comparative political tolerance seems to me the most essential.

In recent years gay film festivals and magazines have appeared in Hong Kong and India; in Malaysia the HIV/AIDS group Pink Triangle is a de facto gay organization, which engages in a constant round of community development activities (and now provides some space for lesbians as well); in Indonesia the gay organization KKLGN (working Group for Indonesian Lesbians and Gay Men) has groups in about eleven cities.[1] Films and novels with gay themes have begun appearing, especially in east Asia.[2] Thailand has the most developed gay infrastructure in southeast Asia, including a Thai gay press (clearly not aimed at tourists) and several well-appointed saunas whose clientele is largely Thai (Allyn; Jackson, *Dear*). Lesbians remain almost invisible when their conditions are compared to those in western countries and except for Thailand there is little public information about lesbian worlds; it is my impression that, except in Indonesia, only tentative steps have been taken to establish a mutual sense of lesbian/gay cooperation.

Such contemporary forms of gay life coexist with older forms (often linked to ritualized expressions of transgender) or hybrid forms—e.g., the annual "Miss Gay Philippines Beauty Pageant" (Remoto 156–59). Yet a certain blurring of the sex/gender order may not be that different from development in the West, as revealed in ideas of the "third sex" which prevailed in the early stages of homosexual consciousness in Europe (see, e.g., Steakley) and more contemporary popular images such as the successful play/musical/film *La Cage aux Folles*. Western images of sex/gender in Asia often stress transgender images, as in the popularity of the play/film *M. Butterfly*, with its story of a French diplomat's love for a Chinese man he allegedly believed was a woman.[3] But to see transvestism as a particular characteristic of Asian cultures is to miss the role of drag in all its perverse and varied manifestations in western theater, entertainment, and commercial sex.

Western fascination with these images may reflect a greater acceptance of transgendered people (more accurately, transgendered males) in many Asian countries. This is suggested in a report that the Indonesian entry to the most recent Gay Games in New York included an all transsexual netball team—the national champions (Wyndham 26). In many countries such transgendered communities are institutionalized and have won an accepted, if marginal, status, often as providers of personal services (hairdressers, beauticians, etc.), which may include prostitution. Thus in Indonesia there is a national association of *waria* whose patron is the Minister for Women's Affairs. In the Philippines local dignitaries will attend *bacla* fashion shows.

There are differences as well as similarities between groups such as Indonesia *waria* or *banci*, Filipino *babaylan* or *bae(k)la*, and Malay *maknyah* or *kathoeys*, which go beyond the scope of this chapter. What they appear to have in common is a conceptualization of the sex/gender order that has no simple equivalent in the dominant language or social arrangements of western societies. In translating the term *kathoey* Peter Jackson makes clear the range of concepts the word conveys: "1: originally a male or female hermaphrodite; 2: male or female transvestite, or transsexual; 3: male homosexual or (rarer) a female homosexual" (*Dear* 301). And referring to similar groups in Polynesia Niko Besnier writes that: "sexual relations with men are seen as an optional consequence of gender liminality, rather than its determiner, prerequisite or primary attribute" (300).

In general, the new-way groups reject a common identity with more traditional identities, and define themselves as contesting sexual rather than gender norms. This is not to deny the significance of gender: as Richard Parker wrote of similar developments in Brazil.

It would be more accurate to suggest that, rather than replacing an earlier system of thought this newer system has been superimposed on it, offering at least some members of Brazilian society another frame of reference for the construction of sexual meanings. In the emphasis on sexuality, as opposed to gender, sexual practices have taken on significance not simply as part of the construction of a hierarchy of men and women, but as a key to the nature of every individual. (95)

The existence of several "systems of thought" leads to a certain ambivalence; thus some Filipinos who belong to gay groups might also see themselves in particular contexts as *bakla*.[4] Clearly the divisions are related—though not identical—to those of class, much as American or Australian men who twenty years ago defined themselves as "gay" were largely from relatively privileged backgrounds.

In much of urban Asia it is easy to see parallels with the West of several decades ago: existing ideas of male homosexuals as would-be women are being replaced by the assertion of new self-concepts; more men are attracted to the idea of primary homosexual relationships, rather than marrying and engaging in "homosex" on the side; there is a development of more commercial venues (but simultaneously, perhaps, there is less public cruising as being "gay" makes homosexuality more specialized); in both organizations and media there is the emergence of a gay political consciousness. The mock femininity of Thai or Indonesian "queens" and the mock-macho pose of hustlers is eerily reminiscent of John Rechy's novel of the early 1960s, *City of Night*, as is the fluctuation between overt queeniness and a certain prudery, public campiness and a great secrecy vis-à-vis families and workmates.

There is, as well, a certain vulnerability and fragility that underlies much of the new gay life—not, of course, without parallels elsewhere. For many of the young men who become part of the growing gay worlds of Asian cities there is rupture with family, village, religion, and social expectations, which can be very painful. It is not uncommon to meet young men whose growing sense of themselves as gay has led to interruptions of study, to breaks with family, to a general feeling of being stranded between two worlds (where an older western man will often be cast in the role of protector). Guilt, self-hatred, even suicide are not uncommon for those who feel themselves irretrievably homosexual in societies that deny open discussion of sexual differences even while allowing for certain variations much less acceptable in the west (Emond).

It is tempting to accept the Confucian and other Asian discourses about the significance of the family, and forget that similar experiences are very common for homosexuals in most countries, even those in northwest Europe that have moved furthest toward official acceptance. American research, for example, suggests the rate of suicide among adolescent homosexuals is far higher than the average (Remafedi). Yes, most homosexuals in Asian (and South American, eastern European, and African) cities are still likely to be more integrated into family roles and expectations than would be true in Sydney, San Francisco, or Stuttgart.[5] But we are speaking here of gradations, not absolute differences, and the growing affluence of many "developing" countries means possibilities for more people to live away from their families, and a gradual decline in pressure to get married. One of the key questions concerns the ways in which gay identities will change as "Asians" recuperate western images and bend them to their own purposes.

To see oneself as "gay" is to adhere to a distinctly modern invention, namely the creation of an identity and a sense of community based on (homo)sexuality. Most homosexual encounters—this is probably true even in the West—take place between men or women who do not define themselves as "gay" or "lesbian," and certainly do not affiliate themselves with a community. The development of such identities and communities began in the nineteenth century, although some historians claim evidence of it—at least in London, Paris, and Amsterdam—in the eighteenth (e.g., Huussen; Trumbach). My focus is very clearly on those men who perceive themselves—and increasingly present themselves to others—as having a consciousness and a politics that is related to their sexuality. They may or may not be behaviorally bisexual; what matters for the purpose of this discussion is their sense of identity. Frequently such men appear more comfortable within an international homosexual world, which they have often encountered firsthand through travel and study, than they are within the traditional sex/gender regime described by anthropologists and still existing in rural areas of their countries.

What characterizes a gay community? Writing of Hungary (where the political restraints until recently were similar to those of authoritarian Asia) Laszlo Toth argues: "There is a specific gay social institution system—from a specific nonverbal communication system to gay publications—which enables homosexuals to communicate with other gays, supporting gay community consciousness" (1). Despite the emphasis on communication, this is an institutional rather than a discursive view of community, recognizing that genuine community requires the existence of specific institutions within which a community-specific language is spoken (true of many homosexual subcultures, and now apparent in the emergence of clearly defined gay slang[s] in Indonesia).

The gay worlds of Bangkok, Jakarta, Hong Kong, Manila, and Seoul are obviously different from those of Budapest, Johannesburg, Hobart, Minneapolis, and São Paulo. Yet in all these cities—covering all continents and both the "developed" and "developing" countries—there are similarities that seem important and that I would hypothesize have more to do with the cultural backgrounds of, say, Thais, Hungarians, and Brazilians. There is a great temptation to "explain" differences in homosexuality in different countries with reference to cultural tradition. What strikes me is that *within* a given country, whether Indonesia or the United States, Thailand or Italy, the *range* of constructions of homosexuality is growing, and that in the past two decades there has emerged an identifiable group of self-identified homosexuals—to date many more men than women—who see themselves as part of a global community, whose commonalities override but do not deny those of race and nationality. This is *not* to present a new version of an inexorable march toward "development," with the end point defined in terms of building American-style gay ghettos across the world. Stephen O. Murray has warned that "there are obstacles to the globalization of an egalitarian (gay) organization of homosexuality even in the relatively industrialized and 'modern' capitals of 'developing' countries" (29). But globalization, in both its cultural and economic manifestations, impinges on the very creation and experience of sexual behavior and identities.

The reasons for these developments lie in both economic and cultural shifts that are producing sufficiently large and self-confident groups of men (and some women) who wish to live as homosexuals in the western sense of the term (i.e., expressing their sexual identity openly, mixing with other homosexuals, and having long-term primary relations with other homosexuals). As such, the tradition that married men are reasonably free to have discreet homosexual liaisons on the side seems as oppressive to the young radicals of OCCUR (Japan) or FACT (Fraternity for AIDS Cessation in Thailand) as it did to French or Canadian gay liberationists of the 1970s. When I was in Morocco in 1995 I met several men who spoke of emigration precisely because they were not willing to engage in the common practice of marrying while continuing to have homosexual encounters outside the home.

It is sometimes assumed that the notion of "a homosexual identity forged through shared lifestyles" has been, as Chilla Bulbeck put it, "almost exclusive to the west" (Bulbeck 5). In fact, the evidence for homosexual identities, lifestyles, and subcultures in a number of "developing" countries, particularly in South and Central America, dates back to the early years of the century and arguably before that, at least in Brazil (Bao; Daniel and Parker; S. Murray: Trevisan). Similar historical work has yet to be done for cities like Bombay, Manila, and Shanghai; almost certainly there are recognizable subcultures whose history has not yet been recorded.

A political expression of homosexuality is far more recent. The first self-conscious gay groups appeared in Indonesia (Lambda, in 1982) and Japan (JILGA, in 1984) just before the advent of AIDS was to change the terrain for gay organizing in ways which would make it more urgent while opening up certain overseas sources of funding. In the past decade there has been a proliferation of gay (sometimes lesbian and gay) groups, and many other AIDS organizations, so there has been a certain amount of gay outreach or even gay community development.

It is clear that the language of HIV/AIDS control, surveillance, and education has been a major factor in spreading the notion of "gay identity" and in facilitating the development of gay consciousness, as it has also contributed to the creation of the self-conscious identities of "sex workers" and "People with AIDS" (PWAs).[6] It is impossible to know how far the dispersal of western-style gay identities would have occurred without AIDS, which has opened up both space and resources for gay organizing and increased western influence through surveillance, objectification, and shaping of sexuality. Consider the large numbers of western or western-trained epidemiologists, anthropologists, and psychologists who have used HIV/AIDS as a reason to investigate sexual behaviors across the world, and by doing so have changed the ways in which the participants themselves understand what they are doing. The relationship is summed up in a flyer announcing a party at the 1995 AIDS in Asian Conference in Chiang Mai (Thailand):

Chaai Chuai Chaai is an NGO based in Chiang Mai. Our aim is to increase safer sex among gay and bisexual men, and male sex workers and their partners, through street outreach, bar outreach and one-on-one peer education. We are a nonprofit voluntary organization staffed and run by the gay community in Chiang mai.

Here the language of gay identity and gay-defined HIV education ("outreach," "peer education") is conflated to suggest a community that many Thais would claim is irrelevant to continuing cultural assumptions.[7] Matthew Roberts has argued that AIDS has been the essential catalyst for these developments, although I suspect he may fall into the trap of assuming a linear development toward the western model: "At Stonewall 50 we will likely find ourselves an open and proud community globally, efficaciously practicing safe sex . . . and with notable advances in our civil rights across the globe" (261).

NEOCOLONIAL "SEX WARS"

A large-scale construction of a lesbian/gay identity as a central social one—what Stuart Hall calls a master identity (280)—developed in the western world from the end of the 1960s on. Clearly, Asians who adopt lesbian/gay identities are conscious of and in part molded by these western examples. In both North America and Europe gay liberation grew out of the counterculture and other radical movements, particularly feminism. To some extent this is also true of the developing gay worlds of the south, but more significant is the global explosion of communications. One example: several years ago I walked into a hotel room in Buenos Aires and turned on the television to see a live broadcast of the Lesbian/Gay Rights March in Washington, D.C. Similarly, the opening of the 1994 Gay Games in New York was on the front page of the *Jakarta Post,* and large numbers of young Asians are learning about lesbian/gay worlds from the proliferation of youth-oriented television and rock videos. (Of course print media served to disperse news of the rise of western gay movements before the days of MTV and CNN, although less effectively.[8])

Michael Tan links the rise of gay identities/organizations to western influence and a growing "middle class" ("Tita") and claims there is "a global Sexual Revolution, involving a gradual shift in transcending the view of sexes-reproduction toward sex and sexuality as consent and commitment, respect and respectability" ("Introduction" xii). Yet as Tan recognizes, "modernity" in the countries under discussion is rather different from its western models, for it coexists with other and sometimes actively competing forces (see Corbridge 199–201). Tan and others have suggested that the absence of the sort of hostilities toward homosexuality in Anglo-Saxon societies may also retard the development of gay political movements. This argument can go overboard, as in Walter Williams's argument that "Indonesian values—social harmony, peacefulness and the national motto 'unity in diversity'—seem to protect gays from mistreatment more completely than western notions of individual rights" (181). Such protection would not extend to those whose "gayness" took on political forms deemed harmful to the Indonesian state.

The importation of certain concepts of sexuality is not of course new: missionaries, anthropologists, government officials, and travelers have all played their roles in simultaneously interpreting and obscuring existing realities. In terms of importing homosexual identity, a significant western influence dates from at least the early years of this century. Western models of homosexuality have come to Asia both through large cultural forces and through the influence of individuals, who were often attracted to "the East" because of its apparent liberality.

This is particularly true of Bali, which from the 1920s on was constructed by rich European homosexuals as a "paradise" because of the seeming beauty and availability of young Balinese men. The life of Walter Spies, as a German painter, most clearly expresses this. Spies was responsible in part for the western discovery and fetishization of Balinese art, and eventually he fell afoul of a colonial moral drive that came just before World War II (Rhodius and Darling 85). Indeed, Adrian Vickers claims: "It was not the Second World War but Bali's reputation as a homosexual paradise which ended the golden era of European Bali" (124, cf. Baranay). Yet after World War II and independence there was something of a rebirth of Bali's reputation, as a number of gay foreigners, among them the Australian painter Donald Friend, settled there for a time. A similar role has since been played by European expatriates in Morocco (Finlayson). Today there is a considerable expatriate gay population in Bali, as there is in Thailand, the Philippines, and Japan, drawn by the lure of "available" young men and "tolerant" social mores.

It is easy to condemn these men in the tones that are increasingly being used in a blanket fashion to demonize all sex tourists, and it is undeniable that there are some very ugly aspects to gay sex tourism. At one level there is the same exploitation of young Asians common in the much larger heterosexual scene (Jennaway; Sturdevant and Stoltzfus): beach prostitution in Kuta (Bali) and takeout bars in Bangkok are not particularly attractive and young men face many of the same threats to health and integrity as do young women. But without denying the ugliness born of larger economic inequities, one has to recognize a somewhat more complex pattern of relationships at work. In many cases young men are able to use their sexual contacts with (usually older) foreigners to win entry into the western world, either through the acquisition of money, skills, or language or, more dramatically, through the possibility of emigration. Some young men have made a conscious decision to use their sexuality as a means for social mobility, settling for a "housewife" role with a richer and older westerner out of a mixture of glamor and calculation.

Nonetheless, these relationships are inevitably shaped by colonial structures, which are almost impossible to escape. Racism and colonial scripts of superiority/inferiority are replicated within structures of desire in ways that neither side is comfortable in admitting. (One reader of this chapter assumed that I was speaking here of active/passive or top/bottom role-playing; I have something more complex in mind. As Genet showed in relationships between servants and master in his play *The Maids,* such roles may well be reversed in an unconscious transgression of colonial assumptions.) Ironically, the assertion of "gayness" among young middle-class Asian men is beginning to erode their willingness to employ the same script an older generation has used to enter the western homosexual world.

There is a danger that both moral indignation and overromanticizing will get in the way of fully understanding the dynamics of western/Asian homosexual contacts. Undoubtedly many westerners desire in Asians (both men and women) deference and servitude that may be unavailable at home, and for some the colonial/racist framework of their relationships allows them to act out their own sense of self-hatred. While there is an extensive literature of the gay expatriate—from the late nineteenth-century Frenchmen in northern Africa to Anglo-American writers such as Angus Wilson and Francis King and, more recently, Christopher Bram, Neil Miller, and Peter Jackson (*Intrinsic*)—there is virtually nothing written from the point of view of the "local," and there is a great need to hear those voices.[9]

But this is only part of the story: the gay men one sees in western-style discos at Legian (Bali) or bars in Bangkok are not the only ones. There are many venues in Bangkok, Tokyo, or Manila that cater almost exclusively to locals; indeed, a number of gay bars in Japan deliberately discourage foreigners, and the one gay sauna in Manila explicitly excludes them. In both cases fear of AIDS is the ostensible reason; the larger underlying motives are clearly more complex and operate on a number of levels. Long-lasting relationships exist between Asian homosexuals, marked by a certain equality, and part of the creation of "modern" gay identity appears to be a desire to open up the possibility of such relationships without their being framed by necessary differences of age, status, or race.

There is another factor now at work: the development of significant communities of "gay Asians" in the diaspora. An Asian gay consciousness has emerged over the past decade in the United States, Canada, Australia, and Britain, expressed through a host of burgeoning social political groups (Chua). In this sense, the image presented in the film *The Wedding Banquet* is remarkably out of date: the film opposes a white gay world to a traditional Taiwanese heterosexual one, but nowhere recognizes the existence in a city like New York of a very significant and increasingly visible East Asian gay community. Gay Asian expatriates are playing a role of some importance in the furthering of gay groups and identities "back home," even though, as Richard Fung has warned, they often seek to "conflate the realities of Asians in the diaspora with those living in Asian countries" (126).

GLOBALIZING INFLUENCES ON ASIAN SEXUAL IDENTITIES

There are three dominant scripts in which the globalization of gay identities is commonly described. The first sees southeast Asia as possessing a "natural" tolerance for sexual fluidity and expression before the onset of colonialism, and places great emphasis on the continuing traditions of both homosexual and transgender cultures. Thus Frederick Whitham writes: "The Philippines, as is generally true of Southeast Asian and Polynesian societies, has maintained a long-standing tradition of tolerance for its homosexual populations" (234). This script led to the twentieth-century view of some parts of Asia—Thailand; Sri Lanka; Bali—as homosexual paradises. Out of this grows the second script, strongly emphasizing the impact of colonialism and tourism in creating homosexual worlds. This in turn feeds a third script, which places its emphasis on the impact of modernity, and argues for the current development of gay identities, communities, and organizations across Asia as part of a larger pattern of economic and cultural globalization. Thus Kevin McDonald, though barely mentioning homosexuality, refers to "the importance of globally produced imaginary communities centered on forms of constitution of the body, consumption and sexuality" (21). As two Indonesian AIDS workers have written: "Globalization and economic growth have allowed Indonesian youth unprecedented access to information and media about sex" (Murdijana and Prihaswan 10).[10]

It is constantly important to find a balance between the view of globalization as a new stage of imperialism and the triumphalist discourse of globalization as the creation of a new world society, characterized by Simon During as "magic":

"General magic" is an appropriate term because it catches the astonishing cross-cultural reach of the desire for broadcasting, music, camera and video products. This general desire is not "natural." . . . Desires are produced by transnational advertising campaigns, while the technologies are shaped by data gathered through ethnographic market research. (341)

While I accept the role of economic and cultural globalization as crucial to the development of new sexual identities, such explanations must build on existing sex/gender regimes and values, just as contemporary gay worlds in the West have built on preexisting traditions and cultures. But as I am skeptical that the recent claims of John Boswell for the existence of church-sanctified gay marriage in the early Middle Ages tells us much about either current Catholicism or contemporary homosexuality, so I suspect that the emergence of gay groups and commercial worlds in modern Asia has relatively little to do with precolonial cultural formations. The comment of Clark Taylor—that "homosexual Mexicans often prefer their way of interacting to the U.S. forms because of cherished, cultural values" (117)—ignores the other factors at play.

This is not to deny the powerful symbolic and psychological reasons for exploring such connections: one of the benefits of a postcolonial approach is to unravel the ways in which colonial practices have denied cultural tradition. It is ironic that in many developing countries religious and gay interpretations present bitterly opposed views of the "traditional" status of homosexuality. Thus in Iran or China—with several thousand years of literary exploration of homosexual love—there is bitter persecution of "decadence." The desire of developing elites to deny their own sexual histories because of imported moralities, and the resulting persecution of homosexuals, are explored for China by Hinsh (165–66; see Ruan and Tsai).

Sexual identity politics grows out of modernity but also shows the way to postmodernity, because it both strengthens and interrogates identity as a fixed point and a central reference. The claiming of lesbian/gay identities in Asia or Latin America is as much about being western as about sexuality, symbolized by the co-option of the word "gays" into Thai, Indonesian, etc., and by the use of terms such as *moderno* (in Peru) and *internacional* (in Mexico) to describe "gayness" (S. Murray 29). As Alison Murray puts it,

Jakarta is now gayer than ever, and despite the dominant discourse, gay is a modern way to be. This has undoubtedly been influenced by western trends and internationalisation of gay culture, and in the process, the distinctive position of the *banci* has tended to be subsumed within the definition of gay. (6)

While such developments are clearly related to affluence, it is nonetheless worth noting the slow development of a western-style gay world in such countries as Japan, Taiwan, and Korea. In these countries, despite both extensive American influence and a considerable commercial world, it does not appear that a large open community is developing—although there is growing media interest in gay issues. (I have been told that the first Korean homosexual to "come out" on television subsequently received death threats.) In both Singapore and Hong Kong one feels a large gay presence about to burst forth; in both cities one meets large numbers of young men who identify as gay, but who are restrained by familial and governmental pressures from adopting the life-style that affluence and global media increasingly hold up before them.

A NEW GAY/LESBIAN POLITICS?

"The personal is the political" holds true for lesbian/gay politics in "developing" countries as much as it does in western countries. But where there is a legacy of colonialism, which has infused sexual relationships as much as other interactions, that slogan takes on particular meanings. In conversations among gay activists, particularly in the southeast Asian region, there has been some discussion of "Asian empowerment," by which is meant a reversal of the traditional assumptions that Asian men are sexually available for westerners. Such conversations suggest particular forms of self-assertion, and involve a rejection not only of the image of Asian men as "available" but also of the dominant stereotype of them as "feminine" or "passive." Just as western gay movements have asserted a certain masculinity in their constructions of male homosexuality, so Asian gays, having to counteract both indigenous and imported perceptions of them as men-who-want-to-be-women, are likely to be attracted by some variant of the western "macho" style. (Yes, gay men are beginning to frequent gyms in the richer cities of the region.) In gay discussion groups in Manila and Kuala Lumpur there is talk of "Asian" men learning to eroticize each other as a way of overcoming a deeply internalized sense of inferiority vis-à-vis Europeans.

The sexual-political relations of colonialism mean that for many gay men in

Asia the phallus is white and must be rejected, sometimes leading to a rejection (more rhetoric than practice) of European men as sex partners in the belief that they inevitably bear certain racial and colonial prejudices (see, for example, Filipino-American poet R. Zamora Linmark's "They like you because you eat dog" [266]). On a more conversationally political level there are only occasional examples of Asian gay groups engaging in activity of the sort associated with their counterparts in the West. Recent success in ending the criminalization of homosexual behavior in Hong Kong seemed to have relatively little to do with gay activism; rather, as had been the pattern in Britain, it followed a recommendation of the Law Reform Commission in 1982, finally ratified by the colony's legislative Council in 1990 ("After 10 Years"). Apart from limited moves in India I am not aware of political agitation to repeal such laws in other ex-British colonies such as Singapore and Malaysia, though the issue has been discussed within both Pink Triangle and People like Us (Singapore). There have been several small radical gay political groups established in the Philippines in recent years, and although not directly connected with any of these groups there was considerable coverage of the suggestion by one Filipino Congressman that there should be explicit representation of homosexuals in the legislature.

The development of political movements among people whose identities are being defined in terms of their sexualities will reflect larger features of the political culture of their societies. Gay politics in both Indonesia and the Philippines reflects the class structures of the countries: in both countries there are powerful upper-class figures whose homosexuality is widely known but who refuse any public identification with a "movement." In Indonesia in particular there is some evidence of the emergence of gay activism among lower-middle-class people who have less to lose. My impression is that there are certain tensions around class position between developing groups, often correlated with access to the English language and the outside world—but at this stage this is only a tentative suggestion based on limited observation.

Although the assertion of gay identities and communities in the west took a particular political form associated with the development of gay liberation movements in the early 1970s, this does not mean that groups in other parts of the world, whose sense of "gayness" is fueled by somewhat different sources, will necessarily follow the same itinerary. We must avoid what Michael Connors has termed the "narcissistic transition narrative in 'diffusion,'" whereby the trajectory of the Third World has already been traversed by the First" (12).

The best example of western-style political activism has come from the Japanese group OCCUR, which has engaged in lobbying various Japanese Ministries, persuading the Japanese Society of Psychology and Neurology to declassify homosexuality as a mental illness, and which succeeded in a court case against the Tokyo Metropolitan Government in winning the right to use public educational facilities. Despite these gains, OCCUR has warned:

There are many obstacles to lesbian and gay organizing in Asia and the Pacific islands which do not necessarily exist elsewhere in the world. These include not only the existence of

governments repressive of human rights, but also problems that stem from cultural, historical and social differences with the West. For OCCUR this has meant resisting a direct
importation of models of lesbian and gay activism developed in the West and developing
instead an original form of activism that reflects Japan's specific social and political context.
(OCCUR)

OCCUR and several other lesbian/gay groups from Asia and other developing
areas participate nonetheless in international networks such as ILGA (International Lesbian and Gay Association) and IGLHRC (International Gay and Lesbian
Human Rights Commission), thus increasing their own links to the West and
furthering the idea of a universal identity with claims to civil and political rights
transcending other cultural and national boundaries. That this is highly contested
was obvious in claims for lesbian inclusion at the recent IV World Conference on
Women in Beijing (1995), and in counterclaims such as that of Singapore's Foreign
Minister at the 1994 Human Rights Conference in Vienna that "homosexual rights
are a western issue and are not relevant to this conference" (quoted in Berry 73).

I am optimistic enough to believe that these sorts of arguments will lose in the
long run. In the words of United Nations Secretary General Butros Butros Ghali:

We must remember the forces of repression often cloak their wrongdoing in claims of
exceptionalism. But the people themselves time and again make it clear that they seek and
need universality. Human dignity within one's culture requires fundamental standards of
universality across the lines of culture, faith and state. (Ghali)

The ways in which the new gay groups of Asia, South America, and Africa will
adapt ideas of universal discourse and western identity politics to create something new and unpredictable—these will be the interesting developments.

Because of this belief, if we abandon the idea that the model for the rest of the
world—whether political, cultural, or intellectual—need be New York or Paris, and
if we recognize the emerging possibilities for such models in Bangkok and Harare,
we may indeed be able to speak of "a queer planet." We may even recognize the
need to question whether Anglo-American queer theorists are saying much of
relevance to the majority of people in the world who are developing a politics out
of their shared sexuality in far more difficult conditions that those within which
western lesbian and gay movements arose.

NOTES

1. KKGLN produces a monthly publication, Gaya Nusantara (contact: Jln Mulyosari
Timur 46, Surabaya 60112).

2. On film see Berry. The best-known novels are probably those of Mishima; few
others have been translated, but see Hsien-yung (Taiwan). Lee (Singapore) and Selvadurai
(Sri Lanka) are in English.

3. See the discussion in Garber 235–48. While she emphasizes the transgender aspects of the play, this is not to deny the other issues raised by the work.

4. For insights into these ambivalences see Garcia and Remoto.

5. This is the theme of a recent Singaporean novel (Koh).

6. I have deliberately limited the discussion of AIDS in this chapter, as I have discussed it at length elsewhere. See Altman 1994a, 1994b.

7. For more discussion of the role of "gay" organizing around HIV/AIDS in Thailand see *Newsletter of the Thai-Australian Northern AIDS Prevention and Care Project (NAPAC)*.

8. Thus a book published in India in 1976 spoke of "gay liberation," although in entirely American terms. See Devi.

9. A western attempt to make "the boys" central to the story is Ashford.

10. This theme was developed in *AsiaWeek* ("Sex: How Asia . . .") and *The Economist* ("It's Normal . . .").

WORKS CITED

"After 10 Years' Debate, HK's Gays Free to Love in Private." *Australian* (13 July 1990).

Allyn, Eric. *Trees in the Same Forest*. Bangkok and San Francisco: Bua Luang, 1991.

Altman, Dennis. *Power and Community*. London: Taylor & Francis, 1994a.

———. "Political Sexualities: Meanings and Identities in the Time of AIDS." In: *Conceiving Sexuality*. Edited by John Gagnon and Richard Parker. New York: Routledge, 1994b. 97–106.

"Anjaree—Towards Lesbian Visibility." *The Nation* (Bangkok) (25 Sept. 1994).

Ashford, Kent. *The Singalong Tribe*. London: GMP, 1986.

Bao, Daniel. "Invertidos Sexuales, Tortilleras, and Maricas Machos: The Construction of Homosexuality in Buenos Aires 1900–50." *Journal of Homosexuality* 24 (1993): 183–219.

Baranay, Inez. *The Edge of Bali*. Sydney: Angus and Robertson, 1992.

Berry, Chris. *A Bit on the Side*. Sydney: EMPress, 1994.

Besnier, Niko. "Polynesian Gender Liminality through Time and Space." In: *Third Sex, Third Gender*. Edited by Gilbert Herdt. New York: Zone, 1994. 285–328.

Boswell, John. *Same-Sex Unions in Pre-modern Europe*. New York: Villard, 1994.

Bram, Christopher. *Almost History*. New York: Donald Fine, 1992.

Bulbeck, Chilla. "Exploring Western Sexual Identities through Other Sexual Identities." Paper presented to Australian Sociological Association Conference, Adelaide, Dec. 1992.

Chua, Siong-huat. "Asian-Americans, Gay and Lesbian." In: *Encyclopedia of Homosexuality*. Edited by Wayne Dynes. New York: Garland, 1990. 84–85.

Connors, Michael. "Disordering Democracy: Democratization in Thailand." Unpublished paper. Melbourne University, 1995.

Corbridge, Stuart. "Colonialism, Post-colonialism and the Political Geography of the Third World." In: *Political Geography of the Twentieth Century*. Edited by Peter Taylor. London: Belhaven, 1993. 171–206.

Daniel, Herbert, and Richard Parker. *Sexuality, Politics & AIDS in Brazil*. London: Falmer,

1993.

Devi, Shakuntala. *The World of Homosexuals*. New Delhi: Vikas Publishing, 1976.

During, Simon. "Postcolonialism and Globalization." *Meanjin* 2 (1992): 339–53.

Emond, Bruce. "Homosexuals Live on Stressful Line of Conformity." *Jakarta Post* (6 April 1994).

Finlayson, Iain. *Tangier: City of the Dream*. London: HarperCollins, 1992.

Foucault, Michel. *The Birth of the Clinic*. Translated by A. M. Sheridan. London: Routledge, 1986.

Fung, Richard. "Looking for My Penis: The Eroticized Asian in Gay Porn Video." In: *Asian American Sexualities*. Edited by Russell Leong. New York: Routledge, 1996.

Garber, Marjorie. *Vested Interests*. New York: Routledge, 1992.

Garcia, Neil, and Danton Remoto. *Ladlad: An Anthology of Philippine Gay Writing*. Manila: Anvil, 1994.

Ghali, Butros Butros. "Democracy, Development and Human Rights for All." *International Herald Tribune* (10 June 1993).

Hall, Stuart. "The Question of Cultural Identity." In: *Modernity and Its Discontents*. Edited by Stuart Hall, David Held, and Tony McCrew. London: Polity, 1993. 273–325.

Hinsh, Bret. *Passions of the Cut Sleeve*. Berkeley: University of California Press, 1990.

Hsien-yung, Pai. *Crystal Boys*. San Francisco: Gay Sunshine, 1990.

Huussen, Arend. "Sodomy in the Dutch Republic during the Eighteenth Century." In: *Hidden from History*. Edited by Martin Bauml Duberman, Martha Vicinus, and George Chauncey. New York: New American Library, 1989. 141–49.

"It's normal to be queer." *Economist* (6 Jan. 1996).

Jackson, Peter. *The Intrinsic Quality of Skin*. Bangkok: Floating Lotus, 1994.

———. *Dear Uncle Go: Male Homosexuality in Thailand*. 2nd ed. Bangkok: Bua Luang, 1995.

Jennaway, Megan. "Pleasuredromes and Paradise." In: *Sites of Desire/Economies of Pleasure*. Edited by Margaret Jolly and Lenore Manderson. Chicago: University of Chicago Press, 1997.

King, Francis. "A Corner of a Foreign Field." In: *One Is a Wanderer*. Edited by Francis King. Harmondsworth: Penguin, 1985. 161–85.

Koh, Andrew. *Glass Cathedral*. Singapore: EPB, 1995.

Lee, Johann. *Peculiar Chris*. Singapore: Cannon, 1992.

Linmark, R. Zamora. "They Like You because You Eat Dog." In: *Charlie Chan Is Dead*. Edited by Jessica Hagedorn. New York: Penguin, 1993. 265–66.

Lunsing, Wim. "Japan's Lesbian and Gay Movements 1982–94." Paper presented to conference on "Organising Sexualities," Amsterdam, June 1994.

McDonald, Kevin. "Identity Politics." *Arena Magazine* (Melbourne) (June–July 1994).

Miller, Neil. *Out in the World*. New York: Random House, 1992.

Muchmore, Wes, and William Hanson. *Coming Out Right: A Handbook for the Gay Male*. Boston: Alyson, 1991.

Murdijana, Desti, and Priyadi Prihaswan. "AIDS Prevention in Indonesia." *National AIDS Bulletin* (Canberra) (April 1994): 8–11.

Murray, Alison. "Dying for a fuck: Implications for HIV/AIDS in Indonesia." Paper presented at gender relations conference. Canberra, 1993.

Murray, Stephen O. "The 'Underdevelopment' of Modern/Gay Homosexuality in Mesoamerica." In: *Modern Homosexualities*. Edited by Ken Plummer. London: Routledge, 1992. 29–38.

Newsletter of the Thai-Australian Northern AIDS Prevention and Care Project (NAPAC)
    2.4. Chiang Mai (1995).
OCCUR (Tokyo). "HIV/AIDS and Gay Activism." (6 June 1995).
Oetomo, Dede, and Bruce Emond. "Homoseksualitos di Indonesia." *Prisma 7* (1991)
    (English version supplied by Oetomo).
Parker, Richard. *Bodies, Pleasures, and Passions.* Boston: Beacon, 1991.
Rechy, John. *City of Night.* New York: Grove, 1964.
Remafedi, G. "Adolescent Homosexuality: Psychosocial and Medical Implications."
    Pediatrics 79 (1987): 331–37.
Remoto, Danton. *Seduction and Solitude.* Manila: Anvil, 1995.
Rhodius, Hans, and John Darling. *Water Spies and Balinese Art.* Zutphen: Terra, 1980.
Roberts, Matthew. "Emergence of Gay Identity and Gay Social Movements in Develop-
    ing Countries: The AIDS Crisis as Catalyst." *Alternatives* 20 (1995): 243–64.
Ruan, Fang-fu, and Yung-mei Tsai. "Male Homosexuality in Contemporary Mainland
    China." *Archives of Sexual Behavior* 17 (1988): 189–99.
Selvadurai, Shyam. *Funny Boy.* Toronto: M & S, 1994.
"Sex: How Asia Is Changing." *AsiaWeek* (23 June 1995).
Steakley, James. *The Homosexual Emancipation Movement in Germany.* New York:
    Arno, 1975.
Sturdevant, Sandra, and Brenda Stoltzfus. *Let the Good Times Roll.* New York:
    New Press, 1992.
Tan, Michael. "Introduction." In: *A Different Love.* By Margarita Singco-Holmes. Ma-
    nila: Anvil, 1994. ix–xiv.
———. "Tita Aida and Emerging Communities of Gay Men." *Journal of Gay & Lesbian
    Social Services* 3.3 (1995): 31–48.
Taylor, Clark. "Mexican Male Homosexual Interaction in Public Contexts." In: *The Many
    Faces of Homosexuality.* Edited by Evelyn Blackwood. Binghamtom, N.Y.: Harrington
    Park, 1986. 117–36.
Toth, Laszlo. "Development of Hungarian Gay Subculture and Community in the Last
    Fifty Years." Unpublished paper, Budapest, 1994.
Trevisan, Joao. *Perverts in Paradise.* London: GMP, 1986.
Trumbach, Randolph. "London's Sodomites: Homosexual Behavior and Western Culture
    in the Eighteenth Century." *Journal of Social History* 2 (1977): 1–33.
Vickers, Adrian. *Bali: A Paradise Created.* Melbourne: Penguin, 1989.
Warner, Michael, ed. *Fear of a Queer Planet.* Minneapolis: University of Minnesota
    Press, 1993.
White, Edmund. *States of Desire.* New York: Dutton, 1980.
Whitham, Frederick. "Bayot and Callboy: Homosexual-Heterosexual Relations in the
    Philippines." In: *Oceanic Homosexualities.* Edited by Stephen O. Murray. New
    York: Garland, 1992. 231–48.
Williams, Walter. *Javanese Lives.* New Brunswick, NJ: Rutgers University Press, 1991.
Wilson, Angus. *As If by Magic.* New York: Viking, 1973.
Wyndham, Susan. "Put on the Street." *Weekend Australian* (18–19 June 1994).

Chapter 2

The Perfect Path: Gay Men, Marriage, Indonesia

Thomas D. Boellstorff

In a 1997 ad for Ciputra Hotels that appeared in the Indonesian national airline's in-flight magazine, a smiling Balinese dancer in bejeweled "traditional" garb stands juxtaposed to glittering hotel facades. The ad proclaims that "Indonesia is also home to Asia's newest hotel concept. . . . While tradition thrives in Indonesia, the world's most modern concepts are equally at home." Presumably, one of these "modern concepts" is the "western" male business traveler, who will feel "at home" under the domestic attentions of the female staff.[1]

It hardly takes a subversive reading to see that the ad constructs Indonesia as a hybrid of tradition, gendered female, and modernity, gendered male. This binarism has a long history, extending from colonialism to modernization theory. Many non-"western" intellectuals have addressed its symbolic violence, including the man many consider Indonesia's greatest living author, Pramoedya Ananta Toer. His novel *Footsteps,* which opens in 1901, is set in the late colonial period but speaks by analogy to the Indonesia of the 1970s and 1980s, when it was written. The protagonist, Minke, has just come from Surabaya to the capital, known informally as Betawi. Alone and poor but on his way to medical school and a "modern" career, Minke frames his arrival as a change of time as well as place:

Into the universe of Betawi I go—into the universe of the twentieth century. And, yes, to you too, nineteenth century—farewell! . . . People say only the modern man gets ahead in these times. In his hands lies the fate of humankind. You reject modernity? You will be the plaything of all those forces of the world operating outside and around you. I am a modern person. . . . And modernity brings the loneliness of orphaned humanity, cursed to free itself from unnecessary ties of custom, blood—even from the land, and if need be, from others of its kind. (Toer 15)

Through Minke's voice, Toer questions the perfect path of modernist teleology, with its assumption that "footsteps" to the future necessarily lead to a homogenized subjectivity that denies the local, the "others of its kind." One can well imagine Minke as the modern business traveler; building his career, reading an in-flight magazine, experiencing the "loneliness of orphaned humanity," and hoping to find a home. But where would Minke's footsteps have taken him if he had flown into Jakarta International Airport in 1999, rather than disembarked on its shores in 1901? How would he think of the relationship between past and future, tradition and modernity, self and other? There is no doubt that the forces of globalization have grown and shifted tremendously in recent decades. But many scholars of transnationalism question whether this growth implies homogenization or instead may result in new forms of difference. As Arjun Appadurai notes, the contemporary moment is marked by disjunctions in the global movement of images, commodities, and persons and by "a new role for the imagination in social life" (Appadurai 31).[2]

On the most fundamental symbolic level, for instance, the Ciputra Hotels ad requires that the woman staring out at the prospective customer not be lesbian. Her heterosexuality structures the very opposition between tradition and modernity on which the ad's semiotic logic rests. This logic is part and parcel of a system of governmentality in which the Indonesian state strives to efface the distinction between itself and society through metaphors of the heterosexual, middle-class family. Such heteronormativity raises the question of why there are *lesbi* and *gay* subjectivities in Indonesia, the fourth most populous nation, at all. By exploring the "homoscapes" in which some non-"western" subjects identify as lesbian or gay—in particular, by exploring the "mystery" of gay-identified men's marriages to women in Indonesia—I hope to clarify the processes of "reterritorialization" and "localization" identified by scholars of globalization.[3] What is the history and social context of these subjectivities? These are the kinds of questions that came to my mind when I first saw this ad on my way to Indonesia to begin fieldwork.

My consideration of these questions took place in a postcolonial frame. By *postcolonial*, whose scope and validity remain ambiguous, I refer to a theoretical stance according to which the emergence of nations in the formerly colonized world poses a new set of questions about belonging, citizenship, and the self. I turn to creative uses of this framework by such scholars as Homi K. Bhabha, Partha Chatterjee, Stuart Hall, Akhil Gupta, and Gayatri Chakravorty Spivak rather than to analyses that reject "postcoloniality" by claiming that it implies that colonialism is "past,' that economic forces are irrelevant, or that all nations follow the same path.[4] One theme of this chapter is that in LGQ studies (i.e., gay, lesbian, bisexual, queer, transgender, and intersex studies) a more serious engagement with postcoloniality as a category of analysis might improve our understanding of sexualities outside the "West."

In this essay I focus on people outside the "West" who use the terms *gay, lesbian,* and *bisexual,* or close variants of them, rather than on the "indigenous" homosexualities and transgenderisms that have hitherto been the almost exclusive concern of the "ethnocartography" of homosexuality.[5] (In the case of Indonesia, the subjectivities I refer to are *gay* and *lesbi.)* While attention to lesbian, gay, and bisexual subjectivities outside the "West" is certainly increasing, Kath Weston's 1993 observation that "in the international arena, the 'salvage anthropology' of indigenous homosexualities remains largely insulated from important new theoretical work on postcolonial relations" continues to be distressingly valid in 1999.[6] This provincialism originates in the perceived incompatibility between postcoloniality, on the one hand, and persistent narratives of a "global movement" within LGQ studies, on the other. While such narratives are politically salutary — indeed, a strategic essentialism may be warranted in some contexts, given the dominance of "development" as a rubric for conceptualizing global change[7]— they have limited LGQ studies' awareness of the ethnocentrism of many of its assumptions about what constitutes activism, visibility, politics, social movements, and even identity. In response, I view this chapter as representing a category of scholarship that might be termed "postcolonial LGQ studies."

I am struck by the predictable manner in which interpretations of non-"western" gay and lesbian subjectivities fall into two reductionisms in LGQ studies. In the first, these subjectivities are said to be "just like" lesbian and gay subjectivities in a homogenized "West." They represent the transcendental gay or lesbian subject, characterized by a supposed essential *sameness* that has been there all along, hidden under a veneer of exotic cultural difference. (Such an understanding recalls Bhabha's analysis of colonial mimicry, "the desire for a reformed, recognizable Other, as a *subject of difference that* is *almost the same, but* not *quite,"* and is represented in texts like *The Global Emergence of Gay and Lesbian Politics: National Imprints of a Worldwide Movement*.[8]) I want to point out how teleologies like this converge with Minke's "footsteps" to modernity, critiqued in Toer's novel.

The second reductionism, the opposite of the first, assumes that these gay men and lesbians suffer from false consciousness and are traitors to their "traditional" subjectivities, victims of (and, ultimately, collaborators with) a global gay imperialism. They represent the McDonald's-ized, inauthentic gay or lesbian subject, alienated from its indigenous *Geist*. From this perspective, these subjectivities have an essential *difference,* hidden under the veneer of the terms *lesbian* and *gay*. So the "footsteps" of traveling LGQ theorists go in circles around the "sameness" or "difference" of non-"western" gay and lesbian people with respect to gay and lesbian people elsewhere. The issue of sameness and difference extends to concerns about postcolonial subjectivity beyond LGQ studies; it is in fact one of the animating concerns of anthropology in the twentieth century. My work has been motivated in part by a search for a way of talking about sameness and difference that avoids these reductionisms. Such a way might point toward less teleological paths of theory and identity in LGQ studies.

Considering the importance of postcoloniality in this way has led me to recall that in the last twenty years there has appeared, outside LGQ studies, a sophisticated body of literature exploring Indonesia from a postcolonial perspective.[9] Yet the scholars who have contributed to it have paid scant attention to *lesbi* and *gay* subjectivities, even though most U.S.-based Indonesianists of the past fifteen years were taught Indonesian by Dédé Oetomo, a Cornell-trained anthropologist who has written on *gay* identities in Indonesia.[10] In this chapter I use ethnographic material from Indonesia to interrogate the complementary lacunae in Indonesian studies and LGQ studies in search of a third framing of *gay* and *lesbi* subjectivities. Historical context plays a role as well. Both *Footsteps* and *Imprints* employ a path metaphor either to critique or to celebrate globalization as developmental and homogenizing. In 1990, however; an Indonesian sociologist discovered in a Jakarta archive a remarkable manuscript written by a man named Sucipto, who had had sex only with men and had participated in a community of like-minded men in 1920s colonial Java. Sucipto titled his writings *The Perfect Path.* The relationship between his "perfect path" and contemporary *lesbi* and *gay* subjectivities cannot be reduced to a Procrustean modernist path. The contingent appropriation of concepts of homosexuality makes for subjectivities that are irreducible to those in the "West," even if the terms are similar. *Gay* and *lesbi* are not just "gay" and "lesbian" with a foreign accent.

An important caveat is that in this chapter I focus on *gay* men (that is, men who self-identify as *gay* in some contexts at least). In some sense "gay" and "lesbian" moved to Indonesia as one concept, "gayandlesbian"; thus homosexuality has implied heterosociality in some circumstances.[11] But despite an impressive record of cogendered community, the *"gay* archipelago" I describe is decidedly gendered male.[12] The case study I employ is the "mystery" of *gay* men's marriages to women. In the larger project from which this essay is derived I explore the specificities of *lesbi* subjectivity in Indonesia from historical and contemporary perspectives, building on existing analyses of Indonesian women's same-sex and transgendered subjectivities.[13]

SAMENESS VERSUS DIFFERENCE, LOCAL VERSUS GLOBAL: RECONCEIVING TWO BINARISMS

I develop my argument for a postcolonial perspective via two binarisms that permeate most discussions of LGQ identities outside the "West": sameness versus difference and local versus global. In regard to the vexed binarism of sameness and difference, the issue is not the world's becoming more the same *or* more different under globalization (neither homogenization nor heterogenization per se) but the transformation of the very yardsticks by which one decides whether something is the same or different in the first place, that is, the reconfiguration of the grid of similitude and difference. In *The Order of Things* Michel Foucault characterizes shifts in western European thought in terms of conceptualizations of sameness and difference.[14] What analytical purchase might be gained by positing, under some circumstances at least, a postcolonial "order of things" in which relationships between same and other were characterized not as boundaries transgressed but as boundaries blurred, not as borders crossed but as borderlands inhabited, not as spheres adjoined but as archipelagoes intertwined?[15] This approach might help theorize the inequalities of globalization (oppression does not require distinct boundaries), and the fact that globalization is not rendering the state irrelevant, in a way that still accounts for the fact that *gay* and *lesbi* Indonesians find their subjectivities authentic.

The second issue is the revamping of the local-global binarism. Building from emic cultural logics of a *gay* archipelago, I argue that *gay* and *lesbi* are translocal subjectivities for which the local-global binarism is conceptually and methodologically insufficient. The isomorphism between difference and distance is broken; sameness is measured not in terms of concentric spheres of decreasing familiarity but archipelagically, so that someone thousands of miles away might be "closer" than someone next door. This phenomenon is not a cosmopolitanism by which national subjects (usually urban elites) imagine themselves as part of a community that transcends the nation, sharing structures of feeling and patterns of migration above local (usually poorer) communities (see Cheah and Robbins). Nor is it a diaspora in which gay or lesbian selves disperse from an originary homeland, or a hybridity in which two prior unities turn difference into sameness via an "implicit politics of heterosexuality" (Young 25). *Gay* and *lesbi* Indonesians construct themselves as part of a community that, while it includes non-Indonesians in complex ways, transforms rhetorics of nationalism and locality as well. The dialectic between immanence and transcendence sets these subjectivities apart from cosmopolitan, diasporic, or hybrid ones.

The production of translocality in *gay* and *lesbi* subjectivities presents a problem for some theories of globalization, for it is not predicated on the movement of people; most *lesbi* and *gay* Indonesians are working-class, do not speak English, have never traveled abroad, and have no contact with non-Indonesian lesbians and gay men.[16] A majority live in the towns and even the households where they grew up. Nevertheless, most see not only their selves but their social places as figurations of a simultaneously national and global community. To explore how translocal subjectivities could arise without the movement of people, my research needed to be translocal as well. I conduct ethnography in three primary urban sites—Surabaya (East Java), Denpasar/Kuta (Bali), and Ujung Pandang (South Sulawesi)—but in a profound sense I do not regard my work as comparative. I am certainly interested in differences and similarities between my sites, but I also view my work as taking place in one site, Indonesia.[17] While extralocal affiliations are common throughout Indonesia, impacted not only by nationalism and capitalism but by world religions like Islam and Christianity, *gay* and *lesbi* subjectivities exhibit translocality to a heightened degree. Significantly, there are local places and organizations for *lesbi* women and *gay* men and a national network but no intermediate Java-wide or Bali-wide organizations. Throughout the remainder of this chapter I show why, while *gay* and *lesbi* Indonesians are aware of their ethnicities, the idea of a specifically Javanese or Balinese *gay* or *lesbi* self is currently unthinkable: there is a meaningful incompatibility between ethnicity and *gay* or *lesbi* subjectivity. Anthropologists looking in Surabaya for gay Javanese people, *orang gay Jawa,* would fail. Instead, they would find people who, in the context of their sexual subjectivities, thought of themselves as *orang gay Indonesia.*

GAY WORLDS AND ARCHIPELAGOES

In the early 1980s some Indonesians began to take the "western" terms *lesbian* and *gay* and transform them until they saw them as authentically Indonesian. Through everyday practices of spatial formation, pleasure, romance, bodily comportment, social imagination, and language (including the use of a slang involving not only lexical substitutions but unique inflections), they have articulated a community that they call the *dunia gay,* or "gay world."[18] For men, this world encompasses a range of places and activities, from strolling in air-conditioned shopping malls to hanging out in parks or by the side of a road at night, forging quasi-private sites in public space called *tempat ngeber,* or "flaunting places." That the *gay* (and occasionally *lesbi)* Indonesians who frequent such sites see them as transformed is illustrated by a contrast drawn by an informant in Bali. We were talking about the importance of friendship when he said, "[Gay men] might become friends in places like the *tempat ngeber* in the town square, but if we meet in a *tempat umum* [public place] like a movie theater or supermarket, we pretend we don't know each other." In terms of semiotics, bodily comportment, and community, he no longer experiences the town square as a public place.[19]

This man's emphasis on *tempat ngeber* as a place to make friends is significant. Under general conditions, when one is rarely far from the watchful eye of family, workplace, or school, *tempat ngeber* are sites where subjectivities are forged. The people who hang out there are only secondarily looking for sex; indeed, many come night after night with long-term lovers or a group of friends. Groups of two or three quietly conversing alternate with crowds of five to thirty engaged in "campy" (*ngondhek*) joking, gossip, and rapid-fire retorts, using slang extensively. Gay men and *lesbi* women define themselves in terms of "desiring the same," unlike transgenders, who see themselves as having the soul of one gender in the body of another. *Tempat ngeber,* then, are literal subject positions, forming both local communities and the persons who inhabit them. Some *tempat ngeber* comprise areas where "open" *gay* men are known to congregate (often under a streetlight), other areas where those who are more "closed" gather, and still others where sexual partners may be found regardless of self-identification. People's movements between these areas—on a given night but also in a general pattern over a period of weeks or months—not only reflect their subjectivities but reconstitute the relationships that form these subjectivities. Since *tempat ngeber* usually exist in public spaces and at night, access to them is limited for women, including *lesbi* women. But they and gay men also form subject positions in homes, salons, food stalls, and church groups; on volleyball teams; and in shopping malls or discos. Some *gay* men and *lesbi* women form organizations with varying degrees of formality and even publish magazines.[20]

It is widely felt that these groups, as well as the less formal subject positions of parks and homes, are linked in a national network. Gay men and *lesbi* women assume that *gay* and *lesbi* communities elsewhere in Indonesia share their subjectivities, differing only in the degree to which their members can be "open" and can interact with transgenders. Some *lesbi* and *gay* Indonesians experience communities outside their own directly through migration as they search for work (or attempt to escape from prying family members). In addition, many cities (particularly Solo, Yogyakarta, Denpasar, Malang, and Surabaya) put on performance events that attract *gay* men and *lesbi* from distant cities for two or three nights of revelry. Rural *gay* men say that these events give them a rare chance to move outside the limited world of pen pals and build a friendship network.

While many rural and some urban *gay* men and *lesbi* women are isolated from other *gay* men and *lesbi* women (owing to the fear of discovery or to their not knowing where others can be found), most have a network of five to twenty friends who play a constant role in their lives. An all-gay volleyball team practices every afternoon on a crowded athletics field; a line of men waits to play, but many sit on the sidelines and exchange news. Agung, a *gay* man, lives with his parents in their boardinghouse. It has twelve rooms on the upper floor; over a period of two years five are rented to *gay* men, two to *gay* couples, and one to a *lesbi* woman. In the hallway between the rooms, conversations on long hot nights give way to meetings and the idea of an organization, until one day the mother decides that she dislikes Agung's crowd, and one by one they move elsewhere. A *lesbi* woman whose parents own a small restaurant finds temporary work for another *lesbi* woman in a nearby shop and advises her on a recent breakup. While the quotidian details of life come and go, *lesbi* or *gay* Indonesians who move from one city to another expect to find people who share their subjectivities and suspect where they may be found. For the larger number who do not move from one city to another, there remains a sense that these everyday experiences are part of an imagined community of *gay* and *lesbi* subjectivity extending across Indonesia.

Moreover, *gay* and *lesbi* Indonesians think that non-Indonesian lesbians and gay men share a set of beliefs, desires, and practices (even though only a few have known such people personally). At the end of interviews I always asked my informants if they had any questions. Some wanted to know if gay bars really existed or if I had met Leonardo DiCaprio, but just as often they responded politely that "I feel I already know everything about your life."[21] *Gay* men and *lesbi* women usually assume that these familiar others are "the same" in terms of same-sex desire and "different" in terms of social acceptance and political rights. (But the meanings of "desire" and "acceptance" may themselves be conflicted, as *gay* men's marriages to women indicate.) Here the role of social imagination, already important in the nation, takes on new significance. For example, in Surabaya most *tempat ngeber* are named after locations outside Indonesia: *Texas, Kalifor, Pattaya* (a tourist beach in Thailand), *Paris, Brasil.* Such names, by permitting embodied visits to locales simultaneously outside and inside Indonesia, sidestep the binarisms of same-different and local-global. Such *lesbi* and *gay* imaginings are not unique to *tempat ngeber,* but they provide a particularly clear example of them.

The *gay* world is a domain of everyday subjectivity and practice that parallels the regular world, but when the places of the *gay* world are linked in an imagined national or transnational community, distant but present, the metaphor shifts from world to archipelago. One group in Surabaya names itself (and its magazine, usually recognized as the national magazine) GAYa Nusantara, an intentional polysemy in which each term has a dual valence. *Gaya* is the Indonesian for "style," but the unusual capitalization highlights the term's similarity to *gay. Nusantara* means "archipelago" and is also a nationalist term for "Indonesia." Because adjectives follow the nouns they modify in Indonesian, while they usually precede them in English, the term *GAYa Nusantara* parses in a fourfold manner as "archipelago style," "Indonesia style," "gay Indonesia," and gay archipelago." While this term is by no means used by or even known to all Indonesians who identify as *lesbi* or *gay,* it manifests a common way of translocalizing these subjectivities "archipelago-style," at the intersection of local, national, and transnational rhetorics of selfhood, sexuality, and community. In other words, the local does not form the ontological ground for these subjectivities, and *lesbi* and *gay* Indonesians do not see themselves in a position of simple exteriority or interiority vis-à-vis non-Indonesian gay and lesbian communities. State ideology frames Indonesia as an archipelago of ethnicities; *lesbi* and *gay* Indonesians co-opt this image by conceptualizing the sites of *lesbi* and *gay* identities as "islands," which at a higher resolution are reframed as a single island in a transnational archipelago of gay and lesbian community. While the Javacentric Indonesian state provides a familiar example of archipelagic inequality, archipelagoes are nevertheless composed of discontinuous sites, none of them subsumed by the others: they are not bounded domains with a necessary center and periphery. How are we to understand subjectivities that connect and confound traditional levels of analysis—and, arguably, lived experience in the "West"—namely, the local, regional, national, and international?

Such interconnections are illustrated by the name and symbol for GAYa Dewata, a group in Bali that is housed in an AIDS organization. *GAYa* comes from *GAYa Nusantara; dewata* is the Indonesian for "gods": the Balinese refer to their island as *pulau dewata,* or "island of the gods." The symbol for this group is an AIDS ribbon inverted and turned around so that it looks like a ceremonial Balinese male headdress. In this image we see discourses of local, national, and international provenance intertwined with AIDS development discourse and with the state ideology that requires every province to have a distinct character.[22] This translocal subjectivity cannot be explained solely in terms of local versus global; the parallels reveal not a common path but a logic of reconfiguration—on local and translocal levels—that does not originate in the "West."

This reconfiguration is best understood as archipelagic in form. Indonesian transgenders frequently ask me, "Are there people like me in America?" *Lesbi* women and *gay* men never ask this question, because their subjectivities already assume the copresence of analogs beyond the local. What we see in Indonesia is not movement toward a uniform global sexual culture; the "foreign" elements are not only localized but translocalized, and this process is far too determined to be reduced to an aggregate aftereffect of localization. Indonesians do not identify as *gay,* then imagine themselves as part of a national community, then construct it as part of a transnational community. The process proceeds on all levels at once, in a historically specific manner sometimes through the explicit metaphor of a *gay* archipelago. Postcolonial lesbians and gay men are not "the same" as "western" lesbians and gay men, and they do not live across a chasm of absolute difference.

DUBBING CULTURE: STATE HEGEMONY, MASS MEDIA, AND THE GOOD FAMILY

The archipelago concept, in the "unity in diversity" form in which it is articulated through the practices and statements of *lesbi* and *gay* Indonesians, is not a timeless cultural archetype but is quintessentially modern, a key structuring principle of the nation-building project. Its reformulation has been a crucial means by which the state has struggled to reinterpret the denizens of Alfred Russel Wallace's colonial-era "Malay Archipelago" as citizens of a postcolonial archipelago.[23] The *wawasan nusantara*, or "archipelago concept," dates from the early period of nationalism, at the beginning of the twentieth century, but it gained new force in 1957 in the context of an international dispute over maritime boundaries.[24] In 1973 the Indonesian government decreed that the archipelago concept "gives life to national development in all its aspects—political, social, and cultural" (Kusumaatmadja 25). Public culture in Indonesia is replete with the image and ethos of the archipelago. Diversity subsumed in unity is a hallmark of the state's rhetoric of cultural citizenship; it is predicated on a distinction between "culture" and "politics" that frames ethnicity (*suku*) as a matter of religion and the arts, while the people (*bangsa*) are linked to politics, commerce, and, above all, modernity.[25]

Fifty-four years after national independence, this Indonesian subjectivity is as fully imagined as any ethnicity, with its own language, ritual practices, ideologies, and symbolic sites. That it is complexly imbricated with the state does not invalidate its everyday authenticity for many Indonesians. It has not supplanted ethnicity but interacts with it in an additive manner, since the valorization of pluralism is central to the state's self-presentation as an archipelagic container of diversity. *Gay* or *lesbi* Indonesians are not necessarily more nationalist than other citizens. At the same time, state rhetorics of the archipelago are not deployed in a utilitarian manner by presocial *gay* and *lesbi* subjects; a man hanging out in *Texas* does not deploy the archipelago concept instrumentally, although it does facilitate his imagining that place and his self as linked to an imagined gay Texas elsewhere. The state stands as an inadvertent idiom for *gay* subjectivity, influencing the daily practices by which the *gay* archipelago is enacted, constituted, and maintained in all its marginality.

The state itself, however, pays little attention to these subjectivities. There is no political persecution of *gay* men and *lesbi* women or banning of their magazines; indeed, government officials have labeled homosexuality incompatible with Indonesian society only once, at the United Nations International Conference on Population and Development in Cairo in 1994.[26] But the state has played an accidental role in fostering these subjectivities, by encouraging the mass media as a means to build nationalism.[27] One afternoon, for example, Darta, an informant, told me this story:

When I first heard the word *gay*, it was in the fifth or sixth grade [c. 1985], on the island of Ambon, where I grew up, near New Guinea. It was there that I first heard about *lesbi*. Earlier, you know—gay wasn't around yet. But *lesbi* was already in women's magazines. I read lots of those magazines, because Mom was a regular subscriber. Mom and I loved reading the articles on sexual deviants. I was always effeminate, and one day she said *I* was *lesbi,* because she didn't know *gay;* the term wasn't public back then. [For "public" Darta used the term *umum,* the same term used by my Balinese informant to distinguish *tempat umum* (public places) from *tempat ngeber.*] But eventually I learned the term *gay* as well. That was also from a magazine. There was some story about historic English royalty . . . Richard someone. When I saw that, I thought, "There are others like me."[28]

While Darta's prior identification as *lesbi* raises interesting questions about the disjunctural character of postcolonial sexualities, the element of his story that I want to highlight is the role played by mass media. Most Indonesians do not learn of the terms *lesbi* and *gay* through non-Indonesian lesbians and gay men or through *lesbi* and *gay* magazines, which they usually access only after identifying as *lesbi* or *gay.* Most learn of these terms through imported programs—movies like *Cruising, The Wedding Banquet,* and *My Best Friend's Wedding;* television shows like *Melrose Place*—as well as through pop psychology advice columns and gossip columns on the sexual lives of celebrities.[29] Many informants recall a moment of recognition when "I knew that was me" or "I knew I was not the only one." Some "western" lesbians and gay men may find such a moment of recognition familiar. However, the subjectivities that these Indonesians recognize (or misrecognize; see Bourdieu) in mass media cannot be reduced to dominant "western" models of sexual identity. Nor does a preexisting internal state of desire find its social label at this moment. Instead, the subject and the archipelagic frame encompassing its desires are mutually constituted.

To situate the moment of recognition or construction, it is once again necessary to bring in the postcolonial nation-state. The Indonesian state has become aware that its mass media policies have crossed a threshold beyond which they encourage not only nationalism but translocal subjectivities that threaten to spin beyond state control. Television stations in Indonesia, for example, rely heavily on imported programming (each imports about seven thousand shows a year), and they frequently dub these shows into Indonesian. In 1996, sensing an opportunity to further its language policy, the parliament, with Suharto's tacit approval, passed a draft law requiring that *all* foreign shows be dubbed (*Republika* [Jakarta], 2 May 1996). An unusual debate between Suharto, the parliament, the army, and other pressure groups ensued, and in July 1997, after months of controversy, Suharto refused to sign the law—the first time in Indonesian history that such a constitutionally questionable act had taken place (*Kompas* [Jakarta], 25 July 1997). When the dust cleared in December 1997, the law had been changed to its exact opposite: all dubbing of foreign television shows was forbidden; only subtitles were permitted.[30]

The government has justified this about-face in terms of cultural contamination and the family. As one apologist explained: "Dubbing can . . . ruin the self-image of family members as a result of adopting foreign values that are 'Indonesianized' . . . whenever Indonesians view television, films, or other broadcasts where the original language has been changed into our national language, those Indonesians will think that the performances in those media constitute a part of themselves. As if the culture behind those performances were also the culture of our people."[31] At the intersection of postcoloniality and globalization, the ability of Sharon Stone or Jim Carrey to speak Indonesian is no longer a welcome opportunity to build language skills and foster the prestige of Indonesian but instead threatens Indonesians' ability to differentiate themselves from the outside.[32] The fear is that the citizen will be alienated, as in Toer's novel, from "others of its kind." How might the emergence of *lesbi* and *gay* subjectivities, on ostensibly personal and social levels, parallel this controversy? How might we think of them in terms of "dubbing culture": an embodiment of subjectivities that, from a modernist perspective, appear disjunctural and inauthentic? How might dubbing culture be less like a path and more like an archipelago?

THE MYSTERY OF *GAY* MARRIAGE

Despite the power of mass media, their influence is neither direct nor determining. Their transformative effects, and those of the archipelago concept, are nowhere more apparent than in the "mystery" of *gay* men's marriages to women. Walking along the dark riverbank in *Texas* one night toward a group of shadows leaning against a railing, I met Andy and four of his friends. Andy identified as *gay,* explaining that his boyfriend of ten years was married with two children. When I asked if the boyfriend should get divorced, he stared in shock: "Of course not. He needs descendants and a wife. I want to get married in five years—I already have a girlfriend. You mean you won't marry as long as you live?" When I nodded, the other men confronted me in astonishment: "How could you not want to get married? You'll be lonely when you get old! Everyone must have descendants."

In this story, *gay* men not only implicate me in their *gay* archipelago but also discuss a central concern of their lives, marriage. Most *gay* Indonesians marry and have children and see these actions as consistent with their subjectivities. Most also assume that gay men in the "West" marry women.[33]   While in Indonesia, I always placed on my desk a picture of my partner that shows him standing with a female colleague. Most gay-identified men would point out this picture and say, "His wife is taller than he is!" My explanation that she was a friend and that neither my partner nor I wanted to marry a woman would be met with disbelief and pity. Many "westerners" have reciprocated with their own misrecognition when assuming, as I once did, that *gay* identities are incompatible with marriage. They have failed to understand that not only the *gay* world but the *gay* self is archipelagic. What is distinctive about these identities vis-a-vis "normal" Indonesian sexuality is not same-sex sex (it is usually taken for granted that both men and women will engage in it, given the chance) but love, abiding romantic interest in the same gender

The *gay* self is not internally homogeneous and integrated; instead, it is composed of multiple subjectivities constituted in, rather than ontologically anterior to, social relations. It is an additive and "dividual" self, consistent with selves identified by many scholars of Southeast Asia and Melanesia but, just as important, embodying state rhetorics of ethnonational identity.[34] *Gay* and *lesbi* Indonesians construct and are constructed by an overdetermined archipelagic idiom. Thus dominant "western" notions of egosyntonic, unitary identity have been reconfigured in the Indonesian context: this homosexual self desires to marry. *Gay* persons are self-reflexive but not self-congruent. Could they become poster children for the ultimate postmodern subject? The mystery is more complex.

Ikbal was a friend of Andy; Ikbal's wife of five years lived in a nearby village with their child, while he cohabited in Surabaya with a male lover, Dodi. Hand in hand with Dodi at *Texas* almost every night, Ikbal frequently lectured other *gay* men on the obligation to marry and the joys it brought. It was a point of pride to him that his wife and parents "knew about him" and that he and Dodi had married cousins so they would never be separated. One day Ikbal insisted that I come to the village to meet his wife. Once there, however, we would stay in a nearby town with his parents until Sunday; he would end up spending only two hours with his wife before we had to return to Surabaya. En route to the meeting Ikbal told me about the months of sexual frustration he and his wife had experienced: they had been able to consummate their marriage only by admitting Dodi to their bed, where he lay alongside Ikbal and, as Ikbal's wife sobbed, stimulated him so that penetration could take place. On this Sunday, when he could delay his visit with his wife no longer, Ikbal warned me to be extra macho: "Now is the time to begin playacting." Apparently his family's knowledge of him was more fractured than I had suspected. As our little minibus, adrift in a green flowing sea of rice paddies, approached the village and a tense afternoon of silent squabbles and awkward smiles, Ikbal looked out the dusty window and almost whispered: "These parts of my life cannot be unified." (The term Ikbal used for "unified," *nyatu,* is derived from "one," *satu.*)

Theoretical physicists may believe in God's creation; social constructionists may believe that they were born gay or lesbian. The mystery of *gay* men's marriages to women is that most *gay* men evince—simultaneously, within a single subjectivity—an archipelagic self to which marriage is not only compatible but pleasurable and a self for which it stymies a desire to integrate one's spheres of life into a single narrative trajectory.[35] Most *gay* men want to marry, but they also scheme how to delay or avoid it and how to maintain *gay* friendships and sex partners once married. This is a mystery not only to the "external," non-Indonesian observer but also to the men themselves; many of them, like Ikbal, experience it as a contradiction. One clue to it lies in the origins of the imperative to marry itself. While marriage is a powerful norm throughout Indonesia, the particular form of this imperative that *gay* men experience certainly does not stem from a primordial localism: I have found strikingly little regional, religious, or ethnic variation concerning *gay* men's ideologies of marriage. In some regions, like Java and South Sulawesi, it is not historically expected that all persons will wed and procreate.[36] Additionally, what limited sources we have suggest that from the 1920s to the 1960s Indonesian men with same-sex subjectivities assumed that their subjectivities, like those of gay men and lesbians in the contemporary "West," precluded marriage to an opposite-sex spouse. What, then, is the origin of the imperative to marry?

A key element of Indonesian state ideology, apart from the archipelago concept, is the *azas kekeluargaan,* or "family principle," which holds that the family is the fundamental unit of the nation.[37] Crucially, this is not the extended family but the nuclear family, whose ubiquitous smiles illuminate television ads and government posters: husband, wife, and two children, with a car, a home with smooth white tile floors, a television set, and other paraphernalia of the new middle class. It is this "public domesticity" that the state equates with citizen subjectivity and summons into being through a range of development practices.[38] Children are necessary for continuing the nation and for supporting their elders in their old age. The state's ideal family converges with the rhetoric of globalization.

Figure 1.
"A poor *hetero* family that does not follow Family Planning. In the end they create not heaven but a 'hell' on earth. How far can this husband and wife guarantee that their children will become successful people later on?"

While a considerable body of work has pointed out the gender inequalities of the new international division of labor, less attention has been paid to its foundation in the naturalization of the heterosexual couple as the basic unit of the postcolonial nation. More effectively than Henry Ford's fabled management of his workers' lives ever could, the heterosexualization of the labor force constitutes the domains of public and private, locates the family as the unit of consumption, and naturalizes gender inequalities. Thus heterosexuality provides a critical suture between capitalist ideologies of production and nationalist ideologies of the nuclear, middle-class family as metonym for the nation. It is a moral economy linking economic production and citizenship. As constituted by these discourses, the unmarried self is an incomplete economic and national subject.[39]

Figure 2.
"A *lesbi* couple who are professionals. They can live together comfortably, with greater plenty, greater prosperity, and... fewer problems on average than *hetero* families."

Albeit rarely, *gay* men sometimes directly critique the conjunction of class, nation, and the imperative to marry, as the following examples from a manifesto published in Jakarta in 1997 show. In figure 1 we see "a poor *hetero* family that does not follow Family Planning." Utensils and toys are strewn about a dirt floor; a mother, weighed down by an infant, screams over a gas stove, while the father is incapacitated in bed by the fighting of the other four children. One child is urinating on the floor; curtains hang precariously from unhinged shutters. "The parents have "create[d] not heaven but a 'hell' on earth. How far can this husband and wife guarantee that their children will become successful people later on?" By contrast, figures 2 and 3 show "a *lesbi* couple who are professionals" and "can live together comfortably" and "a young *gay* couple who, besides being happy, also can enjoy life optimally." The author notes that the *lesbi* couple can live "with . . . fewer problems on average than *hetero* families" and asks, if the *gay* couple "were each married in the *hetero* manner could it be guaranteed that they would live as comfortably as shown above? Only if they were descended from wealth." What is shown in figures 2 and 3 are beautifully coiffed hair, upholstered furniture, clean clothes, smooth white tile floors, television sets, automobiles, two servants (men for the gay couple, women for the lesbians), gardens being watered, and the calm aura of leisure. The message in the Indonesian context is clear: *lesbi* and *gay* couples can "outfamily" the family. But what constitutes the family is not challenged: it remains the modern middle-class, professional household. The hegemony is resisted, but only in its own language and in terms of its own consumerist logic.

Figure 3.
"A young gay couple who, besides being happy, also can enjoy life optimally. If they were each married in the *hetero* manner could it be guaranteed that they would live as comfortably as shown above? Only if they were descended from wealth."

This notion of the family is strongly influenced by shifting economic rationalities. In 1982, following the oil boom, Suharto's technocratic ministers gained ground and enacted economic and fiscal reforms that resulted in massive inflows of capital, which accelerated a shift away from agriculture and toward the service and industrial sectors (see Hill; Winters). This shift led to the rise of a substantial middle class for the first time in Indonesian history; Daniel S. Lev dates its consumerist and self-reflexive consciousness to a special edition of the magazine *Prisma* on the "new middle class" in 1984, during the same period in which *lesbi* and *gay* subjectivities appeared in the form of a national network for the first time.[40] These economic changes did not affect *gay* and *lesbi* subjectivities in a determinist manner, nor were Indonesians suddenly able to travel to or to obtain lesbian and gay publications from the "West." Most *lesbi* and *gay* Indonesians make less than fifty dollars a month—working-class wages even by Indonesian standards. But many observers identify the Indonesian middle class in terms of aspiration and "mode of consumption." In Howard Dick's words: "Among the *rakyat* (lower classes), consumer durables are shared: it is antisocial to restrict the access of one's neighbors. Middle class households, by contrast, confine the enjoyment of such goods to members of the household. . . . In other words, there is 'privatization' of the means of consumption."[41]

With this consumerist ethic comes a modernist, narrative self, defined in terms of autobiography. While far from universal, the notion of the self as something constructed is hardly new.[42] What is at issue in the Indonesian context is the conjunction of a fashioned self with a specific middle-class consumerism. It is not a fantasy of the sultan or the superrich cosmopolitan who selects at will from the world's bounty. It is a circumscribed personhood-as-career in which, given limited resources, one negotiates and budgets one's life trajectory within a marketplace logic that guides the crafting of choices. The self becomes the self's profession: this middle-class subjectivity is a story that the self tells to itself about itself, rather than a story passed down primarily through kinship, ethnic, or religious background, as the stories of the lower and upper Indonesian classes historically were.[43] Like middle-class subjectivities, *gay* and *lesbi* subjectivities are not passed down through tradition; they become their own stories, and the telling of those stories becomes a problem. A palette of possible lives spreads out before the subject, whose only prohibition is not to choose. One self-consumes, struggling to forge one's self-story. Like M. C. Escher's image of two disembodied hands gripping pens, conjuring each other into existence on a drawing pad, the self and the self's story form a loop of personhood in which social others are secondary. As Escher's loop breaks down without the pens with which to draw, so the commodity forms the conduit by which the middle-class self writes its story. In this sense, the *gay* person is self-contingent. Is this the same old liberal, bourgeois subject that has received such scholarly attention?[44] The mystery is more complex.

My goal is not to adjudicate between apparently contradictory notions of *gay* personhood, the archipelagic and multiple (where marriage to women is not a problem) or the consumerist and congruent (where marriage to women is a problem).[45] Noting that both the archipelago concept and the family principle emerge in the shadow of the state, I wish to hold them in tension, as a mystery, because it is precisely in such a multiply mediated contact zone that *gay* subjectivities exist.[46] Neither concept of personhood is exclusive to Indonesia; at issue are the circumstances of their imbrication. In the context of a narrativized self that is also multiple, a *gay* self can be a married, procreating self. When a *gay* man turns to his lover in bed and tells him to marry, he is not confused about who he "really" is, nor is he internalizing homophobia or denying reality. He is expressing and perpetuating an identity best thought of as archipelagic (rather than cosmopolitan, diasporic, or hybrid). While I find the gender politics of this scenario disturbing, particularly for women like Ikbal's wife who have little power in their marriages, it is important to recognize the situated rationality at play in the production of these new inequalities.

The crucial point is that homosexuality (and sexuality more generally) is globalized not as a monolithic domain but as a multiplicity of beliefs and practices, elements of which can move independently of each other or not move at all.[47] In the case of *gay* and *lesbi,* the notion of homosexual identity has moved, but other aspects of the dominant "western" discourse of homosexuality have not. Foucault's genealogy of homosexuality in the "West" locates the intersection of power and knowledge at the confession (*History of Sexuality,* vol. 1). Identity reveals and renders intelligible an interior, private self but is not authentic until exteriorized to an interlocutor who interprets and acknowledges this confession. Only then is the person "out of the closet," even in the remarkable case of the "intralocutor" operative in "coming out to yourself." Many theorists have shown how this model construes homosexual identity as a constant, iterative process of articulation and reception, an incitement to discourse that contributed to the "reverse discourse" of the lesbian and gay rights movement.[48]

But when the terms *lesbian* and *gay* moved to Indonesia, the conjunction of sexuality and confession neither preceded nor followed them. As a result, the ontological status of *lesbi* and *gay* subjectivities does not hinge on disclosure to spheres of home, workplace, or God. *Gay* men and *lesbi* do not "come out of the closet" but speak of being "opened" (*terbuka*) or "shut" (*tertutup*). Construed not in terms of moving from one place to another but in terms of opening oneself, these subjectivities are additive rather than substitutive; opening them does not necessarily imply closing others. In addition, *lesbi* and *gay* Indonesians open not to the whole universe but to the *gay* world; confessing to other worlds in society is irrelevant. We find not an epistemology of the closet but an epistemology of life worlds, where healthy subjectivity depends not on integrating diverse domains of life and having a unified, unchanging identity in all situations but on separating domains of life and maintaining their borders against the threat of gossip and discovery.

This may call to mind the work of George Chauncey and other scholars on the history of homosexual identities in the "West." In early-twentieth-century New York, for instance, the term *coming out,* derived from the notion of a debutant ball, implied coming out to a select community, not to all spheres of life. Furthermore, many homosexually identified people married and did not see their doing so as incongruous. Nonetheless, I would caution against a teleological reading of Indonesians as followers in these footsteps and against a structuralist reading of contemporary Indonesia and historical New York as presenting a mutual set of necessary and sufficient conditions. Such interpretations beg the question of how sameness and difference are measured in the first place. Contemporary *lesbi* and *gay* subjectivities diverge in important respects from earlier homosexual identities in the "West," not least because they imagine themselves situated in an actual transnational archipelago of established lesbian and gay movements. As Ikbal's story reveals, moreover, the epistemology of the gay world coexists mysteriously with a narrative self exhibiting a tropism toward unity.

The fallacy of seeing contemporary *gay* and *lesbi* subjectivities as living fossils is highlighted by what we know about homosexual identities in Indonesia before national independence in 1945. It may seem that people started hanging out in *tempat ngeber* like *Texas* only after the emergence of *gay* and *lesbi* subjectivities. But the following episode from Sucipto's text *The Perfect Path,* mentioned at the beginning of this chapter, suggests otherwise. The year is 1926, and Sucipto, young and homeless in Surabaya, has been walking along the river at night. He pauses to rest on a bridge near the Gubeng train station, near present-day *Texas.* While he is lost in thought, a voice calls out to him. It is a Dutchman, who invites Sucipto to his house and pays Sucipto to have sex with him. After leaving the house, Sucipto returns to the bridge, "thinking about what had just happened. . . . it was completely impossible that a Dutch person could desire things like that. . . . he was of a different race than myself. Apparently my assumptions had been turned upside down . . . . How did he know that I like this kind of thing? This was what astonished me."[49]

The "westerner" of Sucipto's imagination did not have same-sex desires prior to this encounter. Even after learning that a colonial "westerner" can have these desires, Sucipto does not identify with him; he sees him as interested only in commodified sex, incapable of the love that distinguishes the desire Sucipto has shared with other Javanese men. Sucipto sees his homosexuality in the 1920s as a local, Javanese phenomenon; he also sees it as incompatible with marriage and has discouraged his Javanese friends from marrying. Living at the high point of Dutch colonialism, he does not imagine himself as part of a national or transnational community, but in some ways his subjectivity is closer to "western" gay or lesbian subjectivity than to contemporary Indonesian *gay* subjectivity, since normative *gay* Indonesians marry and normative gay "westerners" do not. It is not coincidental that the sociologist who discovered Sucipto's text published it as *Path of My Life,* which seemed "more fitting with its character as an autobiography," rather than as *The Perfect Path.* From his perspective, Sucipto's story could represent not a perfect path but only the path of his life. From this standpoint, self-identity is personal and Sucipto's text an autobiography—particular, not universal.[50] Clearly, a theory of globalization that holds that things become more similar as time marches on is insufficient. Contemporary *lesbi* and *gay* subjectivities are not just the evolutionary end points of Sucipto's subjectivity. They represent a dubbing culture, the production of translocality, the reterritorialization of "western" discourses of homosexuality in the context of already existing notions of same-sex desire.[51]

CONCLUSION

> The term "post-colonial" is not merely descriptive of "this" society
> rather than "that," or of "then" and "now." It rereads "colonization" as
> part of an essentially transnational and transcultural "global" process—
> and it produces a decentered, diasporic or "global" rewriting of earlier,
> nation-centered imperial grand narratives. Its theoretical value therefore
> lies precisely in its refusal of this "here" and "there," "then" and "now,"
> "home" and "abroad" perspective. (Stuart Hall, "The Question of
> Cultural Identity," 247)

In this chapter I have taken in earnest Hall's interpretation of postcoloniality as a flexible, provocative problematic. In doing so, I have produced the beginnings of a decentered, archipelagic rewriting of what might otherwise be interpreted as imprints on a perfect path: the emergence of *lesbi* and *gay* subjectivities in Indonesia. Refusing the perspectives of sameness-difference and local-global, I hope that my analysis opens avenues of inquiry beyond the Indonesian case.

In reference to nationalism, Chatterjee asks: "If nationalisms in the rest of the world have to choose their imagined community from certain 'modular' forms already made available to them by Europe and the Americas, what do they have left to imagine? History, it would seem, has decreed that we in the postcolonial world shall only be perpetual consumers of modernity. . . . Even our imaginations must remain forever colonized" (*The Nation and its Fragments* 5). For Chatterjee, postcoloniality provides a rough starting point from which to deconstruct this dilemma. Such a framework, I argue, proves worthwhile in the context of *gay* and *lesbi* subjectivities as well.

Transposing Chatterjee's question to sexuality, I would answer that there is a vast, archipelagic space in which *gay* and *lesbi* Indonesians might imagine new subjectivities and communities, despite conditions of inequality, oppression, and contradiction. When some Indonesians began to identify as *lesbi* and *gay,* they articulated subjectivities that apparently rejected local traditions and lay outside Indonesian history. But in fact these Indonesians have reconfigured local, national, and transnational discourses in a way that challenges the modernist single trajectory for lesbian and gay identity. Were Sucipto and Minke to meet a contemporary *lesbi* or *gay* Indonesian, they would have difficulty understanding a postcolonial subjectivity that has transformed the boundaries by which one decides who is "the same." The specter of LGQ identities as either homogenized or fractured beyond recuperation by the forces of globalization must give way to a more nuanced postcolonial and translocal perspective, informed by a rubric of postcolonial LGQ studies. There is no perfect path.

ACKNOWLEDGMENTS

To protect their confidentiality, I have changed the names, as well as details of locations and personal histories, of all Indonesians mentioned in this essay except Dédé Oetomo. My research in Indonesia in 1992, 1993, 1995, and 1997–98 was generously supported by a Social Science Research Council International Dissertation Research Fellowship, a National Science Foundation Doctoral Dissertation Improvement Grant, the Department of Social and Cultural Anthropology at Stanford University, the Morrison Institute for Population and Resource Studies, and the Center for the Teaching of Indonesian. During the writing of this essay I received support as a MacArthur Fellow at the Center for International Security and Cooperation at Stanford University. I thank the following individuals for commenting on earlier drafts: Kathleen Coll, Shelly Errington, Erich Fox Tree, Akhil Gupta, David Murray, Dédé Oetomo, and Sylvia Yanagisako. Particular thanks are due George Chauncey, Bill Maurer, and Elizabeth Povinelli for their supportive editorial guidance and to Purnima Mankekar for a careful reading of a final draft. All errors, of course, are my sole responsibility.

NOTES

1. Throughout this chapter the terms "West" and "western" are quoted to indicate that they are hegemonic norms. Like Akhil Gupta, "in speaking of 'the West,' I refer to the effects of hegemonic representations of the Western self rather than its subjugated traditions. Therefore I do not use the term to refer simply to a geographic space but to a particular historical conjugation of place, power, and knowledge" (36). It is precisely this homogeneous image of the "West" that gay and *lesbi* Indonesians experience as *the* West. Throughout the chapter the terms *gay* and *lesbi* are italicized to distinguish them from "gay" and "lesbian" as analytical concepts.

2. In contradistinction to what he terms a priori difference, Daniel Miller describes the "new forms of difference" as a posteriori differences: "This is the sense of quite unprecedented diversity created by the differential consumption of what had once been thought to be global and homogenizing institutions. . . . The idea of *a posteriori* diversity . . . seeks out new forms of difference, some regional, but increasingly based on social distinctions which may not be easily identified with space" (2–3). Excellent examples of the burgeoning literature on globalization and difference include Arjun Appadurai, "The Production of Locality," in *Modernity at Large,* 178–200; Mike Featherstone, "Global and Local Cultures," in *Mapping the Futures: Local Cultures, Global Change,* edited by Jon Bird et al. (London: Routledge, 1993); Featherstone, "Localism, Globalism, and Cultural Identity," in *Global/Local: Cultural Production and the Transnational Imaginary,* edited by Rob Wilson and Wimal Dissanayeke (Durham: Duke University Press, 1996), 46–77; J. K. Gibson-Graham, *The End of Capitalism (as We Knew It): A Feminist Critique of Political Economy* (Cambridge, Mass.: Blackwell, 1996); Paul Gilroy, "Route Work: The Black Atlantic and the Politics of Exile," in *The Post-Colonial Question: Common Skies, Divided Horizons,* edited by Iain Chambers and Lidia Curti (London: Routledge, 1996), 17–29; Akhil Gupta and James Ferguson, "Beyond 'Culture': Space, Identity, and the Politics of Difference," *Cultural Anthropology* 7 (1992): 6–23; Stuart Hall, "The Local and the Global: Globalization and Ethnicity" and "Old and New Identities, Old and New Ethnicities," in *Culture, Globalization, and the World-System: Contemporary Conditions for the Representation* of *Identity,* edited by Anthony D. King (London: Macmillan, 1991); Hall, "When Was 'the Post-Colonial'? Thinking at the Limit," in Chambers and Curti, *Post-Colonial Question,* 242–60; Hall, "The Question of Cultural Identity," in *Understanding Modern Societies: An Introduction,* edited by Stuart Hall et al. (Cambridge, Mass.:

Blackwell, 1995), 596–633; Ulf Hannerz, "Scenarios for Peripheral Cultures," in King, *Culture, Globalization, and the World-System;* Hannerz, *Transnational Connections: Culture, People, Places* (London: Routledge, 1996); Fredric Jameson, "Notes on Globalization as a Philosophical Issue," in *The Cultures of Globalization,* edited by Fredric Jameson and Masao Miyoshi (Durham: Duke University Press, 1998), 54–77; Philip McMichael, "Globalization: Myths and Realities," *Rural Sociology* 61 (1996): 25–55; and Malcolm Waters, *Globalization* (London: Routledge, 1995).

3. See Richard Parker, *Beneath the Equator: Cultures of Desire, Male Homosexuality, and Emerging Gay Communities in Brazil* (New York: Routledge, 1999), 218–21; Appadurai, "Production of Locality"; Jonathan Friedman, "Being in the World: Globalization and Localization," *Theory, Culture, and Society* 7 (1990): 311–28; and Gupta, *Postcolonial Developments.*

4. E.g., Aijaz Ahmad, *In Theory: Classes, Nations, Literatures* (London: Verso, 1992); Arif Dirlik, "The Postcolonial Aura: Third World Criticism in the Age of Global Capitalism," *Critical Inquiry* 20 (1992): 328–56; Ella Shohat, "Notes on the 'Post-Colonial,'" *Social Text* nos. 31–32 (1992): 99–113. For useful discussions of postcoloniality debates see Bart Moore-Gilbert, *Postcolonial Theory: Contexts, Practices, Politics* (London: Verso, 1997); and Hall, "When Was 'the Post-Colonial'?" In response to fears about the term's potential to efface cultural specificity, Hall notes that "Australia and Canada, on the one hand, Nigeria, India, and Jamaica on the other, are certainly not 'post-colonial' *in the same way.* But this does not mean that they are not 'post-colonial' *in anyway"* (246).

5. For an excellent critique of the concept of the "indigenous" see Gupta, *Postcolonial Developments,* chaps. 3–4.

6. Kath Weston, "Lesbian/Gay Studies in the House of Anthropology," *Annual Review of Anthropology* 22 (1993): 344. Examples of the growing literature of lesbian, gay, and bisexual identities outside the "West" include Dennis Altman, "Global Gaze/Global Gays," *GLQ* 3 (1997): 417–36; Evelyn Blackwood, "Tombois in West Sumatra: Constructing Masculinity and Erotic Desire," in *Female Desires: Same-Sex Relations and Transgender Practices across Cultures,* edited by Evelyn Blackwood and Saskia E. Wieringa (New York: Columbia University Press, 1999), 181–205; Donald L. Donham, "Freeing South Africa: The 'Modernization' of Male-Male Sexuality in Soweto," *Cultural Anthropology* 13 (1998): 3–21; Peter Drucker, "'In the Tropics There Is No Sin': Sexuality and Gay-Lesbian Movements in the Third World," *New Left Review,* no. 218 (1996): 75–101; Peter A. Jackson, *"Kathoey* < > Gay < > Man: The Historical Emergence of Gay Male Identity in Thailand," in *Sites of Desire, Economies of Pleasure: Sexualities in Asia and the Pacific,* edited by Lenore Manderson and Margaret Jolly (Chicago: University of Chicago Press, 1997), 166–90; Mark Johnson, *Beauty and Power: Transgendering and Cultural Transformation in the Southern Philippines* (Oxford: Berg, 1997); Martin E Manalansan IV, "In the Shadows of Stonewall: Examining Gay Transnational Politics and the Diasporic Dilemma," in *The Politics of Culture in the Shadow of Capital,* edited by Lisa Lowe and David Lloyd (Durham: Duke University Press, 1997), 485–505; Parker, *Beneath the Equator;* and Saskia E. Wieringa, "Desiring Bodies or Defiant Cultures: Butch/Femme Lesbians in Jakarta and Lima," in Blackwood and Wieringa, *Female Desires,* 206–29.

7. See Gayatri Chakravorty Spivak, *In Other Worlds: Essays in Cultural Politics* (New York: Methuen, 1987), 202; Arturo Escobar, *Encountering Development: The Making and Unmaking of the Third World* (Princeton: Princeton University Press, 1995); and James Ferguson, *The Anti-Politics Machine: "Development," Depoliticization, and Bureaucratic Power in Lesotho* (Minneapolis: University of Minnesota Press, 1994).

8. Homi K. Bhabha, *The Location of Culture* (London: Routledge, 1994), 86. For one example of this first type of reductionism see Barry D. Adam, Jan Willem Duyvendak, and

André Krouwel, editors, *The Global Emergence of Gay and Lesbian Politics: National Imprints of a Worldwide Movement* (Philadelphia: Temple University Press, 1999): "There are impressive parallels in the names of organizations: many countries have known 'gay liberation fronts,' 'revolutionary leagues,' and so on, indicating that movements follow more or less comparable paths, pass through the same phases, and draw names from other social and political movements with which there is some resemblance in terms of ideology, goals, or methods of resistance" (369–70; see also 352, 357). Cf. my discussion of GAYa Nusantara and GAYa Dewata, below.

9. Important examples of this literature include Benedict Anderson, *Imagined Communities: Reflections on the Origin and Spread of Nationalism* (London: Verso, 1983); Anderson, *Language and Power: Exploring Political Cultures in Indonesia* (Ithaca: Cornell University Press, 1990); John R. Bowen, *Muslims through Discourse: Religion and Ritual in Gayo Society* (Princeton: Princeton University Press, 1993); Suzanne Brenner, "Reconstructing Self and Society: Javanese Muslim Women and 'the Veil,'"*American Ethnologist* 23 (1996): 673–97; Brenner, *The Domestication of Desire: Women, Wealth, and Modernity in Java* (Princeton: Princeton University Press, 1998); Amen Budiman, editor, *Jalan Hidupku: Autobiografi Seorang Gay Priyayi Jawa Awal Abad XX* (1927; reprint Jakarta: Apresiasi Gay Jakarta, 1992); Robert W. Hefner, "Islam, State, and Civil Society: ICMI and the Struggle for the Indonesian Middle Class" *Indonesia* 56 (1993): 2–35; Robert W. Hefner and Patricia Horvatich, editors, *Islam in an Era of Nation-States: Polities and Religious Renewal in Muslim Southeast Asia* (Honolulu: University of Hawaii Press, 1997); John Pemberton, *On the Subject of 'Java'"* (Ithaca: Cornell University Press, 1994); Michel Picard, *Bali: Cultural Tourism and Touristic Culture* (Singapore: Archipelago, 1996); Geoffrey Robinson, *The Dark Side of Paradise: Political Violence in Bali* (Ithaca: Cornell University Press, 1995); Danilyn Rutherford, "Of Birds and Gifts: Reviving Tradition on an Indonesian Frontier" *Cultural Anthropology* 11 (1996): 577–616; Laurie J. Sears, *Shadows of Empire: Colonial Discourse and Javanese Tales* (Durham: Duke University Press, 1996); James T. Siegel, *Solo in the New Order: Language and Hierarchy in an Indonesian City* (Princeton: Princeton University Press, 1986); Siegel, *Fetish, Recognition, Revolution* (Princeton: Princeton University Press, 1997); Mary Margaret Steedly, *Hanging without a Rope: Narrative Experience in Colonial and Postcolonial Karoland* (Princeton: Princeton University Press, 1993); Anna Lowenhaupt Tsing, *In the Realm of the Diamond Queen: Marginality in an Out-of-the-Way Place* (Princeton: Princeton University Press, 1993); and Adrian Vickers, *Bali: A Paradise Created* (Hong Kong: Periplus, 1989).

10. See Dédé Oetomo, "Patterns of Bisexuality in Indonesia,' in *Bisexuality and HIV/AIDS: A Global Perspective,* edited by Rob Tielman, Manuel Carballo, and Aart Hendriks (Buffalo: Prometheus, 1991); and Oetomo, "Gender and Sexual Orientation in Indonesia," in *Fantasizing the Feminine in Indonesia,* edited by Laurie J. Sears (Durham: Duke University Press, 1996), 259–69.

11. My thanks to Lisa Rofel for helping me develop this point. I explore the implications of cogendered friendships and activities in Tom Boellstorff, "The Gay Archipelago: Translocal Identity in Indonesia," manuscript, 1999.

12. Globalization generally is highly gendered. See Gibson-Graham, *End of Capitalism;* and Maila Stivens, "Theorizing Gender Power; and Modernity in Affluent Asia," in *Gender and Power in Affluent Asia,* edited by Krishna Sen and Maila Stivens (London: Routledge, 1998), 1–34.

13. See Evelyn Blackwood, "Falling in Love with An-Other Lesbian: Reflections on Identity in Fieldwork," in *Taboo: Sex, Identity, and Erotic Subjectivity in Anthropological Fieldwork,* edited by Don Kulick and Margaret Willson (London: Routledge, 1995);

Blackwood, "Tombois in West Sumatra"; B. J. D. Gayatri, "Coming Out but Remaining Hidden: A Portrait of Lesbians in Java" (paper presented at the International Congress of Anthropological and Ethnological Sciences, Mexico City, July 1993); Gayatri, "Indonesian Lesbians Writing Their Own Script: Issues of Feminism and Sexuality," in *Amazon to Zami: Towards a Global Lesbian Feminism*, edited by Monika Reinfelder (London: Cassell, 1996), 86–97; Alison Murray, "Femme on the Streets, Butch in the Sheets (a Play on Whores)," in *Mapping Desire: Geographies of Sexualities*, edited by David Bell and Gill Valentine (London: Routledge, 1995), 66–74; Murray, "Let Them Take Ecstasy: Class and Jakarta Lesbians," in Blackwood and Wieringa, *Female Desires*, 139–56; and Wieringa, "Desiring Bodies or Defiant Cultures." In my larger project I also examine the male-to-female transgendered identity known as *waria* (Boellstorff, "Gay Archipelago," chap. 2).

14. Michel Foucault, *The Order of Things: An Archaeology of the Human Sciences* (New York: Pantheon, 1970). For a discussion of the strengths and weaknesses of Foucault's archaeological method see Hubert L. Dreyfus and Paul Rabinow, *Michel Foucault: Beyond Structuralism and Hermeneutics* (Chicago: University of Chicago Press, 1982).

15. Here I reference a discussion of sameness, difference, and postcoloniality whose detailed enumeration is beyond the scope of this chapter. For examples see Akhil Gupta, "Blurred Boundaries: The Discourse of Corruption, the Culture of Politics, and the Imagined State," *American Ethnologist* 22 (1995): 375–402; Gloria Anzaldua, *Borderlands/La Frontera* (San Francisco: Spinsters/Aunt Lute, 1987); Renato Rosaldo, *Culture and Truth: The Remaking of Social Analysis* (Boston: Beacon, 1989); and Craig Calhoun, editor, *Habermas and the Public Sphere* (Cambridge, Mass.: MIT Press, 1992).

16. This is true not only in Indonesia. See, e.g., Donham, "Freeing South Africa"; Johnson, *Beauty and Power;* Parker, *Beneath the Equator;* and Took Took Thongthiraj, "Toward a Struggle against Invisibility: Love between Women in Thailand" in *Asian American Sexualities: Dimensions of the Gay and Lesbian Experience*, edited by Russell Leong (New York: Routledge, 1996), 163–74.

17. I have also come to realize that the neglect of *gay* and *lesbi* subjectivities in Indonesian studies stems less from a putative homophobia than from the equivalencies drawn in the "western" academy between disciplines, methodologies, and discursive constitutions of the "field" as a unit of analysis. Historically, anthropologists in these islands have tended to study "ethnicities," the Javanese or Balinese or Minangkabau, rather than "Indonesians."

18. Given the limitations of space, I do not discuss conflicts in these communities in terms of gender, class, region, and so on (see, e.g., Murray, "Let Them Take Ecstasy"; Blackwood, "Tombois in West Sumatra"; Boellstorff, "Gay Archipelago"; and Oetomo, "Gender and Sexual Orientation in Indonesia"). Instead, I focus on processual formations of imagined *lesbi* and *gay* communities (i.e., the conditions of possibility for imagining intercommunity conflict in the first place).

19. For a broader discussion of the "privatization" of public spaces by lesbian, gay, bisexual, and transgendered communities see Gordon Brent Ingram, Anne-Marie Bouthillette, and Yolanda Retter, editors, *Queers in Space: Communities, Public Places, Sites of Resistance* (Seattle: Bay, 1997); and Bell and Valentine, *Mapping Desire.*

20. The distinction between "organizations" and other spaces is less clear than it might seem. Organizations tend to be small (three to ten members), and many cease to exist after three or four years. Those that survive for longer periods have usually obtained international funding, but since the primary impetus of such funding is HIV/AIDS prevention, and since international HIV/AIDS prevention discourse commonly ignores lesbians, *lesbi* groups are rarely able to access such funding, so they find it particularly difficult to sustain themselves. Only a few specifically *lesbi* magazines have ever existed: one, *GAYa*

LEStari, was published four times between February and August 1994 as a supplement to the magazine *GAYa Nusantara.* A specifically *lesbi* magazine, *MitraS,* published three issues beginning in December 1997, but it is currently on hiatus.

21. During colonial times it was hardly unusual for Indies "natives" to have greater knowledge of the "West" than "westerners" had of them. This imbalance persists today and represents a strong thread of continuity in the postcolonial context. At issue is the relationship that this knowledge bears to the *gay* or *lesbi* self.

22. For discussions of this ideology see Pemberton, *On the Subject of "Java";* Picard, *Bali;* and Rutherford, "Of Birds and Gifts."

23. Alfred Russel Wallace, *The Malay Archipelago, the Land of the Orangutan and the Bird of Paradise: A Narrative of Travel, with Studies of Man and Nature* (1869; reprint New York: Dover, 1962). The centrality of nationalism to postcoloniality has been explored thoroughly in Partha Chatterjee, *Nationalist Thought and the Colonial World: A Derivative Discourse* (Minneapolis: University of Minnesota Press, 1993); and Chatterjee, *The Nation and its Fragments: Colonial and Postcolonial Histories* (Princeton: Princeton University Press, 1993).

24. At the First International Conference of the Law of the Sea in Geneva in 1958, Indonesia argued that its borders did not lie only a certain distance from the coast of each island, as was the norm, but included all of the waters "within" the archipelago. The Second International Conference in 1960 recognized the notion of an "archipelagic state" and with it the archipelago concept. See Mochtar Kusumaatmadja, "The Concept of the Indonesian Archipelago," *Indonesian Quarterly* 10, no. 4 (1982): 19.

25. The framing of diversity in unity is common in postcolonial nationalisms (including the United States's own motto, *E Pluribus Unum*). See, e.g., Akhil Gupta, "The Song of the Nonaligned World: Transnational Identities, Late Capitalism, and the Reinscription of Space," *Cultural Anthropology* 7 (1992): 63–79.

26. Gayatri, "Indonesian Lesbians Writing Their Own Script," 94; Murray, "Let Them Take Ecstasy," 142. I explore the significance of the fact that this labeling was linked specifically to femininity in Boellstorff, "Gay Archipelago" (see also Tan beng hui, "Women's Sexuality and the Discourse on Asian Values: Cross-Dressing in Malaysia," in Blackwood and Wieringa, *Female Desires,* 289–97). But there is no a priori reason that greater oppression will not appear in Indonesia in the future. A disturbing precedent has been set by the antihomosexual group Pasrah, to my knowledge the first of its kind in Southeast Asia, which was formed in Malaysia in 1998 following the arrest of former deputy prime minister Anwar Ibrahim on sodomy and corruption charges. At present Pasrah appears to be a front organization with a manifesto but no record of activity.

27. The link between mass media and postcolonial states has been commented on in many contexts. For the case of television in India, for example, see Purnima Mankekar, *Screening Culture, Viewing Politics: An Ethnography of Television, Womanhood, and Nation in Postcolonial India* (Durham: Duke University Press, 1999).

28. That Darta and Darta's mother knew of *lesbi* first was probably due to the wide publicity given the marriage of two women in Jakarta in 1981. See Boellstorff, "Gay Archipelago."

29. About two-thirds of my informants learned of these terms through mass media. Almost all the rest learned of them from friends or by wandering into a *tempat ngeber.* Of course, there is a high probability (which I have documented in some instances) that the people who provided them with the information had themselves learned of the terms through mass media.

30. But the law is regularly flouted. See *Republika* (7 March 1998).

31. Novel Ali, "Sulih suara dorong keretakan komunikasi keluarga," in *Bercinta Dengan*

Thlevisi: Ilusi, Impresi, dan Imaji Sebuah Kotak Ajaib, edited by Deddy Mulyana and Idi Subandy Ibrahim (Bandung: PT Remaja Rosdakarya, 1997), 341–42. My translation.

32. See Dédé Oetomo, "Ketika Sharon Stone Berbahasa Indonesia," in Mulyana and Ibrahim, *Bercinta Dengan Televisi,* 333–37.

33. Even if they learn (from a non-Indonesian like me, from a mass-media source, etc.) that gay men in the "West" usually do not marry women, most Indonesian *gay* men continue to assume that they themselves will. In other words, the "western" norm is not framed as a necessary component of *gay* subjectivity in Indonesia.

34. See Shelly Errington, *Meaning and Power in a Southeast Asian Realm* (Princeton: Princeton University Press, 1989); Clifford Geertz, "From the Native's Point of View: On the Nature of Anthropological Understanding," in *Local Knowledge: Further Essays in Interpretive Anthropology* (New York: Basic, 1983), 55–72; Marilyn Strathern, *The Gender of the Gift: Problems with Women and Problems with Society in Melanesia* (Berkeley: University of California Press, 1988); and Strathern, *Reproducing the Future: Essays on Anthropology, Kinship, and the New Reproductive Technologies* (New York: Routledge, 1992).

35. Sexual dysfunction like Ikbal's is far from universal. Some married *gay* men claim that their sexual experiences with their wives are mutually satisfying.

36. For example, high-status women who are unable to find suitable partners may remain single and childless for life without compromising their femininity. See Nancy K. Florida, "Sex Wars: Writing Gender Relations in Nineteenth-Century Java," in Sears, *Fantasizing the Feminine in Indonesia,* 207–24; and Errington, *Meaning and Power.*

37. There is an extensive literature on the relationship between the postcolonial state and marriage in Indonesia. See, e.g., Sylvia Tiwon, "Models and Maniacs: Articulating the Female in Indonesia," Julia I. Suryakusuma, "The State and Sexuality in New Order Indonesia," Daniel S. Lev, "On the Other Hand?" and Benedict Anderson, "'Bullshit!' S/ he Said: The Happy, Modern, Sexy Indonesian Married Woman as Transsexual," in Sears, *Fantasizing the Feminine in Indonesia,* 47–70, 92–119, 191–202, 270–94; Evelyn Blackwood, "Senior Women, Model Mothers, and Dutiful Wives: Managing Gender Contradictions in a Minangkabau Village," in *Bewitching Women, Pious Men: Gender and Body Polities in Southeast Asia,* edited by Aihwa Ong and Michael G. Peletz (Berkeley: University of California Press, 1995), 124–58; Brenner, *Domestication of Desire;* and Barbara Ratley, "Nation, 'Tradition,' and Constructions of the Feminine in Modern Indonesian Literature," in *Imagining Indonesia: Cultural Politics and Political Culture,* edited by Jim Schiller and Barbara Martin-Schiller (Athens: Ohio University Center for International Studies, 1997), 90–120.

38. Rosalind C. Morris uses this term to refer to a similar configuration of state and marriage in Thailand ("Educating Desire: Thailand, Transnationalism, and Transgression," *Social Text,* nos. 52–53 [1997]: 53–79).

39. Here I draw on a long tradition that explores the relationship between the state, capitalism, and the family. See Dennis Altman, *Homosexual: Oppression and Liberation* (New York: Outerbridge and Diensifrey, 1971); Michael Bronski, *Culture Clash: The Making of Gay Sensibility* (Boston: South End, 1984); Bronski, *The Pleasure Principle: Sex, Backlash, and the Struggle for Gay Freedom* (New York: St. Martin's, 1998); Chatterjee, *Nationalist Thought and the Colonial World;* Chatterjee, *Nation and Its Fragments;* John D'Emilio, "Capitalism and Gay Identity," in *Powers of Desire: The Politics of Sexuality,* edited by Ann Snitow, Christine Stansell, and Sharon Thompson (New York: Monthly Review Press, 1983), 100–113; Frederick Engels, *The Origin of the Family, Private Property, and the State, in the Light of the Researches of Lewis H. Morgan,* edited by Eleanor Burke Leacock, translated by Alec West (1884; reprint New York: International, 1942);

Richard K. Herrell, "Sin, Sickness, Crime: Queer Desire and the American State," in *The Nation/State and Its Sexual Dissidents*, edited by David Murray and Richard Handler (Newark, N.J.: Gordon and Breach, 1996), 273–300; Guy Hocquenghem, *Homosexual Desire*, translated by Daniella Dangoor (London: Allison and Busby, 1978); Andrew Parker et al., editors, *Nationalisms and Sexualities* (New York: Routledge, 1992); Linda Singer, "Sex and the Logic of Late Capitalism," in *Erotic Welfare: Sexual Theory and Politics in the Age of Epidemic*, by Linda Singer; edited by Judith Butler and Maureen MacGrogan (New York: Routledge, 1993), 34–61; and Eli Zaretsky, *Capitalism, the Family, and Personal Life* (New York: Harper & Row, 1976).

40. Quoted in Richard Tanter and Kenneth Young, eds., *The Politics of Middle Class Indonesia* (Clayton, Australia: Monash University Centre of Southeast Asian Studies, 1990), 26. There is a burgeoning literature on the new middle class and consumerism in Southeast Asia, including, besides Tanter and Young's work, Michael Pinches, editor, *Culture and Privilege in Capitalist Asia* (London: Routledge, 1999); Richard Robison and David S. G. Goodman, editors, *The New Rich in Asia: Mobile Phones, McDonalds, and Middle-Class Revolution* (London: Routledge, 1996); and Krishna Sen and Maila Stivens, editors, *Gender and Power in Affluent Asia* (London: Routledge, 1998).

41. Quoted in Tanter and Young, *Politics of Middle Class Indonesia*, 64. Pinches emphasizes the importance of understanding middle classes in Asia in terms of "the processes of status formation through the shared symbols of lifestyle and consumption" rather than solely in terms of raw income *(Culture and Privilege in Capitalist Asia*, 8). See also Gibson-Graham's processual theory of class *(End of Capitalism*, 46–71).

42. See, e.g., Marcel Mauss, "A Category of the Human Mind: The Notion of the Person; the Notion of Self" (1938), in *Sociology and Psychology: Essays*, translated by Ben Brewster (London: Routledge and Kegan Paul, 1979), 57–94; and Michel Foucault, *The History of Sexuality*, translated by Robert Hurley, 3 vols. (New York: Pantheon, 1978–86).

43. More generally, Arjun Appadurai notes that "until recently . . . a case could be made that social life was largely inertial, that traditions provided a relatively finite set of possible lives" ("Global Ethnoscapes: Notes and Queries for a Transnational Anthropology," in *Modernity at Large*, 53).

44. See Jane E Collier; Bill Maurer; and Lilana Suarez-Navaz, "Sanctioned Identities: Legal Constructions of Modern Personhood," *Identities* 2 (1995): 1–27; John L. Comaroff, "Images of Empire, Contests of Conscience: Models of Colonial Domination in South Africa," in *Tensions of Empire: Colonial Cultures in a Bourgeois World*, edited by Frederick Cooper and Ann Laura Stoler (Berkeley: University of California Press, 1997), 163–97; and C. B. Macpherson, *The Political Theory of Possessive Individualism: Hobbes to Locke* (Oxford: Clarendon, 1962).

45. Nor are apparent contradictions inevitably a site of resistance. Stuart Hall notes: "In our intellectual way, we think that the world will collapse as the result of a logical contradiction: this is the illusion of the intellectual—that ideology must be coherent, every bit of it fitting together; like a philosophical investigation. When, in fact, the whole purpose of what Gramsci called an organic (i.e., historically effective) ideology is that it articulates into a configuration different subjects, different identities, different projects, different aspirations. It does not reflect, it constructs a 'unity' out of difference" ("Gramsci and Us," in *The Hard Road to Renewal: Thatcherism and the Crisis of the Left* [London: Verso, 1988], 166). David M. Halperin makes precisely this point with respect to "western" homophobia: "Homophobic discourses are incoherent, then, but their incoherence, far from incapacitating them, turns out to empower them. In fact, homophobic discourses operate strategically by means of logical contradictions" *(Saint Foucault: Towards a Gay*

Hagiography [New York: Oxford University Press, 1995], 34).

46. It is in this context that the existence of the term *biseks* in Indonesia is so interesting. While its range is much smaller than that of *lesbi* or *gay, biseks* is known to a substantial number of men and women. Men and women who identify as *biseks* almost always identify as *lesbi* or *gay* as well; it is a dual subjectivity lexicalizing simultaneous same-sex and opposite-sex interests (i.e., a *gay* man who is married to a woman will sometimes say that he is *"gay* and *biseks,"* but not *biseks* alone). While there are *biseks* subjectivities, there is no *"biseks* world," no *dunia biseks;* these men and women see themselves as part of the *gay* world. In the Indonesian context, what is significant is not that this subjectivity calls into being a different community but that it implies, contrary to the dominant view, that *gay* and *lesbi* subjectivities exclude marriage.

47. "A productive question is to ask how culturally-specific domains have been dialectically formed and transformed in relation with other cultural domains, how meanings migrate across domain boundaries, and how specific actions are multiply constituted. In other words, we need to historicize our domains and trace their effects" (Sylvia Yanagisako and Carol Delaney, introduction to *Naturalizing Power: Essays in Feminist Cultural Analysis,* edited by Sylvia Yanagisako and Carol Delaney [New York: Routledge, 1995], 11).

48. E.g., Judith Butler, *Bodies That Matter: On the Discursive Limits of "Sex "* (New York: Routledge, 1993); Foucault, *History of Sexuality,* vol. 1; Halperin, *Saint Foucault;* Eve Kosofsky Sedgwick, *Epistemology of the Closet* (London: Harvester Wheatsheaf, 1991).

49. Budiman, *Jalan Hidupku,* 111–14. My translation.

50. Sucipto himself never terms his writings "autobiography" or "memoir."

51. Generalizing from a single historical source is precarious but necessitated by the fact that Sucipto's is the only known text of its type from the colonial era. Interviews with informants in their fifties and sixties, although they do not extend quite so far into the past, corroborate important aspects of Sucipto's narrative.

WORKS CITED

Appadurai, Arjun. *Modernity at Large: Cultural Dimensions of Globalization.* Minneapolis: University of Minnesota Press, 1996.

Bourdieu, Pierre. *Outline of a Theory of Practice,* translated by Richard Nice. Cambridge: Cambridge University Press, 1977.

Chatterjee, Partha. *The Nation and Its Fragments: Colonial and Postcolonial Histories.* Princeton: Princeton University Press, 1993.

Chauncey, George. *Gay New York: Gender Urban Culture, and the Making of the Gay Male World, 1890–1940.* New York: Basic, 1994.

Cheah, Pheng and Bruce Robbins, eds. *Cosmopolitics: Thinking and Feeling Beyond the Nation.* Minneapolis: University of Minnesota Press, 1998.

Gupta, Akhil. *Postcolonial Developments: Agriculture in the Making of Modern India.* Durham: Duke University Press, 1998.

Hall, Stuart. "The Question of Cultural Identity." In: *Understanding Modern Societies: An Introduction.* Edited by Stuart Hall and others. Cambridge, MA: Blackwell, 1995. 596–633.

Hill, Hal. *The Indonesian Economy since 1966: Southeast Asia's Emerging Giant.* Cambridge: Cambridge University Press, 1996.

Kusumaatmadja, Mochtar. "The Concept of the Indonesian Archipelago." *Indonesian Quarterly* 10.4 (1982).

Miller, Daniel, editor. *Worlds Apart: Modernity through the Prism of the Local.* London: Routledge, 1995.

Toer, Pramoedya Ananta. *Footsteps,* edited and translated by Max Lane. New York: Penguin, 1990.

Winters, Jeffrey A. *Power in Motion: Capital Mobility and the Indonesian State.* Ithaca: Cornell University Press, 1996.

Young, Robert J. C. *Colonial Desire: Hybridity in Theory, Culture, and Race.* London: Routledge, 1995.

Chapter 3

The Queer Sort of Fandom for *Heavenly Creatures:* The Closeted Indigene, Lesbian Islands, and New Zealand National Cinema

Elizabeth Guzik

> What these monsters stand for, to us, is the symbolic transposition of the place where they stand, the literary topos being literally, in this case, a topographical projection; the *limen*, frontier between the desert and the city, the threshold to the inner recesses of the cave or maze, metaphorizes the symbolic boundary between nature and culture, the limit and the test imposed upon man.—Teresa de Lauretis, *Alice Doesn't: Feminism, Semiotics and Cinema*

> True Siamese twins in spirit [âmes siamoises], they formed a world forever closed; reading their dispositions after the crime, Doctor Logre said, "one would think they were seeing double." With only the resources of their islet, they had to resolve their enigma, the human enigma of sex.—Jacques Lacan discussing the Papin sisters, Christine and Lea, whose case inspired *Sister, My Sister*

While *Heavenly Creatures* may have been a critical success, the film did not exactly have the characteristics of films typically associated with masses of fans like the *Star Wars* trilogy or the *Star Trek* series, both of which conjure up images of devoted, perhaps obsessed, fans flocking to conventions or movie premieres decked out in the milieu-specific regalia and speaking imagined languages, such as Klingon. The monsters in Peter Jackson's film are less clearly marked by makeup, and the strange codes that the girls used to communicate with each other are based on evidence found in the same diaries used to convict the real-world Juliet Hulme and Pauline Parker of the 1954 murder of Honora Parker in Christchurch, New Zealand. A community of fans of this limited release film might well have had a hard time finding one another if not for the advent of the Internet, which provides a fairly inexpensive forum in which fans of any text can create virtual communities that can reach into even the most distant corners of the globe, unhindered by limitations of geography.[1] Adam Abrams' site devoted to the film, titled "The

Fourth World—The *Heavenly Creatures* Website," is filled with extensive information about the film to help the most devoted fans learn all that they can about their favorite movie. The site seems to reflect two pressing questions of fans: Were Juliet and Pauline involved with each other sexually? And, how accurate was the film in representing the real-world events of the 1954 Parker-Hulme murder?

In this case, the fans seem to be asking the very same question that concerns critics, at least as critics attempt to deal with the complex issues raised by Jackson's film. Whatever the actions of Pauline and Juliet of Christchurch, Jackson's film portrays the relationship between the girls as a sexual one. As such, the film inevitably enters into the limited ranks of "lesbian films" that queer women can seek out either in theaters or in video stores when they want to see representations of queer desire on screen. Though a New Queer Cinema may be growing, the women's list of such films is still short enough to assure that those films on the list are often seen repeatedly if only because there are not many of them, creating yet another specialized fan community.

It is the criticism of this last fan group that brings the discussion back to questions of accuracy of representation in the film. Buzz within the lesbian community about the film has had much to do with the fact that *Heavenly Creatures* is another installment in the progression of murderous dyke films. While some lesbians see the film as a clever play on the conventions of the murderous-duo narrative, others are repulsed by the violence and distressed by the connection to a real-world event. Those who are suspicious of representations of killer lesbians have good reason for skepticism. In the 1990s, the 1950s image of the tragic, predatory, or suicidal lesbian in film is transformed into the murderous dyke.[2] Sharon Stone's ice-pick killer *Basic Instinct* has become the poster girl for the femme fatal of the 1990s, who shows interest in the wrong girl instead of (or in addition to) the leading man. Though lesbian visibility on television in the United States has improved, and there have been more films about lesbians who are not killers, the homicidal lesbian remains a mainstay on the silver screen.[3]

However, to examine Jackson's film only from the perspective of yet another white lesbian misses crucial aspects of the film. Despite the presence of a now well-known British Kate Winslet, *Heavenly Creatures* is a predominantly New Zealand production. In his own country, director Peter Jackson is best known for his horror pictures. Too many lesbians in the United States have rushed to analyze the film with lesbian content in terms of what it means to the lesbian community here without paying enough attention to the specific national context from which the text comes. There seem to be several significant factors feeding into this cultural colonialism: the mainstream (white) lesbian community's desperation for representation is only one. The new electronic forms of global fandom also decontextualize films at the same time that they help promote increased global profits for the creators of such texts.

Fandom is crucial to an understanding of *Heavenly Creatures*, in both the diegetic and non-diegetic realms of the film. Its New Queer Cinema themes entered the film into the Dyke Flick canon, and its self-conscious play with the conventions of the killer-dyke narrative and its cinematic fantasia made scholars take notice, creating two specialized and occasionally overlapping fan communities. However, the film itself demonstrates how women on the margins, in terms of both sexuality and nationality, can shape mainstream images, whether from straight romance narratives or from Hollywood cinema, to their own desires. This use of fandom reveals New Zealand's struggle to come to terms with its own national identity while struggling to define a space for itself within the international film community. Because the representations of nationality and sexuality are so intimately linked with the film, and because these tropes seem common to much of New Zealand film, a reading of one is incomplete without the other. The fandom surrounding *Heavenly Creatures* cleanly exposes the contradictory effects of an increasingly global culture: the potential for cultural imperialism of some countries masked by the universality and cultural "neutrality" of forums such as the Internet clashing with the economic rewards of producing a text that can cross over and reach a broader audience internationally and, thus, bring home more profits.

WHEN *FOLIE À DEUX* SPREADS: A MOB OF TWO AND THE PARKER-HULME CASE

> The insight of *Heavenly Creatures* is that sometimes people are capable of committing acts together that they could not commit by themselves. A mob can be as small as two persons. Reading in the paper recently about a crowd of teenage boys who beat an innocent youth to death, I was reminded of this film.—Roger Ebert's review of *Heavenly Creatures*

Constrained by the New Zealand legal system after both girls had confessed to the murder, the lawyers for Pauline and Juliet had to be creative in constructing a defense. They could argue that the two were not guilty only by reason of insanity. The lawyers were then faced with the problem that both girls appeared sane. A psychiatrist for the defense adopted the notion of *folie à deux,* or joint madness. This defense had been used to defend other pairs of queer killers. In the 1930s, *folie à deux* was used in the United States to defend Leopold and Loeb, a famous case later fictionalized in Hitchcock's *Rope* and its New Queer retelling, *Swoon.*

Deeper roots, however, seem to have been laid by Jacques Lacan himself in an article printed in *La Minotare* about the case from Le Mans, France. In "Motives of Paranoiac Crime: The Crime of the Papin Sisters," Lacan explores the characteristics of this shared delirium which caused two sisters (who seemed to be sexually involved with each other, psychologically if not physically) to kill their mistress and her daughter in a hyperbolic frenzy that bears eerie similarities to the Parker-Hulme case:

The attack . . . was sudden, simultaneous, carried out at once to a paroxysm of rage: each seized an adversary, tore her eyes from their sockets (a deed unheard of, it was said, in the annals of crime), and brained her. Next, with the aid of what could be found within reach, hammer, tin pitcher, kitchen knife, they assailed the bodies of the victims, bashing their faces. (Lacan, 7)

Though there are notable differences between the two murders, there are enough similarities to take notice. Both attacks were characterized as excessively violent and unprecedented, both attacks involved massive blows to the heads of the victims, and both attacks involved a cross-class assault. Lacan called the insanity of their mob of two *délire à deux*, in a paper first published in 1933, as popular culture was pathologizing homosexuality in the way that would come to characterize it for the rest of the twentieth century.

One critical aspect of both *folie à deux* and *delire a deux* is the notion that two otherwise sane individuals become mad when in the presence of the other. Lacan notes: "They appeared to three medical experts to have no sign of delirium, nor of insanity, nor any real psychic or physical disorder, a fact which perforce had to be recorded" (7). Juliet Hulme and Pauline Parker also appeared by all psychological evaluations to be perfectly sane once separated. As it was used in the Parker-Hulme case, *folie à deux* suggested that the girls murdered Honora because they were insane when they were together. While I am not convinced that the girls were insane when they were together (and neither was the jury), the fact remains that the notions that underlie *folie à deux* remain central to the lesbian stereotypes that still haunt cinema, television, and literature in the United States today.

As Ebert's review of *Heavenly Creatures* suggests, the notion that one individual can develop a temporary insanity as a result of proximity to another is a theory not restricted to arcane legal defenses of killer-queer couples. The same paradigm has been used to explain the behavior of crowds and mobs that commit violence at public venues such as rock concerts and sporting matches.[4] In his review, Ebert suggests that two can make a mob. Such an assertion raises the question of whether analyses of the influence of the frenzied mob and the seduction of *folie à deux* have something in common.

Jenson's analysis of "Fandom as Pathology" posits that two images of the fan, the isolated and obsessed individual and the crazed and overpowering mob, both present critiques of the modern condition, the alienated individual, and the mass consumers so easily duped by advertising. Not only do both images invoke the fan community represented in Adams' website, but they also raise the specter of the lesbian community as it has been constructed in popular representations.

FANDOM AS A THREAT TO THE MALE-FEMALE-MALE ECONOMY

> Part of the appeal of the male star . . . . was that you would *never* marry him; the romance would never end in the tedium of marriage. . . . It was inconceivable that any fan would actually marry a Beatle or sleep with him (sexually active "groupies" were still a few years off) or even hold

his hand. Adulation of the male star was a way to express sexual yearnings that would normally be . . . repressed. The star could be loved noninstrumentally, for his own sake, and with complete abandon.—Ehrenreich, Hess, and Jacobs in *The Adoring Audience*

The epigraph above is from an article in which Ehrenreich, Hess, and Jacobs examine the fandom associated with Beatlemania, which postdates the 1954 Parker-Hulme case, but clearly predates Jackson's film. Their most compelling point is that the hysterical fandom enacted by teenage girls uses an idol not as a direct object of the fans' desire, but as an image onto which girls can project sexual urges that are being repressed by the dominant culture. Ehrenreich, Hess, and Jacobs focus on the way in which the very impossibility of any actual relationship with the idol allows fans to escape from conventional standards of sexual behavior. In their analysis, the trope of fandom shows the attempted escape from the constrains of hegemonic morality, in the same way that the film *Heavenly Creatures* attempts to do. Juliet and Pauline attempt to escape the mundane prospects of the scripted roles of women in their culture at the time, as Case points out in her analysis of the film:

For Pauline Parker and Juliet Hulme in their lesbian relationship, this fandom offered a zone outside the expectations of compulsory heterosexuality—a possible realm for circulating images of desire between them. . . . Their lesbian relations, then, were inextricably caught up in the virtual realm of fandom. (60)

The girls do circulate images of desire between them, seeming to use their idols as a point of contact or a screen for the desire that society will not allow them to speak of directly.

Fandom as a trope sets up an economy of exchange radically different from that most common to narrative: woman as an object of exchange between two men. Sedgwick's analysis explores the way in which the exchange of one woman between two powerful men allows them to express homosocial desire in a trope prevalent throughout English and American literature and film. In her attempt to define lesbian narrative, Castle posits a different possibility in her attempt to explain the ghosting of lesbian representation in literature. One of the reasons that lesbians are so hard to find in literature as anything other than an apparition, Castle argues, is that desire between women is so destabilizing to the traditional narrative. Desire between two women not only breaks down the male-female-male triangle that Sedgwick explicates, but raises a still more disruptive possibility: the female-male-female triangle. And it is precisely that triangle that female fandom creates. In the case of *Heavenly Creatures*, Juliet-Mario-Pauline is the triangle that poses a threat to the economy of exchange.

At Christchurch Girls' High School, where the girls first meet, Pauline notices the assertive Juliet as she gleefully corrects her French teacher's grammar in class. However, Juliet does not seem to reciprocate that interest until Pauline compliments her for her depiction of Mario Lanza in a drawing in her art class. That same drawing earns the teacher's reproach for failing to obey the rules. After Juliet sticks her tongue out at Miss Collins behind her back, Pauline tells Juliet that she thinks her drawing is "fantastic." In their fantasy world, the two girls connect through their fantasies about idols like Mario Lanza, but physically express their desire with each other. The man, then, serves as a point of contact between two women, only to fall away as the women connect with each other—thus supporting Terry Castle's theorization of the lesbian narrative.

Juliet and Pauline's only sexually explicit scene in *Heavenly Creatures* is firmly situated within the context of fandom and their fantasy world. The sequence begins with the two girls watching *The Third Man* in a movie theater. The first shot in the theater shows the screen and the audience watching the events unfold in black and white. We see the girls exit from the theater, and watch them react in horror to Orson Welles lurking in a dark alley. As the girls scream and run from him, they travel through a world of noir, with oblique camera angles and the lighting so typical of the genre. Welles chases them through the street outside the theater and into Juliet's house. Once they enter Ilam, Welles is shown in black and white, though the girls and the house remain in color. They collapse on the bed, laughing. Pauline's voice-over interrupts, "We talked for some time about It— getting ourselves more and more excited." There is a pause in the voice-over as the camera shifts from its focus on Juliet, who is now supine on the bed, to a shadow cast on the wall moving in from above her. The shadow is of Welles's silhouette, yet as Pauline's voice-over returns, concluding, "We enacted how each saint would make love in bed," the camera cuts to Pauline's face and seems to shift from color to an almost black-and-white tone from the green lighting. She leans down to kiss Juliet, who then becomes engulfed in the same green lighting which washes out her color, so that as they kiss, the two girls appear to have faded into the black-and-white world of noir. As Pauline pulls back from the kiss, the lighting shifts again, Juliet's face appears lit on one side in red, and the other in green as she looks on in horror and ecstasy as the music turns ominous. The camera shifts to Pauline, who morphs into Orson Welles. A gloved hand in brown leather creeps toward Juliet's neck as Welles leans down to kiss her neck. The scene cuts abruptly, punctuated by the sounds of a blade slicing though something, to a plasticine figure of Diello engaged in a sword fight in Borovnia. Shots of Pauline are intercut with his slicings. The girls have shifted, and Pauline is now on her back, looking up at the camera. Welles's still gloved (though now clay) hand reaches for her face. As he leans in to kiss her, he sweeps her off the bed. While he turns her around to lean her against the wall, Pauline shifts into Gina, her plasticine avatar in Borovnia. As the camera zooms out to reveal a wider shot of Borovnia, a scene of plasticine polymorphous perversity unfolds. An orgy is apparently in progress in the castle, with a multitude of gender-indeterminate bodies writhing in sexual ecstasy. Out of the debauchery at the bottom of the screen rises Juliet's fair-haired face, initially lit from above, lending a halo-like glow to her. The lighting returns to the half-green and half-red scheme that began the scene. And as Juliet leans down to kiss Pauline again, it becomes clear that both girls are now shirtless. As they kiss and embrace, Pauline's voice-over returns, saying, "We spent a hectic night going through the saints. It was wonderful—heavenly—beautiful—and ours. We felt satisfied indeed. We have now learned the peace of the thing called bliss, the joy of the thing called sin."

Thus, the most explicit scene of lesbian desire in this film is intimately linked with fantasy and fandom. While the girls' use of the saints, as they referred to their film idols, could be read as a kind of cover used to rationalize their actions as not being lesbian, such a reading is only one of a number of possibilities. The way in which Pauline and Juliet express desire for stars can be seen as a kind of adolescent experimentation, in the same way that Jane Campion's short film *Girls Own Stories* shows teenage girls wearing Beatles' masks kissing the masks. In addition, because of the catalytic presence of Welles, the scene can be read as an indictment of the seduction that American popular culture holds for some New Zealanders. And yet, the scene ends with the girls kissing each other as themselves. It would seem that the girls' use of fandom in Jackson's *Heavenly Creatures* attempts to create a space outside of the male-female-male economy, allowing for a representation of desire between two women, but that same trope also depends upon another hidden trope raised by the film's geographical setting. Their fantasy realm is named the fourth world, and questions of nationality and ethnicity are interlaced with fandom as well.

BEATLEMANIA MEETS NATIONALITY: NEW ZEALAND AND CULTURAL ANXIETY

The Parker-Hulme murder may have occurred in 1954, but the film that brought the case to the attention of international audiences was released in 1994. In the intervening forty years, New Zealand has undergone a number of cultural shifts. Many of those shifts have had to do with Aotearoa's attempts to come to terms with its own complex history and questions of national identity.

New Zealand has a long, complicated history of multiple colonizations. As an island in what is now often called Polynesia, it seems to have originally been settled by a group of people from another island in the region, who came to hunt moa, a now extinct bird. This culture intermarried with the Maori and/or relocated to the Chatham Islands. Some people say that the last survivor of this culture died out in the mid-twentieth century, but there does not seem to be much agreement on this topic. The Maori were the only inhabitants of the island until the late eighteenth century, when European explorers began to attempt to establish posts on North Island. It was through these encounters that the western world began to develop a knowledge of the now-legendary fierceness of the Maori warriors.

In 1840, the Maori signed the Treaty Waitangi, submitting themselves to the rule of the British Government in hopes of maintaining and protecting their land. For the first year under the British, New Zealand was actually a dependency of Australia, governed through New South Wales. While New Zealand was officially declared a separate British colony in 1841, the cultural colonization of New Zealand by Australia has continued to the present day in some ways. For many geographically uninformed Americans sitting down to a screening of *Heavenly Creatures*, New Zealand is linked with Australia in terms of geography and culture.

Even though the New Zealand film industry is slowly gaining international recognition, films from Aotearoa are not necessarily known as New Zealand films. In addition, New Zealand still does not have its own major film school. As a result, the most promising directors are often trained and educated in Australia, and once successful, often find the lure of Hollywood irresistible. Some of New Zealand's most famous filmmakers have moved to America, or are internationally respected as auteurs who are not known by nationality. Such is the case with Jane Campion, who is better known as a feminist filmmaker than as a New Zealand director, in much the same way that Chantal Akerman is better known as an international auteur than as a star of the Belgian cinema.

In recent years, Aotearoa has had to come to terms with its role in the global economy and the revision of history to include a fairer history of this island. There have been a number of cultural productions concerned with retelling history from a perspective more informed by those voices most often left out of traditional histories.[5] In 1993, the elections for Parliament in New Zealand were so close that no one party received a majority on the first vote. In her analysis of the recent focus on history in contemporary New Zealand film and literature, Anne Maxwell notes:

In New Zealand, the interest of history writing has been spurred by the public concern over the "inhuman" effects that have accompanied the nation's recent entry into global markets. If the results of the 1993 general election are anything to go by, there is a widespread feeling that the social turbulence that New Zealanders have experienced over recent years needs to be stabilised so that people can recover their bearings. Part of this stabilising process, it would seem, involves embracing a political system that gives more say to minority parties. (232)

What is most striking in this passage to readers not from New Zealand is the connection between a more stable national government and a political system that gives more say to minority parties. In the United States the exact opposite is usually thought to be the case. It is the more liberal Democratic party that is associated both with social turmoil and with stronger minority representation. Also notable, however, is the perceived connection between socioeconomic unrest at home and Aotearoa's entry into the global economy.

The impact of entry into the global economy is highly relevant to a discussion of *Heavenly Creatures*, a very successful film within New Zealand that also enjoyed extensive international success. This success quickly followed the film from Aotearoa that has been the most successful to date, Jane Campion's *The Piano*. It would seem, then, that national concerns about increasing involvement in a global economy coincided with an increased visibility of Kiwi films in the international cinema market. As a result, cultural anxieties about this new role naturally creep into the films produced in this context.

Quoting from Hancock's historical study of Australia, Schaffer describes the way in which national relationship to both England and Britain is similar to a man's relationship with a mistress:

Reflecting on the ambivalence inherent in the theme of two mistresses, "A country is a jealous mistress and patriotism is commonly an exclusive passion; but it is not impossible for Australians, nourished by a glorious literature and haunted by old memories, to be in love with two soils." (85)

If the splitting of Australia's erotic attachment to two lovers—Britain and England—is the result of its colonization process, then New Zealand must be a site for polymorphous perversity, for New Zealand has a busy bedroom. Thus, we run headlong into the problems with this metaphor. The notion of a countryman with allegiances to two mistresses immediately presumes the citizen to be male, and yet Aotearoa is often gendered as female in its inferior role to Australia. New Zealanders must split their interest among at least four mistresses, and must do so while often being read as female by themselves and those outside the country. It is this complex series of colonizations that influences many of the tropes most common to New Zealand film.

Representations of teenage girls have become a staple for New Zealand film, particularly those directed by women. Such images can be read as the result of the focus of 1970s feminism on relationships between daughters and mothers: "[t]his privileging of the child's (particularly the girl's) point of view seems to be a quintessential aspect of the Australian women's wave" (Robson and Zalcock 60). However, the prevalence of these images also seems to be connected to New Zealand's most recent efforts to contend with its new role in a global economy. In that context, national anxieties about being "the little sister" trying to interject something into the international conversation of more established nations are played out in images in New Zealand film. Though the United States has had little to do with the political colonization of New Zealand, there are fears that the cultural influence of the United States has become too strong. In their analysis of *Crush*, Robson and Zalcock discuss the role that the American character plays in the film and in New Zealand cinema, "Just as Pakeha have intruded into Maori culture, so too, the film suggests, America has intruded . . . and corrupted its life-style and values" (89). It seems not coincidental, then, that the medium through which Pauline and Juliet give themselves permission to explore desire between each other is through the intercession of one of their American saints developed from the films of the United States.

THE CLOSETED INDIGENE: HIDDEN LINKS BETWEEN BOROVNIA AND MAORI

New Zealand is neither Maori nor Pakeha, neither coloniser nor colonized; yet it is all these things and other things as well: biculturalism, both as official policy and as a model of nationhood, is too restrictive to contain the range of experience enacted in and by New Zealand drama. (Tompkins 294)

Lesbian theory's answer to this has been to construct *imaginable* communities. . . . However, by changing the focus of the spectacle—transporting it over state lines, as it were—lesbian theory has neglected to engage the political problem of feminine spectacle in mass society. (174–75)

Thus, fandom as well as New Zealand's complex history of colonization further muddy an already difficult triangle of nationality and sexuality in *Heavenly Creatures*, but it is precisely that triangle that helps to make explicit the way in which much of (white) lesbian theory and culture relies upon tropes borrowed from other cultures without making that use explicit. This film provides only one example of the reason that white lesbians need to look at questions of postcolonialism and nationality in even the most seemingly white texts. Berlant and Freeman attempt to theorize about Queer Nationality and run headlong into this problem. The citizen is an abstract being, safely freed from any distractions of the body and its tendencies toward abjection. Abstraction, however, reads as a male trope in our culture, as Berlant and Freeman point out in their analysis of citizenship: "Female subjects are always citizens in masquerade: The more sexual they appear, the less abstractable they are in a liberal corporeal schema" (174).

Thus, female subjects can only be citizens by masquerading as men. The more sexual a person appears, the less abstractable he or she becomes, and that abstractability is necessary for citizenship. Once a woman makes herself even more sexualized by declaring herself to be someone who practices a sexuality that is read as aberrant, she has further embodied herself. Thus, lesbians and bisexual women declaring themselves to be queer do not remove themselves from the economy of sexual exchange at work in the culture of the United States, but, as the phenomenon of lipstick lesbian chic and the prevalence of girl-on-girl scenes in porn aimed straight at men makes clear, simply make themselves an even more valuable object to acquire. The straight man who could turn a lesbian gains masculinity. The problem with identity categories based on sexual preference is that they inevitably conjure up images of sexual acts—acts that are defined as deviant, and even if women who declare their attraction to other women could remove themselves from the economy of sexual exchange, the perceived deviancy of such acts would still increase their abject or liminal status, and disrupt the possibility of abstraction so necessary for the definition of a citizen.

Instead of even having access to Anderson's imagined communities, lesbians are thus reduced to what Berlant and Freeman define as imaginable communities—places that we can create in our minds, but often cannot even realize the illusion of in the material realm. Often, these imagined communities exist on islands or other far-off lands—whether separated by time or geography, or both.[6] While the imaginability may provide a potential way around the problems with being too abject to be abstract, it can also lead to an inclination to appropriate images, texts, or elements of other cultures without full consideration of the colonializing impulses at work.

In this film, this becomes most clear through the name Juliet gives to her fantasy realm: the Fourth World. However, this is not the only link between Juliet and Pauline's fantasy world and the Maori. As Juliet describes the place to Pauline, she declares that the Fourth World is similar to heaven, but better because there will not be any Christians there. While at the time of the actual murder and trial such statements were used to indict the girls as immoral, today such a remark invokes the specter of colonialism, as so many early colonizers, especially among the islands in the Pacific, were Christian missionaries.

Juliet and Pauline's fantasy world, as described in the diaries, features a pantheon of saints, who faded in and out of prominence depending on the fleeting opinions of the girls. However, the film focuses primarily on Mario Lanza. Viewers most often hear the girls singing his praises (and songs). Early in the film, Pauline returns home from school, and nearly plows over one of the boarders in her house to play Mario's record. As Pauline sings along, her father teases from the other room, asking, "Isn't that Mary O'Lanza, the famous Irish singer?" Pauline, annoyed, corrects Herbert, informing us that he is Italian. Herbert's play on Mario's name not only cross-genders him, turning Mario into a Mary, but also shifts his ethnicity to one that has more explicit history of colonization. Most significantly, Mario is an anagram for Maori. The girls had a number of idols, and the prominence of this particularly named one, as well as the focus on name play in the film itself, questions the relationship between erotic fantasy, Pakeha society, and Maori culture.

Jackson's version of the story may well have been influenced by the research done by Glamuzina and Laurie in *Parker & Hulme: A Lesbian View*. In their investigation of all possible motives for Honora Parker's murder, the authors spoke to a Maori Tohunga, or spiritual leader, who provided an alternate reading of the events leading up to the death of Honora. Maori friends of the authors tipped them off to the fact that Port Levy, where the Hulmes vacationed, taking Pauline along, was a spiritually significant site for at least six centuries. The land at Port Levy that the Hulmes owned had only been sold to a white family within the last hundred years (Glamuzina and Laurie 147). Furthermore, the girls were vacationing there during Easter, a holiday that coincides with a time in the Maori calendar when "a gateway through the clouds may be interpreted as a way to ascend to other worlds" (148). To reach those worlds, the Maori look for the help of gatekeepers who, the Tohunga noted, were quite similar to the saints the girls developed (148). Once she was imprisoned, Pauline Parker studied Maori while she was in prison serving out her sentence (105).

All of these facts seem to be foregrounded in the interpretation of the story that the film offers to viewers. During the film, the first time the Fourth World begins to be embodied occurs while the family vacations at Port Levy. It is during these scenes that the girls narrate their latest installment of the story while the camera assumes the point of view of one Borovnian character, rushing through the sand castle the girls have built. The shift from virtuality to greater realism is complete when Juliet runs away from her parents upset, and the girls are transported into the Fourth World fully realized on the screen for the first time, though it looks more like a fine English landscape garden than a representation of the bush.

In fact, the ambiguity of the fantasy world of the girls seems to embody the busy bedroom of the many mistresses that characterize New Zealand's complex colonial history. The Fourth World alternates between the landscaped English garden, a ship just setting sail, and the faux royalty of Borovnia. All have very different visual styles on screen. The garden appears only once, and features that strange blend of animation and live action that make the film feel Disneyesque and childish, as the scenes from *Mary Poppins* do. The ship scenes show the girls as sisters, happily waving bon voyage while smiling adoringly at their parents, Dr. and Mrs. Hulme. None of the marital problems that the couple evinces in the film are made explicit here. And the Borovnian scenes are the most fantastic, featuring full-size plasticine versions of the character from their fantasy world in a carnivalesque atmosphere. The Gothic elements of the Borovnian scenes are as striking as the nostalgia of the ship scenes, and each raises questions about the connections between fantasy of colonialism.

While fantasy may be one of the most trivialized genres in film and television, often read as the realm of children, representations of lesbians on screens, silver or small, increasingly seem to be emerging in this genre. *Heavenly Creatures'* "ninja turtle style," as B. Ruby Rich describes the grotesque elements, bears a striking resemblance to another pop culture lesbian text with links to Aotearoa. *Xena: Warrior Princess,* with the over-the-top style of producer Sam Raimi influencing it, has become one of the surprise hits of the 1997 syndication market. The show, a spin-off of *Hercules: The Legendary Journeys,* has a dedicated following of women, and a not-so-subtle subtext between Xena and her companion, Gabrielle. The subtext has sparked an article in *Ms.,* a spoof of the lesbian content on *Saturday Night Live,* and a webring of sites devoted to "Seers of the Subtext" featuring carefully paused stills from various episodes that clearly emphasize the sapphic potential of their relationship. Like its parent show, *Xena* is filmed in New Zealand, in part because of the island's legendary scenery, but also because production costs there are so much lower than those in the United States. And like *Heavenly Creatures,* the fan community has been able to produce its culture on the Internet, overcoming any geographical limitations.

Like Pauline and Juliet, Gabrielle and Xena get paired up when Gabrielle insists on following Xena, admiring her exploits and wanting to make stories out of them. Fandom provides the link, and narrative fuels the desire. Just as Berlant and Freeman suggest, Xena's tales are imaginable, lacking some of the historical and textual support that Hercules gets from classic mythology. And both texts have created fan bases that participate in the perpetuation of the global nature of the texts by taking them to the internet.

Both texts rely upon the closeted uses of other cultures to create their more distinctly queer elements: *Heavenly Creatures* uses the Fourth World as a place to express desire between women that cannot be expressed in Pakeha New Zealand,

and *Xena* derives both her name and her signature nonphallic weapon from South Asian cultures.[7] While two texts do not necessarily make a trend, it would seem that only a more thorough examination of the relationship between fantasy and colonialism in queer women's imaginable communities will allow for a reading of lesbian narratives that does not simply reproduce the colonizing impulses of the very culture that such theorizations attempt to escape.

NOTES

1. Glamuzina and Laurie point out that at the time of the Parker-Hulme trial there were no operative television stations in New Zealand. The primary news coverage was by radio and newspaper.

2. See B. Ruby Rich's introduction to *Parker & Hulme: A Lesbian View*, Andrea Weiss' *Vampires and Violets: Lesbians in Film*, Vito Russo's *The Celluloid Closet*, Lynda Hart's *Fatal Women: Lesbian Sexuality and the Mark of Aggression*, and Chris Holmlund, "Cruisin' for a Bruisin': Hollywood's Deadly (Lesbian) Dolls," *Cinema Journal* 34.1 (1994): 31–51.

3. In recent years, films like *Go Fish* and *The Incredibly True Adventures of Two Girls in Love* have supplemented the psycho-killer-dyke fare, but do not yet outweigh the other works.

4. See for example, Joli Jenson's "Fandom As Pathology" among other articles on football (soccer).

5. See Anne Maxwell's "'History' in the New Zealand Novel and Film Today" and Joanne Tompkins' "Re-playing and Dis-playing the Nation: New Zealand Drama," both of which are printed in *Opening the Book: New Essays on New Zealand Writing*, for more on texts that have attempted to come to terms with questions of history and nationhood in Aotearoa.

6. Even a most cursory review of texts that can be read as imaginable lesbian nations in literature and culture makes this clear. From Sappho's legendary island to the culture of the Amazons, even the most historical examples seem to float as illusory communities existing only in imagination because so few historical documents of their existence remain. More contemporary examples might include Katharine V. Forrest's *Daughters of a Coral Dawn* and the television show *Xena: Warrior Princess*.

7. In her analysis of the history of representation of desire between women in the Indian context, Mina Kumar writes:

The Indian lesbian played a bit part in the literature of the Sexual Revolution and the Lesbian-Feminist movement. *The Jewel in the Lotus*, for example, refers to "the aromatic gardens of the Red Fort of Delhi, the fort of Akbar in Lahore and the Kaiserbagh Palace at Lucknow [which] (were full of) zenana women" (406).

It seems an odd coincidence that Xena's name would so directly mirror the name of that used to describe an Indian lesbian woman, if only in fiction. Furthermore, Xena's signature weapon is a circular variation on a throwing star, called a *chakram*, which seems to be a play on or a version of an implement used by the Hindu god Shiva. The *chakram* seems particularly important in the light of Berlant and Freeman's analysis of the imaginable communities, as it is so clearly a weapon designed to counter the traditionally phallic shape of most weapons. In trying to create an imaginably woman-centered image of power, the show borrowed an image from Indian mythology.

WORKS CITED

Abrams, Adam. "The Fourth World – The *Heavenly Creatures* Website." http://www.geocities.com/Hollywood/Studio/2194/creatures.html, accessed 20 Nov, 1997.

Anderson, Benedict. *Imagined Communities: Reflections on the Origin and Spread of Nationalism*. London: Verso, 1983.

Berlant, Lauren, and Elizabeth Freeman. "Queer Nationality." *Boundary* 2, 19.1 (1992): 149.

Case, Sue-Ellen. *The Domain-Matrix: Performing Lesbian at the End of Print Culture*. Bloomington and Minneapolis: Indiana University Press, 1996.

Castle, Terry. *The Apparitional Lesbian: Female Homosexuality and Modern Culture*. New York: Columbia University Press, 1993.

de Lauretis, Teresa. *Alice Doesn't: Feminism, Semiotics, Cinema*. Bloomington: Indiana University Press, 1984.

Ehrenreich, Barbara, Elizabeth Hess, and Gloria Jacobs. "Beatlemania: Girls Just Want to Have Fun." In: *The Adoring Audience: Fan Culture and Popular Media*. Edited by Lisa A. Lewis. London and New York: Routledge, 1992.

Glamuzina, Julie, and Alison J. Laurie. *Parker & Hulme: A Lesbian View*. Ithaca: Firebrand Books, 1995.

Hart, Lynda. *Fatal Women: Lesbian Sexuality and the Mark of Aggression*. Princeton: Princeton University Press, 1994.

Heavenly Creatures. Directed by Peter Jackson. Written by Frances Walsh and Peter Jackson. Performed by Melanie Lynsky and Kate Winslet. Miramax, 1994.

Holmlund, Chris. "Cruisin' for a Bruisin': Hollywood's Deadly (Lesbian) Dolls," *Cinema Journal* 34.1 (1994): 31–51.

Jenson, Joli. "Fandom as Pathology: The Consequences of Characterization." In: *The Adoring Audience: Fan Culture and Popular Media*. Edited by Lisa A.Lewis. London and New York: Routledge, 1992.

Kumar, Mina. "Representations of Indian Lesbianism." In: *The Very Inside: An Anthology of Writing by Asian and Pacific Islander Lesbian and Bisexual Women*. Edited by Sharon Lim-Hing. Toronto: Sister Vision Press, 1994.

Lacan, Jacques. "Motives of Paranoiac Crime: The Crime of the Papin Sisters." *Critical Texts* 5.3 (1988): 7–11.

Maxwell, Anne. "'History' in the New Zealand Novel and Film Today." In: *Opening the Book: New Essays on New Zealand Writing*. Edited by Mark Williams and Michele Leggott. Auckland: Auckland University Press, 1995.

Rich, B. Ruby. Introduction. In: *Parker & Hulme: A Lesbian View*. By Julie Glamuzina and Alison J. Laurie. Ithaca: Firebrand Books, 1995. 1–11.

Robson, Jocelyn, and Beverly Zalcock. *Girls' Own Stories: Australian and New Zealand Women's Films*. London: Scarlett Press, 1997.

Russo, Vito. *The Celluloid Closet: Homosexuality in the Movies*. New York: Harper and Row, 1987.

Schaffer, Kay. *Women and the Bush: Forces of Desire in the Australian Cultural Tradition*. Cambridge: Cambridge University Press, 1990.

Sedgwick, Eve Kosofsky. *Between Men: English Literature and Male Homosexual Desire*.

New York: Columbia University Press, 1985.

Tompkins, Joanne. "Re-playing and Dis-playing the Nation: New Zealand Drama." In: *Opening the Book: New Essays on New Zealand Writing.* Edited by Mark Williams and Michele Leggott. Auckland: Auckland University Press, 1995.

Weiss, Andrea. *Vampires and Violets: Lesbians in Film.* New York: Penguin Books, 1992.

Chapter 4

Im/De-position of Cultural Violence: Reading Chen Kaige's *Farewell My Concubine*

Benzi Zhang

Chen Kaige's *Farewell My Concubine*, the 1993 Cannes Film Festival first-prize co-winner, is a good example of Chinese "queer" film, which explores the issue of cultural violence in relation to homophobic discourse in Chinese culture. Cultural violence, in Foucauldian terminology, can be described as a "strategic field" of forces, where various discourses of power operate concurrently to generate a social body of repression in the name of normality and order. Queer deviance such as homosexuality has long been regarded in Chinese culture as a sign of "transgression" that demands a different order of social normality. In China, homosexuality is never a pure sexual problem, but an issue that raises questions about the violent discourse in which the peremptory heterosexuality has been a predominant force as the ruler of normality. As Chen's *Farewell My Concubine* illustrates, homophobia is produced discursively as well as institutionally by a power that affirms and perpetuates a feudal, patriarchal and quasi-polygynous culture. It is important to understand that in *Farewell My Concubine,* the homophobic anxiety situates itself at a crisscrossing of discourses of historical and cultural violence, in which those detected to be "queer" or "abnormal" are en-gendered as alluring men who are both corrupted and corrupting. Artistically brilliant and ideologically profound, *Farewell My Concubine* bravely explores one of the most disturbing yet undisturbed fields in Chinese culture—homophobia as "second modality of violence," whose ideological mechanism and rhetoric of representation have not yet been fully recognized or explained.

As a fascinating drama, *Farewell My Concubine*, with the strongest storytelling power that the cinematic discourse can provide, presents an intricate story about the lives of two Peking opera stars, Chen Dieyi (nicknamed Xiao Douzi) and Duan Xiaolou (nicknamed Xiao Shitou), against a historical backdrop of the painful upheavals of China in the twentieth century. The two met in a training school for opera performers when they were only little boys. Their friendship develops through a cruel training and hard life, in which violent and brutal punishments are only common treatments. The young Dieyi, a shy and slight boy, is trained to perform as a *dan* (female impersonator)—in a sense he is forced to "become" a woman—that requires him to sing and remember "I am by nature a girl, not a boy" throughout his life. Later, he becomes well known for his exquisite performance in the role of the "Concubine" in a famous opera, from which the film takes its name. His chunky, robust childhood friend, Xiaolou, is fitted to play the role of the masculine "King." For Dieyi, the bond between him and his "stage brother" is both emotional and professional; he attempts to carry his passion for the King over into real life. However, Xiaolou seems to be unaware of Dieyi's feeling and gives his heart to a prostitute named Juxian. Jealous, angry, distressed, frustrated, and confused, Dieyi starts to indulge himself in opium smoking. Their professional and personal bond, however, continues over next several decades of tribulations and violence until the moment when Dieyi, fully dressed up in Concubine's costume, cuts his throat in front of Xiaolou, the King.

The death of Dieyi, which is prepared in the opening sequence and accomplished at the very end of this movie, provides a heartrending frame for the tragic, intensive drama that spans five decades in China's most turbulent times. Dieyi's grace and elegance as an effeminate *dan* is presented against an extreme violent backdrop of tribulation and turbulence—as China moves from warlord era, through Japanese invasion, Communist regime, into Cultural Revolution. Dieyi survives numerous trials, torments, cruelties, and injustices to face his true self by death— finally he chooses death to express himself and to assert his homosexual identity. Set in the whirlwind of historical, social, and political violence, the film highlights the relationship between violence and homosexuality. Chinese culture places man at the center of social domain: he is the master– the source and end of social norms, moral meanings, and political order. In the "old society" of China, a man's masculinity as well as his social status was often indicated by the number of his concubines. A woman is defined absolutely in her relation to men. Different from western culture, in which the woman is "the second sex" and "she is the Other" (cf. de Beauvoir), Chinese culture treats women as "belonging" to/of men, and femininity has no independent status. The original Chinese legend of "Farewell, My Concubine" is about Xiang Yu, a king in ancient China, who loses everything in a battle except his favorite concubine named Yu Ji. Surrounded by enemy troops, he waits for his doomed final moment, drinking and listening to his concubine's dreary chant: "Enemy troops surrounding us / Singing the songs of Chu, the mock us / My lord is doomed / I have nowhere to turn." After her last chanting performance, the concubine cuts her throat and dies in the lap of the King.

Circulated in Chinese society as a "love story" for hundreds of years, "Farewell, My Concubine" is transformed into a cultural discourse invested with male-dominated values, which discriminate against not only women but also effeminate men. Phallogocentrism and Xiang-Yu-like masculinity, with all their institutionalized discursive practices, have been the dominant force of orthodoxy in Chinese culture. Any kind of dissidence or resistance to this masculine orthodoxy has been marginalized, denounced, and persecuted throughout history. Parallel to political and social violence that is "out there" in the world, the oppression of homosexuality usually takes the form of the second "modality of violence," which, as Armstrong and Tennenhouse have noted, is "excised through words upon things in the world, often by attributing violence upon them" (9). The discursive form of violence has put a seal of silence upon the discourse of homosexuality, which is ostracized and underrepresented in Chinese culture and history. According to Jonathan Dollimore, the fact that the resistance to heterosexual orthodoxy and its "literature, historics, and subcultures" are "absent from current debates (literary, psychoanalytic, and cultural)" suggests the existence of a violent force that suppresses the representation of "sexual dissidence" (21). The binary model of Xiang Yu (dominant masculinity)—Yu Ji (subservient femininity), which serves well the patriarchal, heterosexual orthodoxy, has been the dominating ideology in Chinese culture, which has oppressive and suffocating consequences for homosexual discourse. In Chinese culture, homosexuality has a negative connotation of "queer" transgression that subverts the orthodox morality/normality.

"Sexual deviation," Dollimore notes, is often "thought to be a deviation from the truth; this is a truth embodied in, and really only accessible to, normality, with the result that, even if sexual deviants are to be tolerated, 'there is still something like an "error" involved in what they do . . . a manner of acting that is not adequate to reality'" (69). Although homosexuality exists in social reality, the lack of its own "truthful" representation creates numerous misunderstandings that prevent the development of a positive homosexual sensibility in Chinese culture. Homophobia permeates every layer of China's "ideological apparatuses"; the homosexual anxiety is silenced by the hegemony of a semifeudal, patriarchal, and quasi-polygynous culture, which presses sexual deviation to self-negation and self-sacrifice. The lack of voice makes homosexual people, in Homi Bhabha's words, "become what Freud calls that 'haphazard member of the herd,' the Stranger, whose language-less presence evokes an archaic anxiety and aggressivity by impeding the search for narcissistic love-objects in which the subject can rediscover himself" (166). Bhabha's observation makes us aware of the discursive behavior of cultural hegemony that can act as a violent force both to marginalize difference and to constrain individual expression. The "language-less" silence, in the case of homosexual people in China, constricts the development of a speaking subjectivity and makes "failed speech" a pitiable mark of identity for this "muted group."

Farewell My Concubine tries to break the "language-less" silence in search of an appropriate voice to express homosexual experience and anxiety, which are situated in the most painful and violent period of Chinese history. From 1924 to 1977, although the dominating powers were constantly shifting in China, the discourse of peremptory heterosexuality and patriarchy has never been changed or challenged. Similar to the victims of rape, homosexual men meet the worst injustice and violence during that terrifying period of history. Dieyi's tormented fate as gay man is placed in the shadow of her mother, a prostitute who was raped by an old man. The film seems to indicate the connection between Dieyi's twisted sexuality and the mother's rape, which is intensified by the backdrop violence of wars and revolutions. Following Catherine MacKinnon, we can say, "Taking rape [as well as homosexuality] from the realm of the 'sexual,' placing it in the realm of the 'violent,' allows one to be against it without raising any questions about the extent to which the institution of heterosexuality has defined force as a normal part" in sexual politics (219). The juxtaposition between rape and homosexuality in *Farewell My Concubine* suggests that both Dieyi and her mother are violated by a culture that denies homosexuality and female sexuality. In Chinese culture, the representation of violence is particularly difficult and "often characterized by silence, elisions and ambiguities," to borrow Ellen Rooney's words (92); rape and homosexuality are part of the "unspeakable" reality, which lacks concrete representation in cultural forms. "Excluded from representation by its very structure," as Craig Owens has noted, homosexuality and the victims of rape "return within it as a figure for—a representation of—the unrepresentable" (59).

For most of the film, Dieyi remains in female costume and concubine makeup. The transvestite stage of Peking opera seems to offer an imaginary space where Dieyi can both represent and masquerade his genuine sensibility. He seems to become a migrant between two worlds where masquerading becomes manifesting and misrepresentation displaces representation. He is (mis)taken for a woman on stage and "a woman's soul trapped in a man's body" offstage, while he is actually a man—a gay man, a "queer" man. "In all the culturally dominant forms of representation," as Teresa de Lauretis has pointed out in *The Practice of Love*, "desire is predicated on sexual difference as gender, the difference of woman from man or femininity from masculinity, with all that those terms entail—and not as a difference between heterosexual and homosexual, straight and gay sexuality" (110–11). The simple formulation of monological binarism of heterosexual patriarchy deprives Dieyi of the "third space." He is neither the prey of men's sexual desire nor a hunter of women's sexuality. Homosexuality, as Lee Edelman observes, has "been constructed as a threat to the logic of heterosexual, patriarchal representation" (xv). Refusing to be fixed and settled into an either/or trap, Dieyi becomes an enemy to the whole heterosexual structure, a "nomad" who refuses to move from one fixed identity to another (cf. Deleuze & Guattari). In a sense, Dieyi is turned into a woman and then crushed by the same phobic power in the name of normality or morality.

Dieyi is a female impersonator, or *dan* actor, which has a long tradition in Peking opera. "Originally these men were chosen for their looks and ability to appear feminine in women's clothing"; as Roger Baker has noted, "The use of men to play women's roles was the result . . . . of a ban on women imposed by the authorities for moral reasons" (72). When discussing the transvestite theater in England, Stephen Orgel says, "The reason always given for the prohibition of women from the stage was that their chastity would thereby be compromised, which is understood to mean that they would become whores. Behind the outrage of public modesty is a *real fear of women's sexuality*" (26, emphasis is mine). Homophobia and the "fear of women's sexuality" derive from the same hegemonic values cultivated and reflected by the semifeudal, patriarchal, and quasi-polygynous culture that determines what is "normal" in society. Homophobia, as well as the "fear of women's sexuality," is violent and implicated in violence, because it often makes homosexuality and female sexuality convenient and pliable scapegoats for social, moral, and even political problems. In popular literature and the political histories of China, sensual women and sexual dissidents are often presented as villainous, particularly when they are involved in politics; and they are victimized and also punished by the value system of normality, which, ironically, treats polygyny and concubine customs as normal. In the "system that is male-supremacist," according to Andrea Dworkin, "women are defined as sexual chattel," and "systematically kept subservient to men"; "the sexuality of women has been stolen outright, appropriated by men—conquered, possessed, taken, violated; women have been systematically and absolutely denied the right to sexual self-determination and to sexual integrity" (239). In the "old society" of China, unfaithful concubines would be punished violently—death was the most common penalty, as illustrated by Zhang Yimou's film *Raise the Red Lantern.*

The problem of inequality between male and female sexuality is complicated by the issue of homosexuality, which, crossing the assumed boundaries of the respective engendered domains of men and women, not only suggests the repudiation of the masculine "kingdom," but also demands a "dominion" of a different kind of values, norms, and powers, which challenge the binary structure that accommodates the hegemonic discourses such as homophobic patriarchy. In Chinese culture there seems to be a clear demarcation line between female impersonation that appeals to male pleasure and homosexuality that threatens male normality. As a *dan* actor, Dieyi may remind us of Mei Lan-fang, one of the greatest female impersonators in China. Mei was admired for his ability to present convincing, impeccable femininity. As A. C. Scott opines, "Mei's stage technique was 'unsurpassed in its unity of gesture, expression, and exquisite grace and delicacy of line. His voice has purity and quality'" (quoted in Baker 73). However, in China, Mei was always honored as a "man." Dieyi's case is different, because his gender crossing involves more than just stage mannerisms. To use Marybeth Hamilton's words, Dieyi attempts to "display," not to "perform," his real, offstage self—as (in turn-of-the-century terms) "a 'fairy,' a 'third sexer,' a being who straddled the gender divide" (115–16). In what Hamilton calls "a culture that demonized homosexuality," Dieyi's fate cannot be better than an unfaithful concubine. His defiant pertinacity, uncompromising personality, and refusal to give up the right to define his queerness—his "real" identity and "proper" place, which have violently been disavowed by a phobic culture—eventually cost his life.

A homophobic culture often asserts "an exact equation between cross-gender behaviors and homosexual desire" (Sedgwick 59). In China, the violent force of power may also impose other "equations," by which those detected to be traitors and counterrevolutionaries, for instance, can be engendered as queer men who are both corrupted and corrupting. "The interpretation of sexual deviance as political dissidence," as Katrin Sieg argues, can be considered as "communists' strategy of using the accusation of homosexuality in order to discredit the political enemy. It also reflected on the specific, androcentric structure of a centralist state that expected its citizens to duplicate patriarchal relations in the domestic sphere as a sign of political loyalty" (94). What becomes significant, for example, in Dieyi's failed erotic adventures with Mr. Yuan, a wealthy admirer, is the refraction of a suppressive shadow of political violence. Later, at a surprising turn, Mr. Yuan is identified as "a traitor and counter-revolutionary" and executed without a fair trial. While cross-dressing on stage is admired, cross-sexuality offstage is intolerable in both the "old" and "new" societies of China, in which sexual minorities, similar to other power minorities, are among the most susceptible to violence, because over-simplified labeling and "equation" make people learn to loathe homosexuality before they even understand it. The fear of the unknown generates violent suppression of any sign of "queer" transgression or deviation that might demand a different order of social/political normality.

It is widely observed that sexual discrimination in a patriarchal culture can provoke extreme violent acts. The issue of denouncing and persecuting homosexuality, therefore, should be examined in a large context of violent and phobic culture. Let us look at what Christina Gilmartin records in her essay about the violence in China: "Deeply imbedded in Chinese culture, this strong preference for boys has provoked both men and women to perpetrate the crime of infanticide. Even women who had not been pressured by their husbands or relatives to produce a son have been convinced of killing their infant daughters" (216). Infanticide and homophobia are provoked by the same system of cultural values which, as de Lauretis puts it, "produces the human as man and everything else as, not even 'woman,' but non-man" (1984, 121). Such a mentality produces a coercive force, a phobic hegemony that violently disavows the "concrete existence" of homosexuality as well as women's sexuality and their "actual weight in social relations" (Armstrong and Tennenhouse 245). Homophobic culture is a violent force that both marginalizes difference and constrains individual expression. Moreover, since it does not appear to be a historical and legal category, homophobia, as a "second modality of violence" that is different from the "out there" crime of infanticide, takes an invisible privileged-position from which phobic mentality may continue to "demonize," "exclude," or "violate" the interests of women and "nonmen." The issue of homosexuality, as Jill Campbell observes, has "open[ed] up the constellation of interrelated problems – sexual, political, and social" (62). However, beyond the sexual, political, and social discourses that Campbell has envisioned from the perspective of a western culture, homosexuality, as illustrated in *Farewell My Concubine*, has another dimension that is pregnant with symbolism: it represents an unrepresentable "absence" in Chinese culture, which is somewhat mysterious, unapproachable, and therefore queer. Different from the western culture in which you can find the concrete existence or evidence of sexual, political and social discourses for homosexuality, Chinese culture only suggests a kind of society for the "absence" or "non-being-ness" of homosexuality. The issue of homosexuality is related to the suppressed consciousness of modernity that should have developed during the period of Chinese history the film covers—the period of China's modernization. What we are witnessing here, however, is an ironic cultural permutation in which the sensibility of homosexuality is "castrated" and "dismembered" as China moves into a "modern" society on its own terms.

WORKS CITED

Armstrong, Nancy, and Leonard Tennenhouse, eds. *The Violence of Representation: Literature and the History of Violence.* London and New York: Routledge, 1989.

Baker, Roger. *Drag: A History of Female Impersonation in the Performing Arts.* London: Cassell, 1994.

Bhabha, Homi. *The Location of Culture.* London and New York: Routledge, 1994.

Campbell, Jill. "'When Men Women Turn': Gender Reversals in Fielding's Plays." In *Crossing the Stage: Controversies on Cross-Dressing,* edited by Lesley Ferris. London and New York: Routledge, 1993.

de Beauvoir, Simone. *The Second Sex.* Harmondsworth: Penguin, 1987.

de Lauretis, Teresa. *Alice Doesn't: Feminism, Semiotics, Cinema.* Bloomington: Indiana University Press, 1984.

———. *The Practice of Love: Lesbian Sexuality and Perverse Desire.* Bloomington and Indianapolis: Indiana University Press, 1994.

Deleuze, Gilles, and Felix Guattari. *Nomadology: The War Machine,* translated by Brian Massumi. New York: Semiotext(e), 1986.

Dollimore, Jonathan. *Sexual Dissidence: Augustine to Wilde, Freud to Foucault.* Oxford: Oxford University Press, 1991.

Dworkin, Andrea. "Pornography and Male Supremacy." In: *Gender, Race and Class in Media,* edited by Gail Dines and Jean M. Humez. London: Sage, 1995.

Edelman, Lee. *Homographesis: Essays in Gay Literary and Cultural Theory.* New York and London: Routledge, 1994.

Gilmartin, Christina. "Violence against Women in Contemporary China." In: *Violence in China: Essays in Culture and Counterculture,* edited by Jonathan N. Lipman and Stevan Harrell. Albany: State University of New York Press, 1990.

Hamilton, Marybeth. "'I'm the Queen of the Bitches': Female Impersonation and Mae West's *Pleasure Man.*" In: *Crossing the Stage: Controversies on Cross-Dressing,* edited by Lesley Ferris. London and New York: Routledge, 1993.

MacKinnon, Catherine. *Sexual Harassment of Working Women.* New Haven, Conn.: Yale University Press, 1979.

Orgel, Stephen. "Nobody's Perfect: Or Why Did the English Stage Take Boys for Women?" In: *The Violence of Representation: Literature and the History of Violence,* edited by Nancy Armstrong and Leonard Tennenhouse. London and New York: Routledge, 1989.

Owens, Craig. "The Discourse of Others: Feminists and Postmodernism." In: *The Anti-Aesthetic: Essays on Postmodern Culture,* edited by H. Foster. Port Townsend, Wash.: Bay Press, 1983.

Rooney, Ellen. "'A Little More than Persuading': Tess and the Subject of Sexual Violence." In: *Rape and Representation,* edited by Lynn A. Higgins and Brenda R. Silver. New York: Columbia University Press, 1990.

Sedgwick, Eve Kosofsky. "Across Gender, Across Sexuality: Willa Cather and Others." In: *Displacing Homophobia: Gay Male Perspectives in Literature and Culture,* edited by Ronald R. Butters, John M. Clum, and Michael Moon. Durham: Duke University Press, 1989.

Sieg, Katrin. "Deviance and Dissidence: Sexual Subjects of the Cold War." In: *Cruising the Performative: Interventions into the Representation of Ethnicity, Nationality, and Sexuality,* edited by Sue-Ellen Case, Philip Brett, and Susan Leigh Foster. Bloomington and Indianapolis: Indiana University Press, 1994.

Chapter 5

Gender Crossing and Decadence in Taiwanese Fiction at the *Fin de Siecle*

Liang-ya Liou

Taiwanese fiction writers were not absent in the various discourses on gender and sexuality in the 1990s. As a matter of fact, as early as 1980 novels by women writers were both best-sellers and winners of literary awards. Although many of these fictions valorize traditional femininity and idealized romantic love, a growing number of them explore the difficulties and failures of heterosexual love/marriage/family in order to critique patriarchal notions of gender. Shih Shu-ching, Liao Huei-ying, Hsiao Sa, Su Wei-cheng, and Yuan Chueong-chueong are among the best writers who portray women's madness, masochistic self-indulgence, or awakening as a result of patriarchal oppression. Li Ang, on the other hand, is unique among female writers in addressing the issue of female sexuality since the 1960s, which anticipates its emergence as one of the primary feminist concerns in the 1990s. Moreover, Pai Hsien-yung's representations of female sexuality in his 1960s stories of Yu-ching Sao, Ying Shuei-yen, and Mamasam Jin should not be ignored. Pai's coming out a few years after he published the novel *The Outcast Son*[1] draws attention to these early stories and to how he seeks both to sneak in gay men's gender-crossing imagination (Yeh, Chu Wei-cheng) and to participate in feminist discourse.

One of the main characteristics of 1990s Taiwanese fictions is the prevalence of gender crossing and decadence as the theme or subject matter. Fictions delineating female desire and male and female same-sex love are both great in number and frequent winners of fiction awards. Writers who portray female sexuality include Li Ang, Chu Tien-wen, Chu Tien-shin, Cheng Ying-shu, Chen Shuei, Tsao Li-chuan, Lucifer Hung, Chiu Miao-jin, Chang Yuan, Chi Ta-wei, Ping Lu, Du Shiu-lan, and Chang Yi-shuan. As far as heterosexual relationship is concerned, both Chu Tien-wen and Cheng Ying-shu display antiromantic sentiments by deriding love as mere fantasy, and by suggesting that love is less tangible than desire. Women writers tend to depict females as narcissistic and practical, while ridiculing or despising decadent men. Even the extremely self-indulgent heroine of Li Ang's

The Labyrinthine Garden eventually discovers that love is illusory, and the depiction of her awakening underlines her strong female desire. These women writers tend to write from the perspective of the "good" woman. Even so, they redefine "good" as sexually autonomous, and their attitudes toward loose or "bad" women are ambiguous.

Contrary to fictions about heterosexuality, fictions about female same-sex relationship celebrate love. Writers like Chiu Miao-jin, Chu Tien-shin, Chen Shuei, and Lucifer Hung delineate female same-sex love as an integral part of the heroine's self-quest. They also portray how, under the pressure of mainstream heterosexual society, female same-sex relationship is troubled and entangled. In fictions by Chen Shuei, Chiu Miao-jin, Lucifer Hung, Chu Tien-shin, Chang Yuan, Chi Ta-wei, and Chang Yi-shuan, the happiness of lesbian love is often set against the emptiness or insufficiency of heterosexual love. Moreover, in fictions by Chen Shuei and Lucifer Hung, voraciously sensual women sleep around with men without loving them, and are cured of their incapacity for love only through falling in love with women. Chiu Miao-jin, Tsao Li-chuan, and Chen Shuei all depict butch-femme relationships. Tsao Li-chuan's "About Her Gray Hair and Other Stuff," which touches on the generational differences in Taiwanese butch-femme subculture, seeks to trace the history of Taiwanese lesbianism.

Undomesticated female desire induces male voyeurism or backlash. The male narrator of Yang Chao's *A Dark Alley on a Wild Night* is almost a voyeur of female body parts. Fantasies about invading female bodies are also rife in Lo Yi-chuin's *The Dream of My Wife and Dogs*, where the juxtaposition of a dozen raped or deformed female bodies with enticing female nudes suggests both male voyeuristic desire and masculine anxiety about, if not violence against, the New Woman. Cheng Ying-shu's "The Angel's Eyes" is a horror story about a male aesthete's grisly murder of a pure, innocent woman.

Writers dealing with male homosexual subject matter include Chu Tien-wen, Chi Ta-wci, Wu Chi-wen, Lucifer Hung, Lin Juin-ying, Lin Yu-yi, Tsao Li-chuan, Jiang Shuin, and Shu Yo-sheng. Generally speaking, the male same-sex love they portray is less entangled and troubled than the female same-sex love delineated by the above-mentioned writers, although love remains important to the male same-sex relationships they depict. Both Chu Tien-wen and Wu Chi-wen seek to trace the history of Taiwanese male homosexuality. Whereas Chu portrays gay men's underground sexual paradise, Wu depicts gay men's pallid, meager sexual life. Whereas Chu ambiguously contrasts mainstream heterosexual values and male homosexual communal values through a dissembling gay man, both Chi Ta-wei and Lucifer Hung are defiant and seductive in uncovering the repressed and distorted male same-sex desire and exploring male homosexual utopia in cyberspace (Liou, *Engendering* 43–81). Chi deliberately captures the fluidity and tension of male same-sex desire in the family, on the campus, and in the army.

Writers dealing with the subject matter of transsexuality, transvestitism, and bisexuality include Chi Ta-wei, Lucifer Hung, Cheng Ying-shu, Yang Chao, Wu Chi-wen, and Chen Shuei. Influenced by feminist and queer theories, Chi and Hung depict the vacillations of sexual and gender identities in cyberspace, which allows for playful possibilities. Both Yang Chao and Cheng Ying-shu set trans-sexuals in the background of Taiwan, in order to satirize masculinist myths and prejudices against transsexuals in Taiwan (Liou, "Queer Sexchanges"). Both Chen Shuei and Wu Chi-wen delineate the social pressure on transsexuals. Chen's "Sleepwalking in 1994," in particular, shows how the butch may feel obliged to have the transsexual surgery at the femme's request.

The intersection of decadence and gender crossing is no doubt one of the phenomena that incite the most moral controversy and anxiety in 1990s Taiwan. Since 1990s Taiwanese fictions are both agents and products of this phenomenon, they constitute important discourses on decadence and gender crossing. Limited by space, this chapter narrows its discussion to fictions by four "daughters of decadence," using Elaine Showalter's term: Li Ang, Chu Tien-wen, Chiu Miao-jin, and Cheng Ying-shu. I will examine how their works portray gender crossing, how they present the dialectic between love and sex, morality and decadence, and how their imagination of decadence and gender crossing implicates a certain politics of gender and sexuality.

LI ANG

The decadence of Li Ang's *The Labyrinthine Garden* is all the more sensa-tional if we read the novel bearing in mind the shocking sex scandals about pow-erful politicians and magnates in recent years. In a Taiwan society where bour-geois notions of heterosexual monogamy are established as the norm, a "good" woman, even an aristocrat who had studied in Japan and the United States, falls in love with a womanizer/real estate tycoon, thereby experiencing a decadent life accompanied by a series of humiliations as she gets into emotional, sexual, and power entanglements. She has multiple and mutually contradictory identities: a dependent "little" woman (emotionally), a naive, reckless aristocratic woman, a New Woman (economically), a man's plaything, and a loose woman. Apart from that, the text shifts back and forth between the heroine's first-person present-tense narration of her wild abandon and a third-person, past-tense narration of her awakening. Instead of easily fitting in a radical feminist agenda, such ambivalent and ambiguous vacillation is revealing of the complicated interaction among think-ing that is sexual-liberationist-feminist, antipornography-feminist, or patriarchal. Through this "good" woman/aesthete's sexual adventures, Li Ang both explores and reexamines the significance of love, desire, and self in a woman's life.

There is no question about the heroine Chu Ying-hung's worship of the phal-lus/penis in her infatuation with Lin Hsi-gung at first. Although her strong sexual desire is indeed intermixed with a fetishistic love of his beauty, she is particularly fascinated by his despotic arrogance. An inexperienced young woman, she first meets Lin at a pub among a group of the new rich, and while abominating the cheap casual sex of the nightclub world, she is nonetheless immediately captivated by his beautiful tall figure, his youth, and, most importantly, his melancholic dark qualities. She is helplessly subjugated by his tyrannical, self-conceited personality, so that she fantasizes about being his little woman. Feeling "an intoxicated, intense sensation, a wild happiness of extreme abandonment" (44; all subsequent references to the texts are based on their Taiwanese version, and all translations are mine), she is "willing to go to any place and do anything with this strong beautiful man" (45). At their second encounter, she associates him with the white phoenix, so he gains an additional mysterious, legendary quality. He then seeks to conquer her by showing off his Rolls-Royce limousine, his ability to fly first-class to France and the United States for vacation, and his capability of talking to her for hours on international phone calls. Their relationship of master and slave is revealed at the time when Lin suddenly decides to break up with her. He half coerces her into kneeling before him performing fellatio for him, while he flaunts his inflated penis; she, on her part, passively responds, scarcely aware that he treats her as his prey/toy.

Even when Chu acquires a stronger sense of self after she discovers that Lin is a married man who practices casual sex and keeps concubines, she remains hopelessly embroiled in emotional fixation to him. She naively believes that she will eventually captivate him. Paradoxically, she fails to change his sexual practice; instead, her own sexual practice changes. Provoked by Lin's indifference to her, she dissociates her love from her sex; she remains emotionally faithful to him while having sexual intercourse with Teddy Chang. Indeed, it is her insistence on loving Lin that leads her to make rules for her sexual relationship with Teddy: Teddy must be reduced to a penis, and she must refuse Teddy's embrace and caress after the intercourse. Obviously she tries to be the definer of her own sexuality, which implicitly poses a threat to Lin and Teddy, both of whom believe in phallocentric notions of men's sexual prowess. When Lin finally asks to date her again, right before their meeting she once again has sex with Teddy. Imagining Teddy to be Lin, she mounts on his body, feeling that "she herself is launching the attack" (176), turning Teddy/Lin's penis into her prey, enclosing it. Lin seems to be totally unaware of her relationship with Teddy. Her concealing the fact suggests that Lin treats his women as his playthings, although Chu resists Lin's practice secretly. Teddy, on the other hand, feels threatened by her sexual autonomy. When she seeks to resume her sexual relationship with Teddy after jilting him, he humiliates her in ways that reflect his sense of humiliation by her jilting.

Even though Chu is far from being a model feminist, her sexual adventures enable the novel to pursue the dialectic between love and sex: Is it better to have loveless sex (as sexual liberationist feminists would have it), or to have sex based on love (as antipornography feminists would insist)? Here I differentiate Taiwanese sexual liberationist feminism and antipornography feminism only expediently and roughly. Taiwanese sexual liberationist feminism emphasizes that sexual freedom should not be confined to heterosexual, monogamous, procreation-intended sex, that, instead, "deviant" sexualities such as nonprocreative sex, promiscuity, one-night stands, homosexuality, commercial sex, sadomasochism, and fetishism should be allowed as well. Taiwanese antipornography feminism stresses the sexual equality between the two parties of any sexual relationship. Focusing more on heterosexual relationship, it critiques men's sexual violence against women, and men's sexual exploitation of women. Besides, it seeks to replace phallocentric notions of sexuality with feminist ones; i.e., it emphasizes the elements of love and emotion in sexual relationship, and the notion that sexual pleasure may not be confined to penetration.

The answer is rather ambiguous. Chu makes her decadent experiment with Teddy in order to recapture Lin, her love object and her "prey," and to regain sex based on love. Ironically, she soon finds that Lin "has neither Teddy's sexual prowess, nor Teddy's gentle love skill" (226), that "in fact, their sexual love is never so wonderful as she had recalled it so fondly" (226). It turns out that the love in which she has indulged herself is an illusion: Lin's passion cools off very soon, and afterward he makes love to her rather mechanically, which fails to gratify her. Even more ironically, Lin, who likes to boast about his sexual prowess, has been physically depleted due to too much sexual activity. One of the reasons why Lin chooses to have various kinds of sexual games with her at unusual sites (such as in the car, among the weeds, or when they are massaged by a blind masseuse) is because Lin needs more stimulation in order to recover his sexual function. Under the shadow of Lin's impotence, the master/slave, subject/object relationship between them is reticently changed.

On the other hand, conventional codes subject Chu to more social pressure and risks than Lin for her sexual liberation. For all Chu's own belief that her sexual relationship with Lin is based on love, she is generally perceived by people around them as one of the kept women of a womanizer. Masao, the powerful businessman subordinate only to Lin in Lin's enterprise, shows his contempt for her as Lin's kept woman, even equating her to a whore, when he tries to force himself on her under the pretext that he is drunk. She feels more anxious about her unmarried status as she finds herself accidentally pregnant. Eventually she tricks Lin into divorcing his wife and marrying her, only to realize that, given Lin's promiscuity, her status is never secure. Throughout the novel, she compromises herself with patriarchy, but her abortion and her donation of the Lotus Garden, the Chu family garden, signify her autonomy. Toward the end of the book, she calls up her foremother to render Lin impotent as they make love in the Lotus Garden, thereby reversing the master/slave relationship between them. Her act not only manifests a sense of self-identity, but also constitutes a defiant gender crossing.

It is noteworthy that the book portrays several male decadents. Lin is only seemingly decadent, since his promiscuity is partially commercially motivated: he needs to prove through his sexual conquest that he can continue to expand his real estate kingdom, and to compete and build up ties with other men. He practices casual sex partly for the sake of his career. He appears effeminate only when he is in love with Chu or becomes sexually impotent. The real effeminate aesthete in the book is Chu Zu-yen, Ying-hung's father, who displays connoisseurship in managing the Lotus Garden, who also ruins his family by spending all the money collecting expensive cameras, limousines, and stereos after he is silenced under political persecution. He is not an ordinary loser, however; his lavish aestheticism is a form of passive resistance to the government and an attempt to keep the ideals of democracy. Aside from Chu Zu-yen and Lin Hsi-gung, a group of gay men appear in the prologue canvassing in bars for subscriptions for AIDS-patient Charlie. Though humiliated, they still try to promote the gay-rights movement through canvassing. When the figures of these gay men overlap with the view of Chu Ying-hung donating the Lotus Garden, which is shown on the huge TV screen behind them, the narrator seems to imply the possibility of the coalition between feminist liberation and the gay-rights movement.

CHU TIEN-WEN

Chu Tien-wen deliberately draws from the European *fin-de-siecle* imagination of decadence and gender crossing. Both the title and the style of her short story "*Fin-de-Siecle* Splendor" refer to decadent writing (see Ellis Hanson), though the story is relocated in Taiwan. Her short story collection *Fin-de-Siecle Splendor* and her novel *Notes of a Desolate Man* portray aesthetic abandonment, sexual depletion and languor, and gender anarchy. The two books' elaborate, highly ornamented style and overly subtle aesthetic vision make them classics of feminine aesthetic and *fin-de-siecle* decadence in Taiwanese fiction. Set in a daily life under the sway of Japanese, American, and European capitalist commodities, the two books have as protagonists decadent men and Generation X women. Even the marriage of an older generation is shown to reverse the traditional masculinist mode.

Unlike Chu Ying-hung in *The Labyrinthine Garden*, who shows active sexual desire, some girls/women in *Fin-de-Siecle Splendor* seem soft and passive, like traditional "good" women. But they in fact are aggressive and self-centered. All of them indulge in an aestheticizing imagination, and are highly narcissistic. They seem "drugged" as they immerse themselves in private erotic fantasy, but they do not embark on no-win love relationships. In "A Daughter of the Nile," Japanophile Lin Hsiao-yang is a rebel and a loner who adores Seiko Matsuda and herself. Studying at a night school and working part-time at McDonald's, she despises good students and is fascinated by the love fantasy fabricated by Japanese cartoons. In "Take Me Away, Moonlight!" the apparently delicate, quiet Cheng Jia-wei is actually overbearing and adamant. Working in advertising, she lives in a private dream world composed of advertisements and images. She escapes into her fantasy after falling out of love, even wielding a cutting knife to protect her fantasy from intrusion.

Mia in "*Fin-de-Siecle* Splendor" is an extreme example of gender crossing and decadence. Like the protagonist in Oscar Wilde's novel *The Picture of Dorian Gray*, Mia had been narcissistic, fetishistic, charismatic, and unloving. Paradoxically, Mia's radical femininity made her rather masculine in a sense. A model, she indulged in all kinds of fashion, fascinated by the artificial, the surface, the new styles. Influenced by the androgyny of David Bowie, Boy George, and the artist formerly known as Prince, she cross-dressed and captivated a group of girls. She had a quasi-butch-femme relationship with her girlfriend Baby. Then she initiated the trend of imitating Madonna, wearing her bras out and having casual sex with a bunch of boys. She became a Material Girl by the age of twenty. Bored with sex, she wanted to be a Queen Bee whose sole aim was making money. At last she becomes the mistress of old Duan, who is married and old enough to be her father. Enjoying the intellectual sobriety, maternal warmth, and unworldly romance that she gets from old Duan, she turns into a witch who lives on her feminine memories of smells and colors.

The male decadents in *Fin-de-Siecle Splendor* are just as defiantly outrageous as their *fin-de-siecle* European counterparts, although the narrator's tone is slightly critical. The Wallow in the Bitter Sea Gangsters in "A Daughter of the Nile" had been gigolos in a club they ran; they also owned a pub and a boutique selling decadent punk clothes. Ah-shan, one of the gangsters, is shot to death because he takes a rival gang leader's woman. Lin Hsiao-yang, who is secretly in love with him, anticipates his early death when she sees him taking marijuana with a superbly beautiful gesture. In "Take Me Away, Moonlight!" Hsia Jie-fu, an ad agency creative artist from Hong Kong, has such a heightened aestheticizing temper that he is "against the fashion and the designer's collection" (90). Extremely narcissistic, Hsia looks upon every flirtation as an erotic stage on which he "fulfills his desire of performance and self-connoisseurship" (96). In "Buddha of the Body," Little Tong, a gay man in his thirties, encounters Chong Lin in a public bathroom rendered almost vacant after the plague of AIDS. After sex he gazes indulgently at Chong's strong body, calling it "beauty!" "the best thing!" in his thought (53, 56). Having had too much sex, Little Tong often finds himself bored and languid, nauseated by the body. Even so, he still enjoys queering an Indian Buddhist scripture as portraying "an overblown, sensual world" (64); for him, the stories of Buddha's sacrificing his body to feed the tiger and cutting his leg to feed the dove intimate the sex of his gay ancestors. Sexual relationship is no burden to Little Tong. He willingly serves as a Buddha of the Body to a sixteen-year-old gay boy who asks to sleep with him.

Notes of a Desolate Man extends the decadence of "*Fin-de-Siecle* Splendor" and "Buddha of the Body"; though it is more conservative in tone, the novel successfully delineates a *fin-de-siecle* aestheticism and decadence. Chu Tien-wen adroitly chooses for the first-person narrator a cowardly, dissembling, closeted gay man, who serves as a negotiator between the mainstream heterosexual monogamous family values (which are well established before the lifting of the martial law) and the gay men's promiscuous practice within certain circles. Underneath a basically staunch endorsement of mainstream values, there emerges a yearning for transgression and rebellion, which complicates the novel's vision. At the very outset of the novel, Little Shao states in a tone of regret reminiscent of that of Eliot's *The Waste Land*: "This is a time of decadence, this is a time for prophesy" (9). On the one hand, he upholds Levi-Strauss's theory of kinship structure, thereby vilifying homosexuals as freaks; on the other, he also foresees a sexual paradise in Foucault's *The History of Sexuality*, imagining that "in a sexual terrain where every obstacle is abolished, a woman and a woman, or a man and a man, explore sexuality with each other, to see how the horizon of sexual pleasure can be ever expanded. Totally dissociated from the procreative function, sex is sublimated into sex for sex's sake. It is thus a sensual, aesthetic, artistic, and erotic kingdom" (64–65). Certainly a nonreproductive society is doomed to extinction, but the more Little Shao senses the sad fate of the erotic kingdom, the more he savors his aesthetic vision of decadence. Like Little Tong in "Buddha of the Body," Little Shao has reached the state of sexual exhaustion and craves for a stable love relationship. Like Little Tong, too, he remains an aesthete and misses his decadent life in the past despite his denigration of it.

Through Little Shao, the novel celebrates a feminine aesthetic in order not only to challenge the traditional disparagement of femininity and woman, but also to assert the legitimacy of gay men. Even more significantly, the novel accounts for the "cruel" sexual practice within certain male homosexual circles by attributing it to the practitioner's aestheticizing temper. While critical of such aestheticizing, the novel reveals how male homosexual promiscuity does not involve the kind of master/slave relationship that powerful heterosexual womanizers take for granted. The effeminate Little Shao sees himself as having "a feminine soul budding in a male body" (99), with a feminine mentality. For him, although not every gay man is as effeminate as he, they all have an aesthetic penchant for matter, physique, and the appearance. Thus they all have an androgynous soul: "We all have a femininity that is gazed at and a masculinity that gazes" (97). Adoring beauty, these male homosexual circles valorize male icons, who are bound to break many hearts. These male homosexual circles uphold the supremacy of desire, but the object of desire is the male icon rather than the magnate. Physical limitation, however, prevents anyone from being always the conqueror of love. "The principles of the [homosexual] underworld" are "the doomed cycles of betraying and being betrayed" (83) and "never love again, lest you get hurt" (144). As sexuality is disentangled from the social network of marriage, family, and reproduction, gay men can enjoy anonymous sex.

The disagreement between Little Shao and Ah-yao constitutes another dialectic in the book between order and decadence, morality and transgression (see Chang 140–41). Little Shao's refutation of Ah-yao is again shot through with implicit respect and admiration. Little Shao practiced promiscuous, even anonymous, sex after being jilted by his lover; he abandons decadent life only after he meets Yung-ji. In contrast, Ah-yao, who dies of AIDS, has been promiscuous and militant all his life. When Little Shao was still confused about his sexual identity, Ah-yao was already a happy gay man involved in the gay-rights movement. When the post-AIDS Queer Nation adopts defiant and seductive strategies, Ah-yao, who lives in New York, is among the activists who cry out "Act up. Fight back. Fight AIDS" (11). Little Shao, who only wants to have a secure life with Yung-ji, is horrified by Ah-yao's militancy. Shocked by Ah-yao's insatiable sexual desire, he feels sorry that the lonely Ah-yao has to make international phone calls to him after casual sex. Still, Little Shao regards Ah-yao as a hero. Thinking that Ah-yao deserves a panel on the Names Project quilt, in North American gay communal mourning of those who die of AIDS, Little Shao bursts into praise: "You are a warrior, Ah-yao" (35). Even when dying, Ah-yao would not convert to any religious belief, for he thinks "Salvation is a worse way of shirking the responsibility.

. . . Now that he has had a wanton life, has fathomed the bottom of desire, let him go to hell. Any other alternative is bullshit" (22). In Little Shao's recollection, however, Ah-yao is associated with Buddha: he imagines that "Once Buddha became so skinny that he was just like an AIDS patient" (212); and he finds that, after cremation, Ah-yao's throat bone resembles a man sitting Buddha-wise. Despite the fact that Little Shao returns to mainstream order, thereby denigrating practitioners of promiscuity as lechers, he cannot help respecting Ah-yao for bolstering positive images of gayness. Such images enable him to fantasize that Buddha was gay, to imagine that the crucified Jesus is branded with the kisses of his betrayer, and to have a secret marriage with Yung-ji at St. Peter's Basilica in Rome. He also realizes that his monogamous contract with Yung-ji is based solely on the fact that they happen to be highly congenial to each other.

CHIU MIAO-JIN

Whereas the narrator of *Notes of a Desolate Man* is an effeminate gay man, the narrator of Chiu Miao-jin's *Notes of a Crocodile* is a butch woman. They represent respective stereotypes of male homosexuals and lesbians, while their gender crossing is unintelligible and horrifying to mainstream society. As a matter of fact, homosexuality itself is seen as immoral and perverse by the conservatives, since it disrupts the heterosexual scenario and the procreative purpose traditionally assigned to men and women. But butch lesbians and effeminate gay men are doubly discriminated against because they also subvert the rigid gender divide under martial law that aligned man to a robust, virile brand of masculinity and woman to a passive, submissive kind of femininity. The two novels then constitute counterdiscourses to some extent, despite the fact that they also contain mainstream notions of gender and sexuality. More directly than Little Shao, La-tze in *Notes of a Crocodile* critiques the heterocentrism of the mainstream gender paradigm. She sneers at the way mainstream heterosexual society prescriptively equates masculinity with man and femininity with woman, and the way it reduces sex to its reproductive function. Anyone not confined by such a paradigm, La-Tze objects, is "de-masculinized and de-feminized and seen as neutered" (51). In other words, since gender is already heterosexualized, lesbians and gay men are perceived as "queer." "Crocodile" is a metaphor for such a "queer" identity. By depicting the melancholia, resentment, and (self)-derision of a bunch of lesbian and gay college students, the book protests against this heterosexual matrix.

Although La-tze seems more militant and angry than Little Shao, paradoxically she is more constrained by mainstream values. Whereas the dissembling but narcissistic Little Shao has no trouble with his gay identity, the angry but self-hating La-tze is overcome with resentment and despair which affects her love relationships negatively. On the other hand, whereas Little Shao displays his effeminacy and celebrates a feminine aesthetic, La-tze also manifests her masculinity and proposes a "reverse" decadent aesthetic. If Little Shao seems to suggest that every male homosexual has an aestheticizing temper and is hence more or less effeminate, La-tze seems to intimate that every lesbian/homosexual has a violent temper and is therefore more or less masculine. Such violent temper is induced by her/his anger at institutional violence, her/his incapacity to change the system, and her/his helpless internalization of the system's values. Violent temper is directed toward both her/himself and the system. The lesbians and gay men in the novel all feel intense self-hatred, despair, and self-destructive desire due to society's intolerance of their sexual identities. Thus Mong-sheng becomes a drug addict, Chu-kuang attempts suicide many times, Tuin-tuin quits school, and La-tze fools around. La-tze explains to Tuin-tuin how, when she first realized her sexual identity, she felt she was being put into the closet by society: it was as if she suddenly bumped into "an absurd wall" (108); the world changed overnight; she was thrown into a totally alien country, feeling herself silently sinking into sheer isolation. Sensitive to the way homosexuality is perceived as a felony, she experiences guilt and fear over her lesbian identity. Images of violence by society come up frequently. The cruelty of heterosexual society makes her feel that being gay is just like being diseased or murdered or raped or put into the mental hospital or the concentration camp. For her, then, life becomes a miserable hell devoid of any hope or goals.

If the rule for the gay underworld in *Notes of a Desolate Man* is casual sex in a sexual paradise, that in *Notes of a Crocodile* is a playing out of all kinds of sexual dysfunction and inadequacy induced by an oppressively homophobic culture. The book portrays the difficulties of homosexual love by showing emotional entanglements such as an inability to show love, a fear of sex, a fear of being loved, mutual torture, etc. In their sexual practice, lesbians seem more likely in this world to conform to mainstream values than do gay men. La-tze, for example, is almost incapable of confronting and showing her own desire; one of the reasons she runs away from Shuei-ling is that she feels her desire is dirty. Tzu-jo and Tuin-tuin seem to feel the same: in love with each other, they nevertheless separate and try to become heterosexual but never feel happy. Tzu-jo can never be gratified since her love is dissociated from her sex: she loves the male body and woman's soul. Although the two gay men Mong-sheng and Chu-kuang can face their own desire, they fear being loved due to self-hatred.

Although he eventually becomes a drug addict, Mong-sheng in the first half of the book represents the kind of decadent man that La-tze envies—Jean Genet, the French gay writer whom La-tze seeks to evoke. La-tze suggests that Genet is an antiestablishment subculture hero when she mentions more than twice that Genet grew up in prison, regarded convicts as his parents, and deliberately returned to prison by committing theft. Mong-sheng seems like a figure from Genet's fiction, decadently alluring with the assumed wickedness of a motorcycle gangster. (Certainly, his antisocial behavior is more a rebellious gesture of a young literature lover than really vile.) La-tze feels that Mong-sheng's laughter "is showing off to me how he exercises certain power over me, as if he could master me" (42). Mong-sheng behaves weirdly and displays an aptitude for black humor. He sends a packet to her, whom he had met only once before, in red-ink handwriting; the packet contains a stub of a finger, which he claims to be his, cut off because La-tze would not see him. This terrifies her, and she learns only later that it's not true. Mong-sheng is wild and defiantly immoral. In the gay bar named "Nothing," he sings with a man on the stage and has a hot kiss with him, which makes La-tze vomit. He had also performed on the stage the act of defecating and real-life sex with a man and a woman. Moreover, he runs around in the women's restroom urinating and walks around naked in front of a lesbian and a gay man in the men's dormitory.

La-tze's decadent aesthetic is thus different from that of Little Shao. Rather than privileging the beautiful, hers is a "reverse" decadent aesthetic that valorizes the ugly and the immoral. Such an aesthetic is implied in her account of the French film *Mauvais Sang*: "the hero looks like a lizard, close in blood to the crocodile family. The other men in the film are either fat and short or bald; all of them are ugly old men" (27), but the director is one of the greatest aestheticians of our times. Such a decadent aesthetic is further developed in her portrayal of Mong-sheng. He is still a "tall beautiful boy" (31) when La-tze first meets him, but she feels that "it's inappropriate to call him a boy, for I can smell that he has peculiar power to bend people. Such power makes him aged. Except for his superb ability to joke about everything, he has not a single trace of boyish quality in him" (29–30). Identifying with Mong-sheng, La-tze appreciates his decadent humor; she feels familiar and reassured when she receives his message that says, "Don't love you. Want to see you only. Would rape you on midnight next Sunday should you not meet me" (42). For her, his decadent mocking "can be drawn to extreme viciousness at one end and to extreme tenderness at the other" (43).

Like *Notes of a Desolate Man*, *Notes of a Crocodile* depicts the drama of betraying and being betrayed, but here the cruelty often comes from the incapacity for self-love and the fear of being loved. Paradoxically, these difficulties only enhance the intensity of love. When the ambivalent lovers are entangled in sadistic, masochistic, and mutual torturing cycles, their crying signifies not only the pain of love but also a protest against mainstream society.

CHENG YING-SHU

Cheng Ying-shu's novel *Humankind Should Not Fly* and short-story collection *What Good Girls Don't Do* also portray gender crossing and decadence. Unlike *Notes of a Crocodile* and *Notes of a Desolate Man*, *Humankind Should Not Fly* focuses on male-to-female transsexuals. By depicting transsexuals, the novel satirizes heterosexualized gender notions and at the same time ridicules the filthiness of some decadent men. Delineating heterosexual relationship, *What Good Girls Don't Do* is even more critical of decadent men, while it mocks traditional "good girls," satirizes the illusiveness of heterosexual love, and shows the danger of heterosexual liberation.

Humankind Should Not Fly portrays the gender trouble of transsexuals and transgenderists. The two male-to-female transsexuals in the novel show different effects of gender crossing. Jenny, the English transsexual who is as beautiful, "natural," and androgynous as Sharon Stone, confuses the anonymous first-person narrator regarding how to distinguish woman from man, while Nicola (in Ma Shu's story, a story within the novel), who deliberately exaggerates his/her femininity, is seen as affected and a satirical parody of woman. Their notions of gender are also different. Nicola regrets having had the transsexual surgery, which she sees as robbing her of the power of man, while Jenny never expresses similar regrets, even though her bravery toward the end of the novel makes the narrator feel that Jenny remains a man despite the surgical conversion. Jenny's gender crossing both subverts heterosexualized gender and reveals the problem with the effeminate narrator. For the narrator, Jenny the transsexual is a woman, hence his marrying her proves to everyone that he is a man. He is thus puzzled by Jenny's love affair with Gao-sai, the gay man, but eventually he comes to doubt that both he himself and Ma Shu may be transsexual or homosexual. One of the jokes in the novel is that the narrator perceives himself as a "standard," "healthy" male hetero-sexual, but no matter how he tries to prove this through his relationship with women, he is only capable of sisterly affection for them. Even when he has sex with Chien Jong-tze, his female teacher, he only gets his erection through thinking of a gecko. Likewise, Ma Shu sleeps with several women on one single night because he cannot have an orgasm. He has sex with penguins when he is a seaman.

Humankind Should Not Fly is a double-edged satire: it both satirizes the repression and hypocrisy of heterosexist society and ridicules the meanness and ribaldry of some decadent men. The fetish for sex with animals as shown by the narrator, Ma Shu, and Nick, for instance, seems to be derived from their incapacity both for heterosexual desire and for facing homosexual desire. Perceiving himself to be a good man, the narrator often regards deviation from the heterosexual norms as decadent and perverse, but he also participates in it. The narrator is shocked by Jenny's performance of mock oral sex with a bottle, but his own fantasy of seduc-ing ignorant pretty teenage girls is even more obscene. Nick—that is, the presurgical Nicola—also behaves like a good boy until he tries to prove to his companions that he is capable of sexual desire for girls. He reveals his nastiness in coercing an Asian-descended girl into performing oral sex for him.

In both *What Good Girls Don't Do*, which deals with heterosexual relation-ship, and *Humankind Should Not Fly*, decadence is often banalized or vulgarized and shown to be affected, listless, vile, and mean. The decadent men in "The Doves on the Roof" and "Woman's Ordeal," for instance, are both daydreaming bums: one of them keeps making trouble that his wife must repair; the other tempts his girlfriend into prostitution so he can make money as a pimp. The drunkards in *Humankind Should Not Fly* and "The Monster" despise work, and become either so drunk that they pick fights with strangers, or so poor that they have to sell themselves for money. The first-person female narrator of "The Monster" se-duces the fiance of her friend due to her lack of money to buy alcohol, and is humiliated by being half-coerced into performing oral sex. Jenny's decadence seems more positive; the narrator once has the (wrong) impression that she is the kind of "elegant, decadent English gentleman who wears a pale and scornful smile" (106). After she gets addicted to marijuana and alcohol, however, she also appears dazed.

What Good Girls Don't Do even satirizes the reification and violence that an aestheticizing vision may involve. "The Angel's Eyes" is a lurid story, in which a male aesthete uses an elaborate, elegant language to celebrate his wife's sweet innocence and his brutal murder of her. He reifies both her terrible death and her physical beauty; in his diseased imagination, "she is his porcelain doll" (60), and only by crushing her to pieces can he show "her heart-breaking beauty" (60).

In Cheng Ying-shu's portrayal of heterosexual relationship, traditional valorization of beautiful women over ugly ones is overturned, since she depicts the latter as more active and aggressive. The delicate porcelain-doll-like women in *Humankind Should Not Fly*, "The Angel's Eyes," and "The Woman Man Hates" are all vulnerable: one is murdered, another is a battered wife, and the third suffers from melancholia due to an unhappy marriage. The narrator of "The Woman Man Hates" remarks that his mother behaves like Snow White lying in the coffin, or a ballerina playing the role of the dying swan, so brittle that she "is a sheer loser" (127). In contrast, ugly women are more autonomous and physically more powerful. The fat girl in "The Woman Man Hates" bares her breasts when doing her workout in her apartment, which both disgusts and fascinates the peeping narrator. The fat woman in "Woman's Ordeal" is so domineering that she dangles a decadent man's deflated penis and dumps him like an old shoe. In *Humankind Should Not Fly*, the narrator's mother changes from a slim fragile woman to a cow-like ferocious one as she becomes the breadwinner.

What Good Girls Don't Do contains a lot of dialectic between good girls and bad girls, morality and immorality, love and sex. The old-fashioned women in "Bad Neighbors" and "Three Women Secretly Punished a Rapist" all transgress spiritually against their own notions of good women. The self-righteous widow, while indignant at the "Spicy Girl" next door, is nevertheless sexually restless after overhearing the girl's lustful voice in sexual intercourse. The spinster is dazed by the unconscious rapist's inflated penis, which she holds in her hand; she castrates him abruptly only out of fear that people may suspect that she has had sex with him. "Bad Neighbors," "Woman's Trial," and "SOMEWHERE IN TIME" all satirize the illusiveness of love. In "SOMEWHERE IN TIME," falling in love is simply an artificial imitation of the characters and the plot of the film *The Bridges of Madison County*; it is ludicrously distanced from mundane reality. The eldest daughter in "Bad Neighbors" has been seeing her boyfriend for a year without knowing what love is; for her, the hero and the heroine of romance fiction are like idiots. In "Woman's Trial," A-fu-luo-di (a transliteration of Aphrodite?) is enticed by her boyfriend into becoming a prostitute. While she is physically abused, she foolishly convinces herself that she is emulating the heroine of the porn film *The Story of O*; thus she fantasizes about being "an ascetic for love, a martyr for love" (106).

While questioning traditional constraints on good girls and deriding love as an illusion, *What Good Girls Don't Do* also shows the traps and temptation of casual sex. Just like what Chu Ying-hung in *The Labyrinthine Garden* comes to realize, love seems to be less real than desire in *What Good Girls Don't Do*. "Bad Neighbors," "The Monster," "The Secret Room," and "Woman's Trial" all portray lascivious women. In "The Doves on the Roof," the wife who has extramarital relationships also seems undomesticated. But "The Monster" and "Women's Trial" suggest that casual heterosexual relationship, if it involves commercial sex, is potentially dangerous. The female narrator of "The Monster" has a one-night stand with a man because he is rich, but is sexually exploited by him. In "Woman's Trial," A-fu-luo-di moves into her boyfriend's apartment partly because she is homeless, and ends up being sold by him for prostitution and even dumped. Unlike the other women who have or don't have sexual love with men, the fat girl in "The Woman Man Hates" displays an alternative sexual autonomy. She would rather masturbate than fall in love, which, for her, would mean hurting each other.

While *What Good Girls Don't Do* ridicules good women and has reservations about wild women; it portrays women, whether "good" or "bad," old-fashioned or loose, as generally more active and autonomous than women are traditionally portrayed.

CONCLUSION

The ongoing dialectic between morality and immorality in fiction is an attempt to redefine sexual codes. Much Taiwanese fiction in the 1990s deals with the subject matter of homosexuality and/or female desire, indicating an intense interest in gender crossing and decadence. If earlier Taiwanese fiction tends to condemn homosexuality and female desire and take such condemnation for granted, 1990s Taiwanese fiction, even when it continues to denigrate such desires, is more ambiguous and ambivalent in tone. Take, for example, the works I have discussed above. *The Labyrinthine Garden* and *What Good Girls Don't Do* portray, on the one hand, how loose women become men's playthings, and, on the other, how these women's feminist consciousness emerges. *Notes of a Desolate Man* simultaneously vilifies male homosexuality and implicitly criticizes mainstream heterosexual society by relishing homosexual practice. *Notes of a Crocodile* apparently denigrates lesbianism and male homosexuality, but virtually uses it to express anger at and protest against mainstream heterosexual society. In addition, new, unconventional visions are presented, such as feminine, narcissistic women, Material Girls, and the Queen Bees in *Fin-de-Siecle Splendor*, the sexually autonomous fat girls and ugly women in *What Good Girls Don't Do*, and the beautiful male-to-female transsexual in *Humankind Should Not Fly*. Queer gender notions are posited in *Notes of a Desolate Man*, where the male homosexual narrator directly overturns traditional disparagement of femininity and women, and in *Notes of a Crocodile*, where the lesbian narrator asserts violent masculinity. As far as the dialectic between love and sex is concerned, the four female authors seem to affirm the combination of love and sex and are ambiguous in their attitudes toward loveless sex and promiscuity. They portray women's practice of casual sex as an act of rebellion, an act of experiment, or sheer degradation. Paradoxically, heterosexual love often seems illusive; hence the ideal of the combination of love and sex becomes ludicrous. The lesbian relationship in *Notes of a Crocodile*, on the other hand, is difficult and distorted partly due to homophobic social pressure. *Notes of a Desolate Man* seeks to uphold the ideal of the combination of love and sex against promiscuity in male homosexual relationships. But the book also suggests that, historically, male homosexual promiscuity has a quite different cultural context and involves quite different power relations from those of heterosexual promiscuity.

The fictions of Li Ang, Chu Tien-wen, Chiu Miao-jin, and Cheng Ying-shu are only part of 1990s Taiwanese fictions and gender discourses. From a larger perspective, the emphasis on female desire signifies that the meanings of female autonomy have extended to the sexual terrain, where women redefine their sexuality by themselves, thereby posing a great threat to men. Meanwhile, the various genders in 1990s Taiwan go well beyond the traditional gender divide: the sexiest woman may turn out to be a male transvestite, and the most masculine person may be a woman. And it becomes more and more clear that heterosexual relationship may involve quite different power relations from that of homosexual relationship. If the dialectic between love and sex, morality and decadence can give us any food for thought, it may well be that we should confront these differences and be more understanding and tolerant of the differences.

NOTE

1. All my discussion of Taiwanese fictions refers to their Taiwanese version, even though some of them, like Chu Tien-wen's *Notes of a Desolate Man*, may have an English version already. In order to make my discussion more intelligible to non-Chinese readers, I choose not to transliterate the titles of the fictions. And except for the title of Chu's novel, all the translations are mine.

WORKS CITED

Bristow, Joseph. *Empire Boys: Adventures in a Man's World*. London: HarperCollins Academic, 1991.

Chang, Chih-wei. "Homosexual Voices and Homonymic Desires: Chu T'ien-wen's *Huang-jen-Shou-chi*." In: *Queer Archipelago: A Reader of the Queer Discourses in Taiwan*. Edited by Chi Ta-wei. Taipei: Meta Media, 1997. 119–46.

Chen, Shuei. "Sleepwalking in 1994." *Sleepwalking in 1994*. Taipei: Yuan-liou, 1996. 13–44.

Cheng, Ying-shu. *What Good Girls Don't Do*. Taipei: The United Literature, 1998.

———. *Humankind Should Not Fly*. Taipei: The United Literature, 1997.

———. "Three Women Secretly Punished a Rapist." *What Good Girls Don't Do*. 111–22.

———. "The Angel's Eyes." *What Good Girls Don't Do*. 52–63.

———. "The Woman Man Hates." *What Good Girls Don't Do*. 124–46.

———. "The Monster." *What Good Girls Don't Do*. 32–51.

———. "The Doves on the Roof." *What Good Girls Don't Do.* 11–31.

———. "Bad Neighbors." *What Good Girls Don't Do.* 66–96.

———. "Woman's Trial." *What Good Girls Don't Do.* 97–110.

———. "SOMEWHERE IN TIME." *What Good Girls Don't Do.* 169–79.

Chiu, Kuei-fen. *Reading Taiwan/Woman.* Taipei: Meta Media, 1997.

Chiu, Miao-jin. *Notes of a Crocodile.* Taipei: Shih-pao, 1994.

Chu, Tien-wen. *Fin-de-Siecle Splendor.* Taipei:Yuan-liou, 1992.

———. "*Fin-de-Siecle* Splendor." *Fin-de-Siecle Splendor.* 171–92.

———. "A Daughter of the Nile." *Fin-de-Siecle Splendor.* 29–48.

———. "Buddha of the Body." *Fin-de-Siecle Splendor.* 49–71.

———. "Red Rose Is Calling You." *Fin-de-Siecle Splendor.* 155–70.

———. "Take Me Away, Moonlight!" *Fin-de-Siecle Splendor.* 73–154.

———. *Notes of a Desolate Man.* Taipei: Shih-pao, 1994.

Chu, Wei-cheng. "('Comrade' Pai Hsien-yung's) Women, Queers, and Nation: An Articu
lation by Way of Family Romance." *Chung-Wai Literary Monthly* 26.12 (May 1998):
47–66.

Hanson, Ellis. *Decadence and Catholicism.* Cambridge, Mass.: Harvard University Press,
1997.

Hyam, Ronald. *Empire and Sexuality: The British Experience.* Manchester: Manchester
University Press, 1990.

Jeng, Ju-huei. "From Not Having a Unit to Collective Voicing: the Growth of Feminist
Organization Awakening." *The China Times Literary Supplement* (Sept. 10–11, 1998).

Kermode, Frank. "Waiting for the End." In: *Apocalypse Theory and the End of the World.*
Edited by Malcolm Bull. Oxford: Blackwell, 1995. 250–63.

Kumar, Krishan. "Apocalypse, Millennium, and Utopia Today." In: *Apocalypse Theory
and the End of the World.* Edited by Malcolm Bull. Oxford: Blackwell, 1995. 200–24.

Ledger, Sally. *The New Woman: Fiction and Feminism at the Fin de Siecle.* Manchester:
Manchester University Press, 1997.

Li, Ang. *The Labyrinthine Garden.* Taipei: Li Ang, 1991.

Liou, Liang-ya. *Engendering Dissident Desires: The Politics and Aesthetics of Erotic
Fictions.* Taipei: Meta Media, 1998.

———. "Queer Sexchanges: The Representations of the Male-to-Female Transsexual in
Fictions by Yang Chao, Chi Ta-wei, Cheng Ying-shu, and Lucifer Hung." *Chung-Wai
Literary Monthly* 26.12 (May 1998): 11–30.

Luo, Yi-chuin. *The Dream of My Wife and Dogs.* Taipei: Meta Media, 1998.

Pai, Hsien-yung. *The Outcast Son.* Taipei: Yun-chen, 1972.

———. "The Everlasting Yin Hsueh-yen." *Taipei Dwellers.* Taipei: Er-ya, 1983. 1–22.

Showalter, Elaine. *Sexual Anarchy: Gender and Culture at the Fin de Siecle.* New York:
Viking, 1990.

Tsao, Li-chuan. "About Her Gray Hairs and Other Stuff." *Lesbians' Dance.* Taipei:
Titan, 1999. 98–174.

Ware, Vron. *Beyond the Pale: White Women, Racism and History.* London: Verso, 1992.

Yang, Chao. *A Dark Alley on a Wild Night.* Taipei: The United Literature, 1994.

Yeh, Te-hsuan. "Go Camping: Gender Crossing Performances in 'Yung-yuan te Yin Hsueh-
yen' and Nieh-tzu." *Chung-Wai Literary Monthly* 26.12 (May 1998): 67–89.

Chapter 6

Racial and Erotic Anxieties: Ambivalent Fetishization, From Fanon to Mercer

Sonia "Gigi" Otalvaro-Hormillosa

INTRODUCTION

Frantz Fanon raised critical issues that continue to influence questions surrounding postcolonial identity and its location in cultural practices that resist white supremacist hegemony. The contemporary relevance of Fanon's work is a result of his dialectic writing ability in which he engaged his political times with a language through which the future would be created. His status as an intellectual native in colonial Martinique, as well as his efforts in the decolonization of Algeria, provided him with the tools to examine the status of the colonial subject in relation to a variety of issues, ranging from interracial desire to Third World revolution (throughout this chapter, I will most likely refer to the colonial subject in masculine form in order to remain consistent with what appears to be, in my opinion, a masculinist basis in the majority of Fanon's work).[1] The focus of this chapter will be the applicability of interracial desire and Third World revolution to colonial desire, which can be framed in the context of identification and imitation as utilized by cultural theorists who have written on Fanon.

I have chosen a variety of works that can be classified as cultural theory, critical race theory, queer theory, and film criticism, yet many resist classification owing to the hybrid status of their authors. I am conscious of the broad use of the term "hybridity" in circles of cultural studies; my own interpretation of hybridity for the purposes of this chapter is the multiplicity or intersection of identity: for instance, the deviant postcolonial who upholds diasporic consciousness as a potential catalyst in instigating Third World revolution. Stuart Hall describes the diaspora experience as a set of hybrid identities that live with and through, not despite difference. "Diaspora identities are those which are constantly producing and reproducing themselves anew, through transformation and difference" (Hall 234). He ends this article with a quote from Fanon's *Wretched of the Earth* where he insists on perceiving national culture as "a whole body of efforts of a culture that keeps itself in existence" as opposed to a national culture that "delves into the past of a people in order to find coherent elements" (WE, 188). Hybridity creates possibilities for identifications that can lead to cross-race-class-gender-sexuality coalitions in the perpetual struggle against an imperialist system that maintains multiple structures of oppression in place.

Homi Bhabha's work on Fanon includes a densely packed, though useful theoretical interpretation of hybridity similar to Hall's. Commenting on the eyes of the postcolonial woman who writes a history of the poetics of postcolonial diaspora and who resists analogies in relation to sexual difference, Bhabha describes her condition as a "missing person whose structure of difference produces the hybridity of race and sexuality in the postcolonial discourse" (Bhabha, *Location of Culture* 53). It is this hybridity that initiates a process of political thinking that is aware of its own strategy and contingency. In this process, one must be aware of the "priority of the place from which it begins, if its authority is not to become autocratic" (65). This may be quite ironic for Bhabha to state, considering his own status as a postcolonial elite, but by bringing this up, he implicates his own subject position as well as that of the reader. As Hall writes, "The practices of representation always implicate the positions from which we speak or write—the position of enunciation" (220).

Here, I would like to implicate my own socio-geo-racial-sexual-political location in this discourse. I am writing as a queer postcolonial female subject who does not separate sexual politics from racial politics. I advocate Cornel West's "new cultural politics of difference," which resists processes of decolonization that abide by essentialist identity politics at the expense of incorporating heterogeneity along the lines of gender, sexuality, class, and age (West 19–38). Though he may sound as if he were merely naming these categories for the sake of doing justice to the sacred mantra of inclusive identity politics, his arguments remain valid in the context of Third World activism, which continues to be perceived as incommensurate with sexual politics. Kobena Mercer and Isaac Julien articulate their demand for a "radical equality that rests on a precondition of diversity and difference" (Julien and Mercer, "Race" 102). Given their enunciation of gay black male authorship, their statement can be applied to both the queer community and the black community. This will become more clear in my incorporation of their work in this chapter.

One might wonder why most of the authors with whom I am engaging in relation to Fanon are male, despite the fact that some of them may be queer. But the truth is, even if a gay man may seem to do more justice to gender because of his own disruption of gender codes, gaps still exist between the queer male and the queer female; however, with respect to queer men and women of color (even though the category of transgender disrupts this organization), a common space can be shared in which both understand the simultaneous experiences of racial and sexual oppression. For this reason, I have chosen to work primarily with texts by Kobena Mercer and Isaac Julien, whose work is inspired by Fanon. Furthermore, I want to explore the ways in which Fanon's masculinist tradition remains consistent with contemporary gay male discourse. Given my own disidentification with Fanon on issues of gender and sexuality, my identification with queer men of color becomes ambiguous. Do I look to white and colored queer women to fill this "lack"? Will I then be perceived as inauthentic and whitewashed by my heterosexist communities of color? In this chapter, I hope to raise more questions than answer questions regarding the relationship between hybridity and the ways in which identification and imitation, as possibilities for attaining "radical equality," are taken up by authors writing in the tradition of Fanon.

PARADOXES OF CULTURAL CONSUMPTION

Fanon's essay titled "Racism and Culture" from *Toward the African Revolution* reveals what contemporary cultural critics may name as antiessentialist politics. He writes about this at a time when racism seems to have disappeared, yet "the unreal impression was simply the consequence of the evolution of forms of exploitation" (37). Paul Gilroy talks about this newer, more subtle form of racism in the context of England, where citizenship is defined by cultural homogeneity rather than by race and obscures the more obvious forms of exploitation based on race (Gilroy, "End of Antiracism"). Fanon's insight into this matter seems to have paved the way for yet another form of racism that is manifest in practices of cultural appropriation that rely on essentialism, or the idea that there is something inherent about social identities: "Exoticism is one of the forms of this simplification [the determination to objectify, to confine, to imprison, to harden]. It allows no cultural confrontation. There is on the one hand a culture in which qualities of dynamism, of growth, of depth can be recognized" (35). Both the colonizer and the colonized can fall into the trap of relying on "exoticism," which precludes the shifting nature of identity. For instance, he describes the blues as "the modicum of stylized oppression as the exploiter's and the racist's rightful due" (37). I read this statement to be a description of the ways in which the colonizer will always try to access the world of the colonized. Trinh Minh-Ha describes this "tolerance" for an-Other's language as a "reputable form of colonial discrimination, one in which difference can only be admitted once it is appropriated, that is, when it operates within the Master's sphere of having" (Minh-ha 84).

The colonizer wants ownership of the blues, to the Negro's world of misery, and will defend nativism so that his perception of the Negro remains undisturbed, as Fanon states in *Wretched of the Earth* (243). His views on exoticism, in relation to the tendency of the native to look to a distant exoticized past Africa, are enforced effectively through his own poetics in "On National Culture": "It is not enough to try to get back to the people the past out of which they have already emerged; rather we must join them in that fluctuating movement which they are giving shape to... Let there be no mistake about it; it is to this zone of occult instability where the people dwell that we must come" (227). It is in this zone of occult instability where the narcissism on which the colonial relationship is based must be destabilized.[2] In the introduction to *Black Skin White Masks*, Fanon constantly lays out the colonial operation of identification, in terms of how the black wants to be white and how the white man "slaves to reach a human level." On the previous page, he asserts that there are two camps, one black and one white, but that "these metaphysics are often quite fluid" (8–9). This fluidity of the metaphysical nature of black and white camps can be examined in the appropriation of cultural styles and their implications in a neocolonial context.

In "Black Hair/Style Politics" Kobena Mercer provides a clever metaphor for cultural identity in terms of hair style and its politics (Mercer 247–64). Throughout the article, Mercer lists examples of appropriation and commodification of black styles by the dominant culture. For instance, the popularity of dreadlocks and the dashiki can be seen as forms of commodity fetishism in which portions of the dominant culture adopt those styles in order to show their disaffection from western norms. He lists other examples that have more to do with musical styles, an ironic example of which is the popularity of ska and be-bop (in a addition to the shaved-soul-boy look) among white skinheads in seventies Britain. In a brief history of black hair styles, which he describes as a crucial "art form articulating a variety of aesthetic 'solutions' to a range of 'problems' created by ideologies of race and racism" (248), Mercer criticizes the exoticism based on an idealized notion of a pure Africa that inspired the Afro and 'locks; furthermore, this form of nativism led to the denunciation of the supposed "artifice" of other hairstyles such as hair straightening or lightening, which were considered to be rejections of natural black beauty. While the former are considered to be more "natural," Mercer argues that this assertion of difference in comparison to the "artificial" is "contradictory because the difference hinges on the inversion of the same." The basis for his argument lies in the fact that all hair styles are artificial to some extent since each requires careful and conscious cultivation. He prefers the conk because its ambiguity and artifice reflect the contradictions of interculturation from which the more "natural" styles are exempt.

This reading is relevant in light of Fanon's deconstruction of the white artifice inscribed onto the black body, and which ultimately leads to colonial alienation. Mercer's metaphor of hairstyle as identity is an illustration of the detrimental uses of essentialism and/or authenticity in which some cultural subjects are privileged over others because of their adherence to a fixed notion of identity, thus he contests the artifice of the construction of those notions. The contradictions of interculturation clearly mark a type of hybridization that has resulted from histories of migration and displacement. The fact that his metaphor is actually a body part creates a dialectic with Fanon's analysis of the reduction of the Negro to the biological realm. Mercer articulates the complexity of the "semiotic guerrilla warfare" and the lawlessness of the chaos of commodity fetishism in which white imitations of black styles reveal an appropriation of what I would call an idealized racial physicality that imitates surface reality rather than identifies with the historical-reality commodified and fetishized racial subject. In reference to skinhead appropriations of black style, he asks, "What are the bases for the post-imperial mode of mimicry, this ghost dance of white ethnicity?" In the more contemporary and popular context of pervasive hip-hop appropriation, he asks, "Who, in this postmodern melee of semiotic appropriation and counter-creolization, is imitating whom?" (281). I include these questions here because they are crucial interrogations into the forms of neocolonialism that reveal the paradoxical relationships that constitute contemporary race relations. Furthermore, they shed light on the potential problems that arise in "hybrid practices" governed by privileged positions that have been shaped by history (i.e., white middle-class hippie-crits, or yippies as others may refer to them, hip-hopsters, and so on).

Fanon's Manichaean concept of the world in which white has been constructed as beauty and virtue with black as its Other in the form of negation (BSWM 45) sheds light on the irony of cultural appropriation as exemplified by neo-Nazi skinheads, whose ideology maintains the Manichaean divide, and who paradoxically consume black styles. One of the major recurring themes in *Black Skin White Masks* and *Wretched of the Earth* is the racial anxiety that simultaneously masks both desire and fear of the black body and manifests itself in violence toward that body, as illustrated by the history of lynching; hence, the simultaneous violence of neo-nazism and the love of be-bop, ska, and the bald-head look. I don't want to suggest that all practices of cultural "exchange" operate in such a neocolonial racist way. This would rely on essentialist claims that would permit only Cubans to dance salsa, or African-Americans to dance hip-hop, or Chinese people to eat Chinese food, etc. There is a difference between exploitation and appreciation; nonetheless, various forms of cultural exchange suggest that identification via colonial desire is at work. Bhabha argues that three conditions underlie the process of identification: "to exist is to be called into being in relation to an otherness, its locus, its look . . . ; the very place of identification is a place of splitting . . . ; identification is never the affirmation of a pregiven identity—it is always the transformation of the subject in assuming that identity" (Location of Culture 44–45). Several pages later he arrives at the following conclusion: "By following the trajectory of colonial desire... it becomes possible to cross, even to shift the Manichaean boundaries" (62). In the midst of his highly theoretical language, Bhabha fails to provide concrete examples of how this potential can affect change. I myself recognize this potential for what I interpret to be a hybridity arrived at through colonial desire, but I am wary of my own problematic participation in this elite-cultural studies discourse, which risks remaining abstract and useless in relation to economic realities and the cultural productions that sustain oppressive hierarchies. Nonetheless, Bhabha's statements lead to us to question the internal dynamics of racial identification within each subject who allows the Other(s) within to emerge.

EXOTICISM IN GAY CULTURE

Placing colonial desire in the context of gay subculture, Kobena Mercer and Isaac Julien explore issues of identification or lack thereof among men of different ethnicities in the gay community. The analysis of cultural appropriation, which in many cases relies on exoticizing notions of Other cultures in a queer context, can reveal the complexity of the implications that arise from multiple border crossings as they are experienced *on the margins of the margins* of racial and sexual politics. In some articles that Mercer and Julien wrote together, they argue that the politics of representation in the sex-cultural production of pornography, which to some degree has been colonized by white feminists and white gay men in the era of increasing political importance of this issue, are critical in understanding how "ethnicity is a crucial factor in the social construction of manliness, suggesting the racial dialectic of projection and internalization through which white and black men have shaped their masks of masculinity is a key point at which race, gender, and the politics of sexuality intersect" (Julien and Mercer, "Race" 99). Furthermore, whiteness's ethnic location remains invisible in the gay community just as it does in the mainstream, and despite the influences of the black liberation movement on the gay and lesbian liberation movement in the sixties where Black Pride was translated into (appropriated by?) Gay Pride, contemporary mutual reciprocity between the two does not exist (Julien and Mercer, "True" 192). In terms of possibilities for Black Gay Pride, it is unfortunate that the neglect of queers of color by dominant cultures of the gay community and communities of color has continually persisted. Significantly enough, it was the Black and Puerto Rican drag queens who led Stonewall, the historical moment at which queers rebelled against the customary practices of police raids into gay and lesbian bars, which were often accompanied by severe police brutality. Though organizations such as the Mattachine Society and the Daughters of Bilitis existed, organizations with predominantly white middle-class memberships, and other privileged members of society that looked down on bar culture, which primarily consisted of working-class queers and/or queers of color (D'Emilio), I would argue that most people today associate gay and lesbian liberation with Stonewall rather than with these organizations. Unfortunately, there is little mention of the fact that the leaders of this revolutionary moment were queers of color, and that their activism probably had a great deal to with the likelihood that they were already involved in antiracist struggles that served as a catalyst to instigate change in other areas of their lives.

The role that ethnicity plays in queer relations can be better understood vis-à-vis Lewis Gordon's treatment of the racial and sexual matrices of desire and his insistence on their significance for a better understanding of social roles that are informed by "bad faith" forms in which groups are structured in the overdetermined Manichaean structure such that one group is hot/masculine/active/white and the other is cold/passive/feminine/black (Gordon 74–75). Mercer and Julien argue that the new "macho" styles that have been appropriated by gay white men to challenge stereotypes of the effeminate weak queer carry racist and fascist connotations of white masculinity that maintain this overdetermined racial structure in place, regardless of whether or not those styles merely serve to eroticize masculinity ("True Confessions" 192). Mercer and Julien also offer a critique of the masculinist form of the sixties black liberation movement that was exclusive of women and gays and lesbians, and that ultimately led to the autonomous organization of black feminists in the seventies. In contradistinction to the machismo that is prevalent among a large number of black male youth and contemporary rap artists, Mercer and Julien favor alternative constructions of black masculinity as exemplified by the styles of figures such as Little Richard, Prince, and George Clinton, who "play with stereotypical codes to 'theatricalize' and send up the whole masquerade of masculinity itself" ("True Confessions" 200). Even though their study is on masculinity, I would also add a figure such as M'shell Ndegeocello, a black bisexual r&b artist, who disrupts gender codes, specifically those of straight black femininity, in songs in which she is explicit about female-to-female desire or that include a subversive treatment of biblical passages; for instance, in "Leviticus" from *Peace Beyond Passion* (this is a reference to the passage in the bible that considers it an abomination for men to lie with other men) she tells a story of a gay black man whose mother would always pray for him and who eventually gets beaten to death. Later in this chapter, I will explore issues surrounding homopho- bic violence and issues of anxiety via Fanon within racial communities that cause this violence.

Returning to the issue of colonizing agendas in relation to the politics of representation in pornography, I would like to comment on an article by Richard Dyer titled "Coming to Terms" in which he articulates—as a gay white male—the political importance and defense of pornography as a genre, specifically gay male porn, due to its roots in bodily effects, which can give us knowledge that other genres cannot (Dyer 289–98). He argues that gay male porn is structured around a linear narrative that culminates in visual coming. Though gay male porn is marginal to the mainstream, he maintains that this desire to come, which is placed in a narrative structure in which gay male desire to be penetrated is sidelined, does not disturb the status quo. I am tempted to describe this statement as Fanonian in the sense that substitution rather than transformation takes place, as is the case with the national bourgeoisie who merely replace rather than transform the colo- nial power structure during the moment of decolonization (Fanon, *Wretched* 148– 205). Dyer claims that a common feature of gay male porn is to include another porn within the porn, which collapses the distinction between representation and that which it is a representation of. Furthermore, "Porn is . . . part of how we live our sexuality; how we represent sexuality to ourselves is how we live it . . . Gay porn seems to make that all clearer, because there is greater equality between the participants which permits a fuller exploration of the education of desire that is going on" (296). In conclusion, he calls for more criticism of porn that addresses the educational function of porn.

One author who might differ with Dyer's claims about the "greater equality between the participants" in gay porn is Richard Fung, who examines the educa- tional function of porn in "Looking for My Penis: The Eroticized Asian in Gay Video Porn" in which he criticizes the racist representation of Asians in main- stream gay male porn (*How Do I Look?* 145–68). While he acknowledges Dyer's assumption that more equality among participants exists in a gay context than it does in a straight context, for Fung this is only true when all of the participants are white. Fung addresses the role of colonial discourse that has placed Asians on the desexualized end of the sexual spectrum and Africans on the hypersexualized end of the spectrum while whites fall neatly in the middle. He also makes an important point regarding the contradiction of the simultaneous coexistence of Orientalist stereotypes relating to specific groups based on nationality (i.e., the Japanese as kinky, Filipinos as available) and the more general Orientalist stereotype that lumps all Asians into one group, thus perpetuating the notion that all Asians are the same. Responding to Fanon's quote regarding the eclipse of the Negro by his penis, he asks whether or not homoerotic desire is possible for the Asian male because of his apparent lack of a penis. He provides examples of gay porn that privilege gay white male desire in which Orientalist stereotypes of Asian passivity are reinscribed. In the same way that two women are often used in heterosexual male porn, not for the purpose of illustrating female-to-female desire, but for satisfying the straight-male ego and gaze, Asians have occupied a similar subordinate role in gay male porn.

One interesting example is a porn that takes place in a dojo (that also suggests a gay white male appropriation of a suitable "exotic" setting for bondage and discipline) where a dream sequence allows one of the white characters to fulfill his fantasy of submission and passivity by occupying the role of an Asian; hence, Fung sees this as an equation of Asian with anus. Furthermore, racial stereotypes often go with classist stereotypes that portray the Asian as the lower-class houseboy or servant, thus playing on the material conditions of Asian immigrants (165–68). Fung is concerned with these issues because as Dyer has noted, porn teaches us about how we act out our sexuality; in Fung's examples, porn does exactly that: it reveals the racist and classist nature of the gay mainstream where negative or absent representations of Asians have skewed sexual relations among Asian men. Fung makes an important point about the effects that this has on gay Asian immigrants whose initial contact with gay culture occurs in a racist context. These representations provide an interesting comparison and extension of Mercer's and Julien's work on the different dynamics of representation of racial Others in the gay mainstream. They also complicate issues around identification and appropriation in gay culture, which appear to allow for more gender flux and equality at the expense of creating positive images of queers of color.

"AMBIVALENT RACIAL FETISHIZATION"

In an article titled "Skin Head Sex Thing: Racial Difference and the Homoerotic Imaginary," Mercer reveals the shifting nature of his multiply constituted subject position in his reflexive and reflective revision of an earlier reading of Robert Mapplethorpe's photographs of black male nudes, which may be read as pornographic by some, but have been appropriated into the world of art photography (*How Do I Look?* 169–222). Inspired by Michel Foucault's antinaturalist account of the "distinction between author-function and ideological subject position," he justifies his more recent ambivalent relationship to the photographs by contesting the inherent meaning of cultural texts. Mercer treats the cultural text as something that is experienced" across the relations between, authors, texts, and readers, relations that are always contingent, context bound, and historically specific." Consequently, different kinds of readers and contexts have the potential to create a variety of meanings of the same text. In his initial reading of Mapplethorpe's work, specifically a piece called "Man in Polyester Suit" in which the viewer only sees black hands and a black penis (as the indicator of the model's race) coming out of a tacky polyester suit, Mercer interprets this to be an inscription of the Manichaean oppositions of nature/culture, savage/civilized where the significance of the tacky suit is proof of the black man's failure to access "culture" (170–79).

What appeared to Mercer to be a reduction of black bodies to sexual objects echoes Fanon when he writes: "One is no longer aware of the Negro, but only of a penis. The Negro is eclipsed. He is turned into a penis, he is a penis" (BSWM 170). Furthermore, Mercer adds that the two-dimensionality of the text, which allows for "a cool detached gaze (on the part of the white male spectator) that erases the historical context and enables the projection of fantasy which saturates the black male body in sexual predicates," points to the fears and anxieties around the black penis as a threat to white male power. He specifically refers to what Bhabha calls a "colonial fantasy," which articulates power and mastery over the racial Other (see Bhabha, "The Other" 18–36). His reactions to such texts have been ambivalent because he is angry about the negative/colonial images, but he also feels a desire to look. While his earlier reading was guided by feminist critiques of the objectifying male gaze, in his revision he is less sure about the effects of the photographs because he considers major factors, such as Mapplethorpe's status as a *gay* white man who died of AIDS as well as the hybridized aesthetic practices of black queers, which have led to more critical dialogues, readings, and multiple positions from which to enunciate.

It is especially significant to consider the fact that Mapplethorpe acknowledged the historical absence of the black nude from the western aesthetic nude canon. Mercer argues that Mapplethorpe doubles the text by imposing what is considered to be the "polluted world of racist image" onto the "'purified' realm of the aestheticized ideal." Hence, the presence of the black male subverts the normative aesthetic, which leads to the potential reversibility of the gaze. It appears to be the case that in the actual act of writing, Mercer reveals the process of continual transformation in his own analyses. While making a clear distinction between Mapplethorpe as a gay white male and the straight white male spectator, Mercer also recognizes this as the point at which he departs from his previous alignment with feminist theory. While not completely divorcing himself from feminist theory, he enunciates his privileged position as a phallocentric gay male who is able to assert more agency in his own consumption of the text because of his access to the gay male gaze, but which still remains ambiguous and contradictory in light of the racial component—hence, his interpretation of Mapplethorpe's "ambivalent racial fetishization," where ambivalence is defined as the moment at which politics and the contestation of power are most intense, in which he (Mercer) acknowledges his dual location as object and subject (187–90).

Toward the end of this article, he seems to show appreciation for Mapplethorpe's photographs of the black nude because of its decoding of the aesthetic ideal, but he does not return to the famous photograph that initially inspired his criticisms—"Man in Polyester Suit" in which elements of the Manichaean divide manifest themselves in a very obvious manner. In the discussion that follows the article, Mercer reveals the danger of the "doubling" in Mapplethorpe's work in the sense that it can either result in identification—on the part of the black male—with the master/slave narrative in which machismo results as a reaction to the narrative and is then displaced onto others, or in internalization in which stereotypes are played out in gay relationships; however, Mercer resists internalization per se because of its anti-Fanonian rejection of sociogenesis in which the colonized is always constituted objectively and subjectively (219).

On the one hand, I agree with Mercer's claims to the "subversive potential" of the photographs, but I question the large numbers of economically disadvantaged black queer males who have absolutely no access to elite cultural studies discourse around artistic and sexual practices (i.e., how would the African-American 16-year-old male transvestite prostitute who lives on the street as his/her only means for survival respond to terms such as "ambivalent racial fetishization"?). After all, he acknowledges that these kinds of readings are available only to those "in the know." Throughout this text, Mercer stresses the importance of the role of the reader, which highlights the possibility that the same signs in cultural texts, such as Mapplethorpe's photographs, can produce different readings (i.e., their potential to be read as homoerotic or homophobic texts).

It is useful to place Mercer's shifts in political identification in the context of Gordon's paradigm of the antiblack world as an "ideal type" in which the highest nonmixture is white and masculine and the lowest nonmixture is black and feminine (78). In his analysis, Gordon makes the connection between the black man and the (white?) lesbian, because while both are feminized in an antiblack world, they pose a similar threat in demanding power that has been constructed as white-masculine-phallus; however, there would seem to be a disconnection between the black man and the black lesbian considering that she, by virtue of her location in an antiblack world, does not have whiteness (as does the white lesbian) or a physical phallus (as does the black man) that places them in a position to demand white phallic power. It seems that within this configuration in which there exists an inherent gender inequality among black men and black women and white men and white women, the black lesbian poses a potential threat only to the black man, rather than to the white man, due to the feminization of black women and men, which places them on a more equal playing field in relation to each other as opposed to the black lesbian's relationship to the white man.

Gordon stresses that the antiblack world as an ideal type is a subjunctive reality, in which the triple task of the critic includes "interpreting the two poles as perspectives and interpreting her or his own relation as a critical relation to such a world" (84). Hence, my own interpretation of what appears to be a shift in Mercer's politics to a simultaneous identification with white-masculine-phallus-power and disidentification with feminist politics where he previously made the connections between the objectified female body and the fetishized/feminized black body (Mercer, "Skin" 174). I think it is important here to take into consideration Gordon's statement that "for although our antiblack world is also a misogynist world, a misogynist world is not necessarily an antiblack one" (76). This seems to point to the relative autonomy of misogyny from racism in contrast to the dependence of racism on misogyny. Furthermore, Mercer's initial association of racism with misogyny and later identification with Mapplethorpe reveals the primacy of cross-race phallic camaraderie, which is heightened in the context of a male homoerotic and potentially misogynistic realm. I don't mean to essentialize Mercer, I am only using the paradigm of an antiblack world as an ideal type to articulate the potential for hybrid spaces to break down the Manichaean divide as well as the potential danger of discursive inaccessibility that arises from the more privileged spaces of hybridity.

As a multiply constituted subject, Mercer enunciates from various interlocking positions in which he provides us with a piece of writing that is an excellent example of precisely what he argues for: the fact that a text can produce multiple meanings. Depending on the reader's position, this article can be read either as a phallocentric text as evidenced by the implications of his revision, or as an "ambivalent" text that maintains allegiances to the various political positions he embraced throughout this process. Taking into consideration my own subject position as a queer woman of color and my identification with other queer women of color, one might be tempted to reduce my reaction to a rejection of what would be considered a phallocentric text given the disidentification between the black man and the queer woman of color in the context of an antiblack world, though there is still a part of me that identifies with Mercer's text. My own "ambivalence" to the text rejects an essentialist reading of a text by a queer man of color who acts as a possible bridge between the queer white man and the woman of color, who might normally resist any sort of allegiance with the gay white male world given their respective locations in an antiblack world. Furthermore, I am also aware of my own privileged status as a queer woman who grew up during the early years of the AIDS pandemic and consequently did not experience the deaths of loved ones as a powerful vehicle for cross-race identification, which Mercer's text also seems to imply.

AMBIVALENT READINGS OF FANON

Applying Mercer's ideas on ambivalence as a result of the various meanings that a single text can produce, I find myself questioning the limits of Fanon's discourse and the extent to which I am invited into his text. While there are points at which I agree with Fanon, specifically his pieces on national culture and consciousness in *Wretched of the Earth* (even though I question these to some extent, given Fanon's critique of the national bourgeois elite who more often than not were male) or the piece on racism and culture in *Toward the African Revolution*, the sections in *Black Skin White Masks* that attempt to explore neurotic interracial dynamics (i.e., those relationships inspired by "bad faith" in the sense that they are based on racist assumptions) or the psychopathology of the black are points at which I depart. For instance, I felt as though the chapter on the woman of color and the white man did not do justice to the multiple spaces in which women of color find themselves in relation both to society and to men of color. The chapter could have provided a more in-depth analysis of the subjectivity of the woman of color in order to reveal the struggles within the community of color rather than the primacy of the psychopathology of the black man. As Hazel Carby has written in her criticism of white western feminist hegemony, despite the fact that patriarchy is a system that exploits women and men of color, women of color are oppressed differently by men of different colors.

When writing about the man of color and the white woman, Fanon illustrates the ways in which manhood, black or white, is a symbol of patriarchy and can override race: "Once this ritual of initiation into 'authentic' manhood (sleeping with a white woman) takes place, they took the train for Paris" (BSWM 72). By placing the word authentic (read: white) in quotation marks, Fanon suggests that black men strive for white manhood—hence, white patriarchy. This seems like a crucial point at which Fanon could have elaborated upon different systems of patriarchy to illustrate the complex multiple spaces in which the woman of color must wage her wars. In the same way that he draws conclusions about the man of color in the previous chapter, the same could have been done in relation to the woman of color. Though these are chapters in which gender-neutral language is clearly not utilized (despite the argument that in the French translation, he did use gender-neutral language in the rest of his text), the ways in which they are presented privilege male subjectivity over female subjectivity, which is the natural outcome of gender-neutral language, in the same way that race-neutral language can privilege white subjectivity over colored subjectivity.

Another point at which Fanon could have engaged more with internal struggles among the colonized is in his treatment of the veil. In "Algeria Unveiled" from *A Dying Colonialism*, Fanon writes about the transformation of the Algerian woman as an integral part of the revolution. "The Algerian woman is at the heart of the combat. Arrested, tortured, raped, shot down, she testifies to the violence of the occupier and to his inhumanity" (DC 66). I interpreted this statement to be an illustration of the ultimate form of colonial degradation which only the woman can experience owing to her status as the gendered colonized being. Unlike the man, she can be sexually exploited and raped in the most humiliating manner. She is the concrete manifestation of what happens to a culture that is penetrated by outside forces. Men suffered beatings, torture and possibly rape at times, but women also experienced torture, beatings, and rape, while the latter occurred much more frequently.

At the beginning of this chapter, Fanon equates rejected veils with the acceptance of rape by the colonizer, as it is viewed by the Algerian public. He writes quite matter-of-factly about this, almost to the extent that he denies any agency to Algerian women who may have rejected the veil for subversive purposes within their community other than for the acceptance of rape by the colonizer. Later in the chapter, he writes, as though with full authority on the subject, that "the veil protects, reassures, isolates. One must have had heard the confessions of the Algerian women or have analyzed the dream content of certain recently unveiled women to appreciate the importance of the veil for the body of the women" (DC 59). As I was reading this, I felt as though I were reading Freud again or scientific material written by white men on women and/or people of color. It also reminded me of the anthropologist or cultural critic that takes up issues in relation to "others" in a totalizing manner, as if they can understand them better than they can understand themselves. While taking into consideration the fact that this was written at the time of the Algerian war when national unity was a necessary tool in gaining independence, and also a time when Algerian women may not have been in a position to write about these issues, I also see this type of work as a reflection of the pervasive silence about brown-on-brown, or black-on-black, or yellow-on-yellow violence in relation to domestic violence committed by men on women (I am not denying that the reverse occurs or that it occurs in same-sex relationships, but more often than not, the woman in a heterosexual relationship is the victim). This leads to contemporary trends that equate feminism, or any other ideology that challenges the patriarchy on which racial solidarity is justified, as something that is foreign, something that is "white," or western, and that ultimately relies on essentialist notions of culture.

In "Interior Colonies: Frantz Fanon and the Politics of Identification," Diana Fuss makes the argument that the Algerian woman comes to bear the burden of representing national culture in the absence of nation (Fuss, *Identification*). She argues that there is a "fetishistic logic of displacement" on the part of Fanon. In this chapter of her book, she describes the colonial history of identification by exploring "Algeria Unveiled" and the importance of making the distinction between identification and imitation. Fuss argues that this was crucial for Fanon because it is in the dialectic space between the two that politics emerge. Analyzing the role of mimesis, as a form of mimicry that is the deliberate performance of a role, in the psychopathology of colonial relations in the context of "Algeria Unveiled," Fuss considers Bhabha's definition of mimesis in which the "mimicry of colonial others can be disruptive in ways which colonial discourse doesn't intend and cannot control." Furthermore, Bhabha sees that there is a slippage between mimicry and mockery, and performativity and parody, such that the mimicry of subjugation can provide opportunities for resistance and subversion. Hence, the Algerian woman's imitation of the European woman for the purpose of acting as a secret agent in the revolution as an example of mimesis—or imitation—and a refusal to identify with the colonial forces (i.e., defying the Algerian view that the lifted veil signaled the rape of the colonizer), as well as the colonizer's inability to distinguish between imitation and identification (147).

Fuss criticizes Fanon for essentializing black women in his conclusions about the "continuum between the revolutionary and the Algerian woman"—as opposed to "that coefficient of play, of imitation, almost always present in this form of action when we are dealing with the Western woman"—in which the Algerian woman learns her role "instinctively" (DC 50) because it suggests that masquerade is a natural function of femininity. I interpret her criticism to suggest that global politics of gender emerge in that dialectic space between identification and imitation, which is not understood by the colonist nor by the man of color: she asks, "Did the opportunity to dress in European clothes permit some Algerian women to engage in cross-national, cross-racial, cross-class, and cross-cultural identifications with white bourgeois European women?" (150–52). Given the fact that Jean-Paul Sartre wrote the preface for *Wretched of the Earth,* which suggests that Fanon considered the possibilities for people of color to work with progressive whites, it might have been the case that progressive white women played an even more specific role with women of color in this process; however, it seems as though the masculinist basis that is apparent in Fanon's work on gender (as described above) precludes any analysis of the sort.

By comparing the Algerian woman's "instinctive" imitation to the Algerian man who, under torture is forced to imitate the colonist for purposes of colonial identification such that imitation for Algerian men is perceived to be depersonalizing and alienating, Fuss claims that there is a "gender incongruity structuring Fanon's theory of colonial mimicry" because black women are described as essential mimics while black men are not (154). I would argue that this masculinist perspective, like the colonial perspective, cannot adequately distinguish between identification and imitation as it is experienced by women of color who may find white female allies in their own struggles. While I don't want to suggest that privileged white western women's struggles for equal pay are commensurate with Third World women's struggles against such atrocities as the business of mail-order brides or female genital mutilation, to name a few, it seems as though Fanon is too quick to dismiss possibilities for the transnational politics of gender, sexuality, and class.

I am including Fuss's work here to explore alternatives for reading gender and sexuality in Fanon vis-a-vis other work by gay black male theorists. In discussing "The Negro and Psychopathology" from *Black Skin White Masks,* she makes interesting criticisms that seem to work against and with Fanon. For instance, Fanon's treatment of the white woman's desire for rape, masked by anxiety, for the black man is questionable for Fuss because he does not problematize the associations of white femininity with the pathology of masochism. This pathology is present in the violent lesbianism and self-mutilation—both of which become blurred in the racist narcissism of the white woman—which are prerequisites for this anxious desire. In Gordon's illustration of the antiblack world where there is a divide between good/white/masculine and evil/black/feminine, the white woman has masculine power due to her whiteness and is both a lesbian by virtue of her desire for the feminized black man and a masochist because she is not supposed to desire what is evil/black/feminine (Gordon 81); hence this desire is masked by a constructed anxiety of being raped. Despite the discrepancies of the problematic association between pathology and white femininity, Fuss considers the fact that Fanon was very much aware of and concerned about the stereotype of the black man as rapist, and that by writing this material, he was providing a counternarrative. By focusing on the white woman as a comparison to the black man, the black woman is rendered invisible once again. In fact, it is in this chapter that Fanon says, "I know nothing of her [the black woman]" (BSWM 180). Fuss makes an important point about the absence of a thorough analysis, on Fanon's part, of the ways in which violent colonial masculinity maintained the economic and political system by the systematic rape of black women (156). Regardless of whether or not clinical documentation about women of color was available, as some might argue, this does not justify the glaring absence of this crucial analysis. It is clear that the Negro in "The Negro and Psychopathology" is the Negro man since the white man and the white woman are used as comparisons to the black man. The fact that so much of the psychoanalysis in this chapter occurs on the level of fantasy gives Fanon even more of an opportunity to engage with the woman of color. The obvious danger of gender-neutral language reveals itself most clearly in this chapter.

In connecting gender and sexuality, Fuss extends her critique to the implications of what she considers to be a homophobic Fanon. While the anxiety of the white woman can be seen as a masked desire for rape contextualized in an antiblack world, the anxiety of the white man masks a homoerotic desire since the black man is feminized in this world—hence the homosexual moment of colonization that is framed and legitimized within a homophobic society.[3] Fuss interprets a particular footnote in "The Negro and Psychopathology" to be a sign of his homophobia. Fanon argues that because the Oedipal complex is foreign to the Antilles, there are no homosexuals; however, he acknowledges the presence of men who dress like women, who date other men (but who cannot resist other women), and who can "take a punch like any he-man" as a contrast to the more neurotic cases of homosexuality in France where black men, many of whom survive economically by prostitution, are in a subordinate position to white men (BSWM 180). Going back to the neurosis of the anxious homosexual white man, Fuss concludes that this is an indication that Fanon equated homosexuality with white racism. Working from this premise, she suggests that Fanon's disidentification with homosexuality is positive in the sense that it was an attempt to deconstruct anthropological associations between "primitive" and "invert"; it also reveals the Eurocentricity of the construction of sexuality. Again, she considers his "homophobia" in its historical context as Fanon's impassioned response to the pathologization of the sexuality of people of color; however, she also claims that Fanon offers little, if any, room for queers of color who are both antihomophobic and anti-imperialist.

Fuss's reading of Fanon points to various issues, one of which carries deep implications for queers of color. Furthermore, she provides more proof of the ambivalence that should accompany any reader of Fanon who respects him enough to criticize the limits of his discourse. The footnote concerning the men who dress like women in Martinique who are not labeled as "homosexuals" is significant because on the one hand, one could accepts Fuss's reading, which leads her to believe that it exposes the Eurocentric nature of the ways in which "homosexuality" is conceptualized. One could also read it as Fanon's essentialist account of Martinican queerness.[4] Here, it is significant to point out that Fanon primarily spoke about interracial homosexual relationships, which are neurotic in an antiblack world just as interracial heterosexual relationships are in this world. By stating that the men who dress up as women in Martinique, who are also vulnerable to the advances of women, lead "normal sex lives," Fanon legitimizes this essentialist Martinician queerness by virtue of the fact that it operates in a heterosexual paradigm. This footnote, which refers to what appears to be healthy black male homoerotic desire (among other gay black men), seems to suggest that Fanon conceptualized relationships in a framework in which gender hierarchy exists. I'm not sure if Fanon would appreciate this kind of speculation, since it is only a footnote, but it seems like a crucial point to bring up considering the amount of attention it has received by other cultural critics as well as the extensive work that black gay male theorists have written about Fanon. These writers also suggest that Fanon's text could be read as either homophobic or homoerotic. Could it be a narcissistic celebration on the part of the gay black man, by someone like Mercer, who might be perceived to identify with the privileged gay white male world? On the other hand, if one accepts it as a homophobic text, can we speculate that this textual violence masks an anxiety, on Fanon's part, around issues of homosexuality as something that is both desirable and threatening to the straight black mind/body? It seems ironic that Fanon's disidentification with homosexuality has created spaces for queers of color to interrogate a variety of issues (despite the fact that he may not have intended this), such as the Eurocentrism of gay culture. By bringing this up, I hope to expose potential parallels between Fanon's work on the relationship between the black man and the white man and the internal struggles within communities of color around issues of gender and sexuality. In the next section, I will engage with the work of Isaac Julien, whom I consider to be an interesting example of a figure who has incorporated Fanonian thought into racialized queer discourse.

CONTESTING THE BLACK ESSENTIAL (HET) SUBJECT

Isaac Julien's films address the invisibility of black queer subjects in the mainstream queer and black communities. *Young Soul Rebels* is one example of Julien's treatment of hybridity in terms of the space in which multiple identities interact. In an interview titled "Performing Sexualities," he talks about the hybridity that can be experienced in various sites of pleasure and desire, such as music, clubs, and film (Harwood and Oswell 124–35). Julien considers film to be one of the few domains in which spectators can occupy and identify with various subject positions since the role of fantasy in film allows this to happen. He argues that "this hybridity in the field of vision of cinema is disturbing and makes people feel very uncomfortable . . . there is a certain amount of incommensurability between different identities" (134). For instance, he refers to the fact that when *Young Soul Rebels* came out, which was marketed as a black film, many gay white men who saw the film had to confront some of the violence and verbal homophobia of straight black audiences while watching it.

In an article titled "Black Is, Black Ain't," Julien questions the implications of the rise of rap as the signifier of hetero black masculinity in black studio films, which has made it difficult for hybrid representations of blackness to emerge in the mainstream. He sees this as a reflection of the Afrocentrism that permeates rap culture and large constituencies of the Nation of Islam that espouse narrow versions of masculinity. In Julien's opinion, homophobic black culture is reproduced in two of the major black institutions, namely the family and the church. In an article titled "True Confessions," written with Kobena Mercer, they refer to the disavowal of AIDS and homosexuality in the black community in terms of the popular belief that these are a "white man's disease" (199). Julien traces this disavowal partly to the influence that some of the major black leaders had on black popular consciousness, such as W. E. B. Du Bois, who wrote homophobically about Claude McKay's novel on gay and lesbian nightlife in Harlem. Another piece of evidence he provides is the fact that George Bass, the executor of the Langston Hughes estate, continuously tried to prevent discussion of Hughes's sexuality; in particular, *Looking for Langston* (another film by Julien) was censored by the Hughes estate when it arrived in the United States for a film festival.

Young Soul Rebels exposes the dialectic between homophobia and racism as products of the anxieties that are based on the consistent denial of the Others within each subject. In the opening scene, a gay black man is murdered as he cruises (looks for anonymous public sex) in a park. This is significant because the viewer does not know if the murder was based on homophobia or racism. Later in the film, we find out that the murderer was a gay white man. It seems as though Julien establishes the Fanonian concept of colonial violence in terms of the homosexual encounter between the white man and the feminized black man in order to deconstruct the binaries that make up an antiblack world. Music plays an important role throughout the rest of the film, specifically in the presence of disco clubs in the late seventies and early eighties which Julien describes as hybrid spaces in which people across class, race, gender, and sexuality would meet (125). In one of the club scenes, the gay black character meets the gay white character who is very active in Left Socialist politics of Britain. The working-class status of both of these characters is significant because it reiterates the point that Mercer and Julien have made in their articles concerning their disidentification with the white working-class Left as well as with gay and lesbian politics, which were racist in their own right.

Julien's treatment of working-class culture in the film also addresses the "ambivalent attraction and disavowal around the desires and fears of black sexuality" (128). Julien was inspired by his exposure to the East End of London where black and white working-class youth simultaneously experienced intimacy and violence toward each other. He refers to the white skinheads, who were envious of black styles and who were trying to negotiate this in their dress and music, as an example of the intimacy that manifests itself in the performances and masquerades of the racial constructions of masculinities that Mercer and Julien write about in "True Confessions." As a critical response to other popular black films such as *Jungle Fever*, which portrays black middle-class culture's narrow views on pathological interracial relationships, Julien intends *Young Soul Rebels* to paint a picture of the transgressions that occur on the margins of society (Julien, "Black" 255–63). The gay characters meet at nighttime spaces, such as the disco and in outdoor cruising areas, where pleasures and transgressions of racial and sexual boundaries merge.

Looking for Langston serves a similar function, in terms of addressing desire across racial and sexual lines, which undermines dualistic notions that keep them exclusive of each other; however, it is articulated from a diasporic perspective, in the sense that Julien is a British filmmaker who is commenting on a major figure from the Harlem Renaissance. Julien refers to Hall's notion concerning the importance of imaginary reconstruction and the partnership between one's present and one's past. Hall discusses the emergence of young black cultural practitioners whose work comes from a "diaspora aesthetic" in which given meanings are disarticulated and rearticulated symbolically (235). Given the importance for all colonized cultures to reclaim and reconstruct the past, the responsibility for queer postcolonial subjects is heightened by their multiply constituted subject positions. *Looking for Langston* combines archival footage of the Harlem Renaissance with poetry by gay black male poets from the past and present, music, and artistic montage. Issues of colonial desire are present in late-night bar scenes where black and white queers meet. Throughout the film, these men are always in tuxedos, which implies that class privilege facilitated these encounters. Toward the end of the film, there is a scene in which the police and a gang of black and white men attempt to break into the underground bar in order to raid the bar and bash the queers. This scene reveals the way in which homophobic oppressors can unite across race just as oppressed queers can unite across race.

Julien's representation of homophobic violence in black communities seems to be one of the ways in which machismo justifies itself. Mercer describes this phenomenon as such: "In order to gain some degree of power within the conditions of powerlessness that slavery entailed, black men 'internalized' aspects of white patriarchy, such as the attempt to master and control others as indicative of one's masculinity. . . . Black macho reproduces oppression by displacing it onto others" (Mercer, "Skin" 220). With regard to Fanon's questions concerning anxiety and violence, it seems logical to interpret Julien's films as a rearticulation of Fanon's ideas in the context of homophobia in the black community which masks the anxiety that depends on the denial of (racialized? queer?) Others within. One can also read the machismo that permeates various communities of color as a response to white masculine supremacist power, as interpreted by Mercer.[5] Working from this premise, it seems likely that those who have internalized the myth of black phallic and physical superiority over whites reject their queer brothers of color, who, in a sense, have given up their phallic privilege—their most powerful defense against racism—by assuming a passive, "feminine" role. Of course, one only needs to go to a gay club to see that the stereotype of the "feminine" faggot falls apart with the presence of excessively muscular gay men who eroticize their masculinity to the point of exaggerating a kind of hypermasculinity, which, in a queer context, reinforces Fanon's views on racist narcissism. This is apparent in the exoticism of macho gay black men and Latinos who capitalize on society's images of them as the slick, exotic lovers or in the white supremacism of buff gay white men who appear to be quite fascist in appearance. I base these criticisms on my extensive exposure to gay male culture in cities where queer visibility is very high, such as New York, Miami, San Francisco, and London.

COLONIAL DESIRE AND SADOMASOCHISM

Julien's film *The Attendant* places colonial desire in the context of queer s/m practices. The film is less than ten minutes long, but it is filled with images that reinscribe the Manichaean divide for the purpose of subverting the binaries that constitute it. It is significant that the film takes place in a museum space in which the black attendant reminds us of the absence or subordinate role of the person of color in predominantly white museum/gallery spaces.[6] The spectator enters the museum space and encounters paintings that depict images of the slaves on the Gold Coast of Africa. Julien intends the viewer to follow the gaze of the black attendant, who is tormented by his closeted queer desire as he encounters gay white leathermen who enter the museum. Closing time approaches, and the attendant is left alone in the museum as the paintings come to life and become images of contemporary representations of gay s/m scenarios. Throughout the rest of the film, tableaux appear in which white and black gay men are engaged in bondage and discipline scenes. At one point, the viewer sees a frozen image of the attendant being dominated by one of the gay white leathermen who entered the museum (the attendant is in his security uniform and the white man is dressed as an aestheticized leatherman-slave); moments later, the roles are reversed, but the men remain in the same clothing. While this is happening, the attendant's wife, who also works at the museum, hears whip noises and groans that resemble sounds from gay male porn, but she does not say anything. Her function is to act as the heterosexual alibi that legitimizes her husband's closeted desire. In addition to her presence, there are angels that appear in the film. There is usually a group of five gay white angels and one black angel at the center who appear at different points throughout the film. In the midst of the kinky sex, I interpreted these images to be a reminder of the AIDS pandemic, which, initially, predominantly affected black communities and gay male communities throughout the world. The central presence of the black diva challenges the myth of AIDS and homosexuality as the "white man's diseases."

In "Confessions from a Snow Queen," Julien refers to the slave iconography that is "borrowed" for the purpose of s/m practices, suggesting an ironic critique of the privileged status of gay white male culture that allows itself to appropriate this iconography; however, he does not fully engage with this particular issue, which seems to be a significant theme in gay male sexual practices (121–26). In Richard Fung's analysis of queer Asian male representation, he suggests that the dojo scene in one of his examples of racist gay porn is an appropriation of a suitable "exotic" setting in which bondage and discipline can take place. In Julien's case, it seems as though his own appropriation of gay white males' aesthetic appropriation of slave iconography in leather gear, which is used for s/m scenarios, reclaims a space in which black queer subjects can articulate their "unspeakable masochistic desires for sexual domination." He criticizes potential responses by both the black community and the queer community to the participation of black queers in s/m. On the one hand, he sees politically correct straight black readings of the film as being devoid of fantasy and as an attempt to fix and reduce the film to a simplistic version of racist/sexist white domination. On the other hand, he argues that black queers continue to remain invisible subjects in the creation of (white) discourses around queer s/m.

Quoting Pat Califa, who claims that in s/m "the uniforms and roles and dialogue become a parody of authority, a challenge to it, a recognition of its secret sexual nature," Julien insists that black queer subjects should have a choice in acting out their pleasures in the realm of desire and fantasy rather than be inhibited by assumptions of pathological black self-hate. He asks, "Could not the representation of interracial s/m be read as a practice of a racial and sexual dynamic which, in displaying the codes of a (Fanonian) master/slave dialectic, presents a transgressive simulacrum, one which both parodies and disrupts the codes of societal and racial power?" ("Confessions" 123). The title of this article suggests that Julien has reclaimed his own title as a "Snow Queen" (a queer who is in love with the [white] image) who challenges the black essential subject's avoidance of the psychic reality of black/white desire. If I hadn't been exposed to Julien's other works, such as *Looking for Langston,* in which black-male-on-black-male desire is positively affirmed, I might question Julien's primary attention to black/white desire as well as his statement about black queers' masochistic tendencies to be dominated (by whites?). His take on interracial s/m seems to suggest that the further one travels into the margins, more possibilities emerge in which one can act out colonial desires in the process of decolonizing sexuality and destabilizing the Manichaean divide. I don't mean to suggest that everyone should put on leather gear and go around engaging in interracial s/m practices (although, you never know, the possibilities here could be endless), but I do think that it is significant for Julien to carry on the tradition of Fanon in the sense that he explores the dynamics of desire on the margins just as Fanon wrote about interracial desire (as well as in the context of male homoerotica) at a time when it was considered much more taboo than it is now. It is also important to look at Julien's work in light of the work that has been done by gay white male theorists, some of whose work reveals their privileged status in writing about s/m.

In the chapter, "The Gay Daddy" in his book titled *Homos,* Leo Bersani prefaces his views on queer s/m in a Fanonian style by attributing the intolerance of gayness to the political anxiety about the ways in which gays play with revolutionary and subversive social arrangements. Julien and Mercer imply a similar anxiety at work, but they do so within the context of the black community. S/M is an example of a revolutionary social arrangement. Bersani quotes Michel Foucault, who wrote about s/m as a creative enterprise of the desexualization of pleasure, in the sense that pleasure was not limited to genital stimulation in these practices. The references to AIDS in *The Attendant* serve the same function of imagining newer and safer forms of pleasure in the era of the pandemic. Bersani acknowledges Pat Califa's view concerning the parodic and subversive nature of s/m practices and claims that the reversibility of roles in s/m questions assumptions about power that naturally inhere in one sex or race; however, he adds that this kind of parody presupposes an acceptance of those power structures and that rather than parody the structures, s/m practices parody the exclusion of those structures. For instance, many gay men have responded to stereotypical images of effeminate gay men by appropriating masculinity as a challenge to homophobic and heterosexist assumptions about the weak faggot.

Going back to Foucault, Bersani works from his (Foucault's) premise that the pleasure of s/m is derived from the insertion of depoliticized master/slave relations such that the model of dominance and submission becomes a source of pleasure when it is aestheticized. He concludes that the "removal" of the masters and slaves from the economic and racial superstructures that are being parodied in s/m confirms the eroticism of the master/slave configuration. "It is a power's body, a laboratory testing of the erotic potential in the most oppressive social structures . . . S/M profoundly—and in spite of itself—argues for the continuity between political structures of oppression and the body's erotic economy" (89–90). Furthermore the pain that goes with s/m allows the ego to self-shatter and to renounce its power to the world. These arguments are very problematic in the context of racial politics precisely because they seek to remove the material basis of oppression for the purpose of gay white male pleasure. They reinscribe the all-powerful white male gaze, which objectifies, appropriates, and fetishizes without any respect or acknowledgment of the actual histories and current oppressive conditions of its object of desire. In contrast to Julien's work, which seems to be reflective of a double appropriation, in the sense that he is appropriating the slave iconography of leather gear, which was initially appropriated by white hypermasculine leathermen who eroticized their masculinity in their challenges to homophobia, Bersani has made a completely ahistorical argument that fails to engage the subject positions of queers of color, many of whom are in a constant process of decolonizing sexuality. The purpose of advancing Foucault's romanticized views about s/m as an aestheticized practice that is divorced from the historical and contemporary materialist conditions of people of color perpetuates the privileged status of gay white men.

By acknowledging the continuity between the political structures of oppression and the body's erotic economy as well as the inherent eroticism of the master/slave narrative, it seems as though Bersani admits to his own location as a white man. His position as a gay white man in an antiblack world, who celebrates queer hypermasculinity and by doing so reveals a segment of gay male culture's fascist tendencies, allows him to view s/m as a "laboratory" in which the ego can self-shatter and renounce its power to the world. Whose ego and whose power is he referring to? Could it be the white male subject who has never had to question his ego and power? The limits of Bersani's discourse are obvious when it is applied to a person of color who has been denied power in an antiblack world and who is already in a process of reconstructing an ego that has been shattered by persistent hegemonies. Is Bersani's insistence on the inherent eroticism of dominance and submission his own articulation of the white man's inherent inclination to exert power over others? Placed side by side with Julien's analysis, one might question the differences between the two texts considering the privilege of the authors, which manifest themselves in their idealization of s/m. Furthermore, one might ask if both merely reproduce the binaries that constitute the Manichaean divide in the sense that Bersani implies the white man's inherent erotic aggression and Julien implies the queer black subject's inclination to be dominated; however, I am inclined to differentiate Julien from Bersani since the former destabilizes queer theory and race theory by expanding on the influence of Fanonian discourse with a critical queer eye.

CONCLUSION: DESEXUALIZING THE VIOLENCE

What are the origins of violence in the colonial encounter? Throughout this chapter, I have explored the violent uses of exoticism in the context of practices of cultural appropriation and have extended it to the male erotic domain. By taking up Julien and Mercer, I have done justice to Fanon by remaining faithful to the masculinist discourse that persists in many analyses of race and sexuality. While I am appreciative of Julien's and Mercer's work and their critiques of the essential black (het) subject, which in itself disturbs the Manichaean divide, I am well aware of the privilege that informs their hybrid positionalities, one of the consequences of which paves the way for identification with (queer) white-masculine-phallus power. Nonetheless, thanks to them and other queers of color, we can talk about sex and race in transgressive ways rather than be subject to older prohibitions (though still in place) that precluded the simultaneous theoretical exploration of sex and race due to the stigma of their coexistence, which can be traced to the historical objectification and spectacular use of the colonial Other's body.[7] In particular, I find Julien's work on interracial s/m quite remarkable considering the multiple borders that must be radically transgressed in such an enterprise.

Mercer's and Julien's work remains consistent with Fanon's preoccupation with the colonial, violent, homosexual relationship between the white man and the black man; however, their gay male discourse, which should be read as texts whose meanings constantly shift according to each specific context as Mercer suggests, runs the risk of transforming race/queer discourse in such a way that further excludes women. While transformative in some ways, they merely substitute the privileged heterosexual position with a queer position and maintain the status of the all-knowing male subject. I wasn't necessarily expecting to find the woman (queer or straight) in their discourse, but it leads me to question the extent to which violence can be maintained as the basis for analysis of the colonial situation. In an antiblack world, the white man rapes the black man and the black woman because both are feminized in this world. But what happens if difference had encountered difference before the master created difference in the first place, such as possible coalitions across gender among women, or coalitions across race among nonwhites? Would we still talk about colonial violence today in the same way that we speak of race relations in the context of either white police brutality of black male youth or interracial queer male s/m? Given the glaring absence of an analysis of the relationship between violent masculinity and the woman of color in Fanon's work, as discussed by Fuss, we must constantly ask ourselves where to locate the woman of color in race discourse. This absence is dangerously ironic because her rape (is) was real and physical rather than symbolic. I do not intend to undermine the atrocities of the lynchings of black men and women, I am only pointing to the irony of the lack of attention given to the physical rape of the woman of color since so much emphasis has been placed on the symbolic sexual moment of colonization. Her absence in Fanonian discourse is a huge gap that cannot be ignored. She is the lack of the black man. Her absence is her desexualization, since the Negro that Fanon predominantly writes about is the Negro who is eclipsed by the penis. As black male queers pick up where Fanon leaves off, cross-race phallic camaraderie runs the risk of subordinating racial solidarity to male homoerotic solidarity which potentially borders on misogyny. When half of the race has been desexualized through its absence, how will it be possible for the entire race to decolonize its sexuality?

As a person who identifies as a hybrid subject, I recognize the need to constantly question positionalities that privilege themselves over other hybrid positionalities. I realize that it is utopian to think of a world in which privileging subjectivities over others ceases to exist. There will be limits to every "hybrid" text. Looking at race and sexuality in an antiblack world is especially problematic because the antiblack world is structured around "binary systems of thought," as Trinh Minh-Ha would describe them. This is the source of popular conceptions of race that do not account for the color relationality along the racial spectrum. Furthermore, the dualistic nature of the analysis of an antiblack world leads to the reproduction of dichotomous ways of analyzing other structures of oppression that interact with race. When queerness is placed in the context of race, one might be tempted to turn to the black gay male subject because in an antiblack, both the racial subject and the queer subject are constructed as male It is important to continue the work that Fanon started, because the limits of his discourse are potential sites in which queers who are both anti-imperialistic and antihomophobic can create discourses that are more inclusive. In this chapter, I have explored the black/white Manichaean divide as a point of departure for what I hope to be an analysis of a transnational politics based on race, class, gender, and sexuality, where the woman of color is the locus of the feminization of global poverty. The woman of color is at once desexualized and sexualized. Can she end the violence? In putting a twist on Gayatri Spivak's question, I ask can brown women save brown men from white men?

NOTES

1. The issue of gender-neutral language will be raised in later sections of this chapter.
2. Here I refer to narcissism in the Fanonian sense in which the native turns to an exoticism that precludes the dynamism of culture and the white upholds white supremacist beliefs (*Black Skin White Masks*).
3. Lewis Gordon, Professor of Philosophy, African American Studies, and Religious Studies, commented on this in his lectures throughout the course of a graduate seminar in Religious Studies on Frantz Fanon during the fall semester of 1997 at Brown University.
4 Here, I use a definition of queerness that describes life-styles in which people

engage in same-sex practices and/or do not subscribe to heteronormativity.

5. In "Chicano Men: A Cartography of Homosexual Identity and Behavior" from *The Lesbian and Gay Studies Reader*, Tomas Amalguer provides an account of similar dynamics in the colonial constructions of Chicano masculinity in which the aggressive, masculine, Spanish conquistador contrasts the passive, feminine Indian. He argues that this has a profound effect on the perception of Chicano gay men such that those who assume the active role are accepted by society while those who assume the passive role are not, because they (the passive) supposedly give up the privilege to which they have access in a highly gender-stratified society (Abelove 258).

6. For an aesthetic representation of this issue, see Fred Wilson's "Guarded View," an instillation that consisted of four black mannequins (with missing heads) dressed in the security guard uniforms of the most prestigious museums in New York City (the Museum of Modern Art, the Guggenheim, the Whitney, and the Met). This was part of the "Black Male" Exhibition at the Whitney in 1994. Pictures of this instillation can be found in *Black Male* (edited by Thelma Golden).

7. See "The Other History of Intercultural Performance" from Coco Fusco's *English Is Broken Here* for an account of the historical roots of the inscription of the "primitive" in the western practices of creating a spectacle of the racialized Other.

WORKS CITED

Abelove, Henry, Michele Barale, and David Halperin, eds. *The Lesbian and Gay Studies Reader*. New York: Routledge, 1993.

Bersani, Leo. *Homos*. Cambridge, Mass.: Harvard University Press, 1995.

Bhabha, Homi. *The Location of Culture*. New York/ London: Routledge, 1994.

———. "The Other Question: The Stereotype and Colonial Discourse." *Screen* 24.6 (1983): 18–36.

Califa, Pat. "Unraveling the Sexual Fringe, a Secret Side of Lesbian Sexuality." *The Advocate* (27 Dec. 1979).

Carby, Hazel. *The Empire Strikes Back; Race and Racism in 70s Britain*. Birmingham: University of Birmingham, Centre for Contemporary Cultural Studies, 1982.

Cham, Mbye, ed. *Ex-Iles: Essays on Caribbean Cinema*. Trenton, N.J.: Africa World Press, 1992.

D'Emilio, John. *Sexual Politics, Sexual Communities: The Making of a Homosexual Minority in the U.S. 1940–1970*. Illinois: The University of Chicago Press, 1983.

Dent, Gina and Michelle Wallace, eds. *Black Popular Culture*. Dia Foundation Monograph 8 (1992).

Dyer, Richard. "Coming to Terms," in Ferguson: 289–98.

Fanon, Frantz. *Black Skin White Masks*. New York: Grove Press, 1967.

———. *A Dying Colonialism*. New York: Grove Press, 1967.

———. *Toward the African Revolution*. New York: Grove Press, 1964.

———. *The Wretched of the Earth*. New York: Grove Press, 1963.

Ferguson, Russel, Martha Gever, Trinh T. Minh-ha, and Cornel West, eds. *Out There: Marginalization and Contemporary Cultures*. New York: The New Museum, 1995.

Fusco, Coco. *English Is Broken Here: Notes on Cultural Fusion in the Americas*. New York: The New Press, 1995.

Fuss, Diana. *Identification Papers*. New York: Routledge, 1995.

Gilroy, Paul. "The End of Antiracism," in Rattansi and Donald.

Golden, Thelma, ed. *Black Male: Representations of Masculinity in Contemporary American Art*. New York: Whitney Museum of American Art, 1994.

Gordon, Lewis R.. *Her Majesty's Other Children: Sketches of Racism from a Neocolonial Age*. Lanham, MD: Rowman and Littlefield Publishers, 1997.

Hall, Stuart. "Cultural Identity and Cinematic Representation," in Cham: 234.

Harwood, Victoria, David Oswell, and Kay Parkinson, eds. *Pleasure Principles: Politics, Sexuality, and Ethics*. London: Lawrence and Wishart, 1993.

How Do I Look? Edited by Bad Object-Choices. Seattle: Bay Press, 1991.

Julien, Isaac. *The Attendant*, Normal Films 1992; *Looking for Langston*, Normal Films 1992; *Young Soul Rebels*, BFI 1991.

———. "Black is, Black Ain't: Notes on De-Essentializing Black Identities," in Dent: 255–63.

———. "Confessions from a Snow Queen." *Critical Quarterly* 36.1 (1994): 121–26.

Julien, Isaac, and Kobena Mercer. "Race, Sexual Politics, and Black Masculinity: A Dossier," in Chapman: 102.

———. "True Confessions," in Golden: 192.

Mercer, Kobena. "Black Hair/Style Politics," in Ferguson et al.: 247–64.

———. "Skin Head Sex Thing," in *How Do I Look?*: 169–222.

Minh-ha Trinh. *When the Moon Waxes Red*. New York: Routledge, 1991.

Rattansi, Ali and James Donald, eds. *Race Culture and Difference*. London; Newbury Park, CA: Sage Publications in association with Open University, 1992.

West, Cornel. "The New Cultural Politics of Difference." In: *Out There: Marginalization and Contemporary Cultures*. Edited by Russel Ferguson, Martha Gever, Trinh T. Minh-ha, and Cornel West. New York: The New Museum, 1995. 19–38.

Chapter 7

Race, Class, and the Homoerotics of *The Swimming-Pool Library*

James N. Brown and Patricia M. Sant

> In delirium the libido is continually recreating History, continents, king-
> doms, races, and cultures. (Deleuze and Guattari 1983: 352)

> He was a well-made little fellow, smooth and brown, with luxuriant
> curly hair, and he had a beautiful sad expression.—I found his skin as
> smooth as a dream. It was the beginning of all this thing.—I formed the
> impression that I was in the presence of a superior kind of person.
> (Hollinghurst 1989: 132)

Alan Hollinghurst's first fictional text is concerned with intersections of race, class, and generations through the agency of desire. This chapter will examine the portrayal, in *The Swimming-Pool Library*, of a textual "history" of privileged exploitation/exploration of (under)classed and raced bodies in terms of the critique of the interconnectedness of imperialism, capitalism, and the "Oedipal cell" explicated by Gilles Deleuze and Félix Guattari in *Capitalism and Schizophrenia* ([1972], 1983; [1980], 1987). The application of the anti-Oedipus was introduced into mainstream "post"-colonial theory[1] by Gayatri Chakravorty Spivak (1988) and recently expanded on by Robert J. C. Young (1995) to include consideration of *A Thousand Plateaus*; the anti-Oedipus was introduced to French gay theory by Guy Hocquenghem's *Homosexual Desire* in 1972. These studies will be drawn upon in this chapter to promote its argument that *The Swimming-Pool Library* may be understood as a critique—and celebration—of successive and diverse subcultures of English homosexuality in the twentieth century within the theoretical parameters mapped in Deleuze and Guattari's two-volume study.

The Swimming-Pool Library interweaves a history of English homosexual desire with a concurrent history of exploitation of black bodies to illustrate the fetishization of the African male and the complicity of English male desire for the African (male) Other with the (ongoing) project of English imperialism. A fortuitous accidental meeting in a lavatory between the suggestively named twenty-six-year-old Will Beckwith,[2] a gay man who flaunts his sexual difference in the "camp" manner characteristic of some homosexual men throughout the twentieth century, and the aged and equally mannered Lord Nantwich leads to a proposal from the latter that the former write his biography. Will's narrative represents the irrepressible wit, the hedonism, the taken-for-granted class privilege characteristic of one aspect of the London gay community prior to the seismic shock waves reverberant from the cultural construction and public perception of the HIV/AIDS pandemic as "the gay plague" (see Treichler 1987, Watney 1987, Weeks 1990, Edelman 1994); simultaneously, in the absence of a community ethos of caring and responsibility, it records the equally uninterrogated class- and race-based sexual exploitation of underaged youths that were the consequence of these kinds of attitudes prevalent in some sections of the London gay community of the early 1980s. The Nantwich diaries chronicle examples of that Orientalist idealization, even worship, of the African (public and private) body of which Edward W. Said ([1978] 1991, 1993) especially has written; the policing and "territorialization" of these bodies were the primary responsibilities of the colonial régimes of power operative during the period between World Wars I and II.

This brief introduction to the discursive structure of *The Swimming-Pool Library* sketches Hollinghurst's mapping of the inextricability of race and (homo)sexuality in the lives of white Englishmen across the broad sweep of the twentieth century. Will's maintenance of an urbane, supercilious persona expressive of excessive narcissism, a superficiality of appearance and judgment, and a carefully cultivated absence of self-scrutiny and self-awareness fails, nonetheless, to mask the sense of the mutability of the gay world he inhabits and depicts. At the beginning of the text he says:

My life was in a strange way that summer, the last summer of its kind there was ever to be. I was riding high on sex and self-esteem—it was my time, my *belle époque*—but all the while with a faint flicker of calamity, like flames around a photograph, something seen out of the corner of the eye. (5–6)

This "faint flicker of calamity" may be private or public in reference but, introduced as it is early in the text, it identifies the intangible sense of immanent downfall that permeates the ensuing narrative. "Calamity" in one generation resides at the heart of one of the text's two first-person narratives; of the life of Will Beckwith it gestures toward both the closure of the text and an "afterward," which remains unwritten only within the limits of the text but which illuminates the inevitable postpandemic reading of that text.

The narratives of Nantwich and of Will richly detail their views of the (already past) present of the cultures they inhabit and dominate as being inscribed within a feudal order, regimes entirely enclosed upon themselves and composed of prefects and fags, English colonizers and the African colonized, upper-class (homo)sexual nomadic predators and working-class youths. This vision of an

England radically split between not many but two classes informs the narrators' views of the whole of twentieth-century English male behaviors: the gaze of the upper-class narrators of *The Swimming-Pool Library* sees the English bourgeoisie only as philistines, the agents of puritanical, arbitrary, punitive and destructive impediments to the "natural order" of things essentially English, or (even worse, as portrayed by Will's brother-in-law, and by James, his gay-identified best [and only] friend) as pathetically ineffectual and boring members of a lower species.

The Swimming-Pool Library suggests an an-Oedipal, upper-crust, homosexual network suffusing the key institutional social bodies—home, school, colonial-service training and practice, the political and legal fraternities, English class-dictated (homo)social bonding, "Old Boys" Clubs, and general social ties—which wield power throughout and across all elements of society. The text meticulously—and playfully—alludes to a century of such bonding and networking. It names one of Nantwich's 1920s friends "Sandy Labouchère"; it makes teasingly elusive mentionings and visions of Oscar Wilde's disciple, Ronald Firbank, and his preciously styled prose works; it details Lord Beckwith's retrospective musing on the opinions of E. M. Forster on the premiere of Britten's *Billy Budd* and a fleeting glimpse of a decrepit Peter Pears at a current production; it describes (in Nantwich's diaries) the gay London (under)world of the twenties, thirties and forties; and it reveals Will's belated realization of his grandfather's complicity in the antigay pogroms of the fifties (of which Nantwich had been a key victim). The name of the swimming pool, the Corinthian, suggests both the influence of classical Greek homoerotic textual (particularly Platonic) inscription on the minds of generations of English schoolboys and the "seduction of the Mediterranean" (Aldrich 1993) to which large numbers of homosexual men in the nineteenth and twentieth centuries succumbed;[3] and the hotel that figures prominently in the text is named the Queensbury. Ironically, for a former staff member of the "Cubitt *Dictionary of Architecture*" (6), Will seems blissfully ignorant of this long lineage of which he and his generation of gay men are but the latest beneficiaries; indeed, he cares nothing of his private or "public" families' histories.

What we might see here is an example of Deleuze and Guattari's "schizoanalysis" in which a deterritorialized unit is at play and the mechanisms of desire have escaped the individualization of capitalism. Should we view the narratives of Nantwich and Will Beckwith as coterminous, we would perhaps have a view of "schizophrenization" at the "molecular" level of our desiring machines, and see the text as exemplary of that "process which Deleuze and Guattari, echoing Laing, call a 'voyage' of discovery, and in doing so the 'truth of the subject' will become clearer" (Weeks 1993: 33). But exactly what "truth of the subject" is comprehensible as clearer? "Clearer" than what? Within the parameters of Hocquenghem's gay-revolutionary thesis,

the question which the gay movement raises is not so much that of the particular sexual object as that of the functioning mode of sexuality. It is not through the object and its choice that the non-exclusiveness of desire is revealed, but through its very system of functioning. (Hocquenghem 1993: 139)

The unrelenting gaze and lust that Will Beckwith projects at "the variety of the male organ" (139) and his eager pursuit of young men calls to mind (humorously, in its literalness) Hocquenghem's suggestion that "there is a lot to be said for the so-called 'homosexual' system of pickups and mechanical scattering—a system which is so obsessed by sexuality that it often stands accused of lacking soul or feeling" (139). This "mechanical scattering" Hocquenghem eulogizes as "a system in action, the system in which polyvocal desire is plugged in on a nonexclusive basis" in the course of the homosexual cruise, during which the individual is "on the lookout for anything that might come and plug in to his own desire" (131). In terms of the anti-Oedipus, this "homosexual pickup machine" is "infinitely more direct and less guilt-induced than the complex system of 'civilized loves'" and has the potential "to take off the Oedipal cloak of morality under which it is forced to hide." The consequence is that "we would see that its mechanical scattering corresponds to the mode of existence of desire itself" (Hocquenghem 1993: 131–32).

Hocquenghem's idealistic reading of the anti-Oedipus typifies the post-1968 euphoria from which it was born and explicates Will's unrelenting quest for innumerable sexual encounters, all of which he sees either as conquests who succumb to his superior desirability, or as objects into which he can plug as a desiring machine. Although *The Swimming-Pool Library* opens with Will's infatuation with Arthur, a young black man whose race, youth, and inarticulateness all provide Will with perverse pleasure, it soon moves beyond this enclosed and increasingly tedious sexual object to describe Will's growing (if erroneous) security in his attractiveness to the white working-class youth, Phil ("my little philanderer"). Despite Will's extravagant protestations of "being in love" with Phil, he nevertheless feels free to examine and experience "the Corry's" apparently inexhaustible parade of genitalia, which seems to him the ex-colonies' personal gifts to him, in the very heart of the imperium: in the showers he is free to enjoy directing his desiring gaze at "a dal-coloured Indonesian boy with—an exceptionally extensive cock," near which "Carlos's Amerindian giant swung alongside the compact form of a Chinese youth whose tiny brown willy was almost concealed in his wet pubic hair, like an exotic mushroom in a dish of seaweed" (193). And yet, even as Will samples this smorgasbord of exotic genitalia on offer and seduces Phil and numerous other boys and men of color or of working-class origin, his obsession with Arthur continues, in part perhaps because Arthur deserts him, in part because Arthur proves to be a murderer and drug pusher, but perhaps primarily because Will's homosocial conditioning has resulted in a fascination with raced bodies exemplified in the lives and cultural production of so many illustrious gay men throughout the century, here represented by the fictional Nantwich and the late Ronald Firbank (the much-nostalgized author of the 1925 cult classic *Prancing Nigger*, another coded critique of upward-class mobility and black sexuality).[4] The former's chronicle of a lifelong lust for black men—his schoolboy infatuation with Webster, "the first negro I had ever known," his fascination with and seduction of African-American servicemen in Britain during the war, and his enduring, possessive love of a Sudanese boy, Taha, whom he met when Taha was sixteen and brought back with him to London at the end of his service overseas—metonymically represents the seductive force of Africa and "the African" for the twentieth-century Englishman and the primary psychological motivation (no less powerful when repressed than when expressed) for the colonization of Africa by England.

Jacques Lacan (1994), Edward Said (1991), and Homi K. Bhabha (1983) have all produced influential studies of desire as desire for the Other; Said and Bhabha have applied Foucauldian and Lacanian analyses of power and the desiring gaze to the imperial impulse. More recently, Robert J. C. Young has refocused critics' attention on the interconnectedness of the discourses of race and sexuality in the pursuit of imperial conquest. Bhabha's "The Other Question," in particular, elucidates the apparatuses of power by which a fetishized "Other" is constructed to stand in for a generalized desire for a sexualized possession and appropriation of the colonized. Elsewhere we have explicated, through a political application of Lacan's theory of the *object petit a*, the imperialistic creation of a metonymic representative of the colonizer's desire for the generalized, racialized and male Other (Brown and Sant 2000, 2001); here we wish to highlight the appropriateness of this Lacanian formulation to Nantwich's fetishization of the black youth, Taha, during and after his patriotic stint in the Sudan. In this narrative of appropriation, seduction, (presumably unresisted) abduction and consequent devotion to the sixteen-year-old Nubian male we may read, in Nantwich's compulsive pursuit of pleasure in unlikely and déclassé venues, especially lavatories, not a less narcissistic (or more romantic) essentialized attachment but rather an an-Oedipal "scattering" or schizophrenizing. Read this way, *The Swimming-Pool Library* thus enables an interrogation of the validity of Hocquenghem's reading of "homosexual scattering" as predicated on a partial reading of the explication of indiscriminate homosexual desire, which he extrapolated from the anti-Oedipus, and also of the ways in which *Capitalism and Schizophrenia* might illuminate chronologically intertwined and thematically inseparable strands of that desire.

It is germane at this point to question the sense(s) in which the term "colonial desire" (the title of Young's critical text) can be validly applied to the sexualized fields of desire demonstrated by Nantwich and Will Beckwith. That all desire is a territorialization is a primary concern of the anti-Oedipus; the point in question would seem to us to be consideration of how and whether this territorialization works at both micro- and macrolevels. The (degree of) Oedipalization of these men is also a matter for interrogation: neither seems to have had parents; both make reference only to male relatives of the second-last generation. Although Nantwich was thoroughly acculturated by the "homosexual continuum" of both British Public School and civil service networks, he was from an early age attracted (as we have seen) to "Negroes," and hence perhaps in some sense aberrant. On the other hand, he may represent another in a long line of fetishizers of negritude represented in this text by, for example, Firbank's *Prancing Nigger* and *The Flower beneath the Foot*, and continued by Will's unceasing bemusement with Arthur's misfortunes. In this reading we would understand Will's forceful repossession of Arthur's body at their next meeting (237) as exemplary of the need of the white colonizer to reestablish, by violence, re-territorialization of the black colonized body; and we would comprehend the political significance of Will's being severely beaten by white skinheads ("You can tell he's a fuckin' poof—Yeah! Fuckin' nigger-fucker" [202]) when he ventures out to the London slums to seek Arthur ("I wanted to touch him, support him, see again how attractive he was and know he still thought the world of me" [200]). This symbolic violence enacted on the body of the white man in search of his black lover could, in this reading, represent a racist, homophobic reaction by the dominant male populace to the presence among it of the previously—and currently—colonized, raced and threatening male body; it would also suggest an instinctive comprehension of the homoerotics of race that underpinned the colonial project as well as the continuing homoerotics of class and race exploitation, cross-race desire, and homosocial bonding.

Nantwich's and Will's romantic passions for classed, raced, male bodies may be understood as validation of Hocquenghem's reading of homosexual desire in terms of Deleuze and Guattari's anticapitalist, antipsychoanalytic texts: black men are the objects of romantic and self-destructive idealization; but the romance of race never impedes the omnipresent, overpowering need for another sexual conquest, another sexual experience. In Will's case the working-class, underage Phil fills in nicely for the absent Arthur, for example, and becomes the object of another of Will's elaborately constructed romantic dramas. But this *mélodrame* (as Nantwich would term it [240]), when interrupted by Will's finding Phil in bed with an older man of Phil's own class, is easily dismissed and forgotten, Phil having been, at most, a conquest whom Will could flaunt to impress his gay acquaintances with his own desirability, and no impediment whatsoever to Will's promiscuous initiation of various kinds of sexual activity with other men.

Nantwich's drama is more tragic than melodramatic. His initial enchantment, in the Sudan, with Taha is described in his diary entry for May 29, 1926:

and the boy, a supple, plum-black sixteen, with his quiet nervous movements, dreaming eyes occasional smile, so inward and yet candid.—Him I chose for quite contrary reasons, so that his charm, however fickle or professional, w[oul]d be an adornment to each day. And here he comes now. He has the most lyrical hands, and—his long graceful fingers suggest to my woozy fancy the playing of the harp. (241)

The assumption that he has his servant's complete devotion results in intense distress in Nantwich when, after years in Nantwich's service in London, Taha announces that he is about to be married. Nantwich's assumption of complete ownership of Taha and of reciprocal love indicates Nantwich's idealization of Taha and (by the standards of his class) his foolish besottedness. He seems never to have considered the consequences of having lived openly with a black man; and, when he is entrapped during the postWar, antihomosexual pogrom initiated by

Denis Beckwith, he is consequently unprepared for his own imprisonment, Taha's death at the hands of a white gang, and the necessity to construct a different future, which ensue.

Nantwich's future involves the establishment of working-class Boys' Clubs in the West End, occasional visits to the Corry, trips to his Club (which rejoices in the name of "Wicks"), immersion in literary texts, and his recruitment of his domestic servants from a steady stream of ex-convicts. However democratic Nantwich's postimprisonment interests may seem, he remains aristocratic in his attitudes and actions, recruiting, for example, Taha's son, Abdul, as cook, and attractive young waiters to work at his club. Furthermore, Nantwich is engaged, with a fashion photographer of appropriately dubious morals, in casting the club crew in gay pornographic films that he produces and distributes.

Nantwich sees himself not as exploiter of youth or race, but as a savior of the disadvantaged and facilitator of careers. Questioned on his filmmaking activities by Will, he replies bemusedly: "I don't think race comes into it, does it? I mean, Abdul is black and the others aren't—but I don't want any rot about that. Abdul loves doing that sort of thing—and he's actually jolly good at it. He's a pure exhibitionist at heart" (287). And to Will's amazement at seeing "half the staff of a famous London Club about to copulate in front of the camera," Nantwich responds, "I think you'll find a good many of them do it—though not always on film I agree. They're a close little team, there at Wicks's, and they like to do what I want. But then I got them all their jobs" (287).

What, then, has this text to do with Deleuze and Guattari's stunning critique of capitalism and schizophrenia? We would argue that this text is neither an apology for nor a celebration of gay London life as it was lived until HIV/AIDS changed it forever. Rather, we see *The Swimming-Pool Library* as an unsentimental view of the London gay life at the same time as it provides a vision of a "homosexual continuum," an antiarborescent, chronological linking of gay-acting people of notice/notoriety from Ronald Firbank (an old film clip of whom ends the text) and Charles Nantwich to Will Beckwith and his six-year-old nephew, Rupert. Indeed, the chronological mapping of gay intergenerational connectedness extends further than this: the narratives are interspersed with Nantwich's reminiscences of "little private bars, sex clubs really, in Soho before the war, very secret," and of his Uncle Edmund, who "had fantastic tales of places and sort of gay societies in Regent's Park—a century ago now, before Oscar Wilde and all that—with beautiful working boys dressed as girls and what-have-you" (288). One reading of the text would be, then, that the gay world of aristocratic England has retained an identity and a continuity from the invention of homosexuality in the late nineteenth century (Foucault 1990: 43) to 1983, and one that was on the whole benign, close-knit and philanthropic (in every sense).

This imperfect but functional intergenerational gay lineage is threatened by only one enemy, bourgeois puritanism, and in this text it is personified by Denis Beckwith, Will's grandfather. Whether inspired by ambition or a characteristic burst of patriarchal or patriotic zeal, Beckwith had, as Director of Public Prosecutions, collaborated with the Home Secretary and the police to become the driving force behind the 1950s antigay pogroms, of which Nantwich was the most illustrious of victims. Following calls in the House of Commons for reform of sexual offense law, Denis Beckwith left the DPP and took a peerage, Nantwich's postprison narrative wryly reported, resisting expanding upon the multiple ironies attendant upon this exaltation of the DPP to the House of Lords. It is here that we can pinpoint the text's attack on the Oedipalized cell of the triangular family and its suggestion that Oedipalization does nothing but harm to those it touches. "Capitalist ideology's strongest weapon is its transformation of the Oedipus complex into a social characteristic, an internalization of oppression which is left free to develop, whatever the political conditions," wrote Hocquenghem, adding that "[a]fter capitalist decoding has taken place, there is no room for any form of homosexual integration other than that of perverse axiomatisation" (93). And so it is here: Will Beckwith is shamed by the knowledge that all of society except himself knew of the "public service" on which his family's elevation to the peerage was based; and, almost immediately in the text, this shame is metonymically enacted on Will's body as, for the first time, he is anally penetrated, and by Abdul, Wicks's black cook and Taha's son, in a brutal and double humiliation that, perversely and significantly, leaves Will both "gurgling with pleasure and grunting with pain" (307).

This metonymic race-, class-, and power-role reversal may equally underline Hollinghurst's textual concern with the results of colonialism. As Young has argued, following Deleuze and Guattari, "[d]esire is a social rather than an individual product; it permeates the infrastructure of society," Deleuze and Guattari having "already separated desire from the subject by defining sexuality as 'the libidinal unconscious of political economy'" (Young, 1995:168). Thus, argues Young, "[r]acism is perhaps the best example through which we can immediately grasp the form of desire, and its antithesis, repulsion, as a social production: 'thus fantasy is never individual: it is *group fantasy*'" (168–69). Nowhere is this "group fantasy" implied more directly than in Nantwich's explanation to Will of England's desire for colonized bodies in Africa in the years between the World Wars: "'There was this absolute adoration of black people,' Charles [Nantwich] said, 'you could say blind adoration, but it was all-seeing.—I don't know. I think it was more of a sort of love affair for me than for most of the others. I've always had to be among them, you know, Negroes, and I've always gone straight for them'" (283). The attraction Nantwich feels for "Negroes" is not unlike that which Firbank felt for "niggers," or which Will feels for Arthur; and in all these cases this attraction can be seen to have brought about their ruin—social ostracization and disgrace in Firbank's and in Nantwich's lives, physical/facial in Will's case (his nose was broken and his facial beauty destroyed by the skinheads' attack; Nantwich's *post facto* comment is "Well, at least I saw it before they spoilt it") (216).

The Swimming-Pool Library can, thus, also be read as a movement from feudalism to capitalism as described by Deleuze and Guattari. In the earlier instance, social production works as an inscription: "The primary function incumbent on the socius has always been to codify the flows of desire, to inscribe them, to record them, to see to it that no flow exists that is not properly dammed up, channeled, regulated –" (Deleuze and Guattari 1983: 33). The situation changes, however, with the advent of capitalism: "the *capitalist machine*—finds itself in a totally new situation: it is faced with the task of decoding and deterritorializing the flows" (Deleuze and Guattari 1983: 33). Young points out that capitalism differs from earlier historical forms in having to "first of all do away with the institutions and cultures that have already been developed" so that an "encounter between the deterritorialized wealth of capital and the labor capacity of the deterritorialized worker" can be engineered; the result is the reduction of everything to the abstract value of money which enables capitalism "to decode flows and 'deterritorialize' the socius. Having achieved a universal form of exchange, it then reterritorializes— 'institutes or restores all sorts of residual and artificial, imaginary, or symbolic territorialities' such as states, nations or families" (Young 1995: 169). Deleuze and Guattari state:

There is a twofold movement of decoding or deterritorializing flows on the one hand, and their violent and artificial re-territorialization on the other. The more the capitalist machine deterritorialized, decoding and axiomatizing flows in order to extract surplus values from them, the more its ancillary apparatuses, such as government bureaucracies and the forces of law and order, do their utmost to deterritorialize, absorbing in the process a larger and larger share of surplus value. (1983: 33–34)

So little is disclosed concerning the apparatuses of colonial rule in *The Swimming-Pool Library* as to make questionable an argument for the applicability of this thesis to the colonization of Africa (about which we learn only through the lens provided by Nantwich's diaries). It is, however, clear from this individual case that in the metonymic example of Taha a violent deterritorialization has occurred: Nantwich has appropriated him as private property and taken him back to England, where he is killed by white men. Applied to England itself, this theory explains not only the rationale and *modus operandi* of the postwar antigay pogroms but also their intent. What was left of the feudal order after the war had to be destroyed, and their "surplus value" extracted, by capitalism's forces through the agency of government bureaucracies and "the forces of law and order." What the taxation office failed to take, then, the police did, acting on the widely held, popular belief (one certainly not refuted by this text) that the aristocracy was decadent, corrupt, and probably "queer" as well. Nantwich was, then, a great prize, perhaps the proof of Beckwith's policy that launched him into Lords, where he promptly took his place among those whom he had fought so virulently to destroy. Will's "ancestry" is, then, recently, disgracefully and even cynically purchased at a very high cost to those members of English culture with whom Will identifies. Indeed, speaking early in the text about Marsden, "my grandfather's house," Will admits that "[i]t was not until years later [than his childhood visits] that I came to understand how recent and synthetic this nobility was—the house itself bought up cheap after the war, half ruined by use as an officers' training school, and then as a military hospital" (7). Not only is Will's "nobility" a sham predicated upon a shameful act against gay men, but his only other claim to nobility—his physical beauty—is, then, ruined by the end of the narrative.

Apolitical as he is, Will sees no need to worry about anything other than the recovery of his beauty, but Nantwich, as if to point up the reverse colonization on which the text's ironies hinge, says about England: "There are times when I can't think of my country without a kind of despairing shame. Something literally inexpressible, so I won't bother to try and speechify about it" (286). Always the romantic, Nantwich in old age continues to see himself as different from other English colonizers, about whom he tells Will, with no ironic intent:

There was a tendency to treat Africa as if it were some great big public school—especially in Khartoum. But when you were out in the provinces, and on tour for weeks on end, you really felt you were somewhere *else*. If you'd had the wrong sort of character you could have gone to the bad, in that vast emptiness, or abused your power. I expect you know about the Bog Barons in the south—truly eccentric fellows who had absolute command, quite out of touch with the rest of the world. (283)

Predictably, Will responds that" [i]t sounds like something out of Conrad" (283), a comment with which Nantwich doesn't bother to disagree.

No one of Nantwich's generation could, however, have foreseen the spatially specific ways in which the deterritorialization of colonization would—literally— "change the face of Britain"; and it is immediately following this exposition of his difference from other colonizers that Nantwich expressed his sense that "[t]here was this absolute adoration of black people." Where Deleuze and Guattari have produced "a theory of capitalism to which the operation of colonialism as a form of writing geo-graphy is central" (Young170), the geography to which English colonialism is central is, perversely, a (reverse) territorialization of that space that had represented the heart of England. Young refers to Frantz Fanon's account of "the enterprise of deculturation" as inspiration of "the theoretical paradigm of the *Anti-Oedipus* and its articulation of the mechanisms that the native population undergoes under colonial enslavement" (170):

For this its systems of reference have to be broken. Expropriation, spoliation, raids, objective murder, are matched by the sacking of cultural patterns, or at least condition such sacking. The social panorama is destructured: values are flaunted, crushed, emptied. (Fanon 1964: 41, 43)

The colonial subject has been territorialized, deterritorialized, and now, it may seem, inevitably reterritorialized (unthinkably) in the psychic and social reality of England. The Oedipal desire to conquer, to contain, to possess "the black man" in "the colonies" had by the 1980s become the fact of blackness within the English metropolis itself; and where once the colonizers were able to assuage their consciences and their lusts with imaginary illusions and the rationale of a "civilizing" mission, they have been replaced by the skinheads who police the boundaries of the ghettos the English have built to contain the Other that has appeared so unpredictably in their midst. Will's brutalization while in quest of Arthur can then be read as a procedure by which such reactionary behaviors are produced as the basis for normative social experience:

In Deleuze and Guattari's argument, this procedure also operates equally for the subjects of the West: the metropolitan-colonial relation has thus once again been turned round so that global colonialism becomes the historical structure of capitalism, whether at home or abroad. (Young 1995: 172)

But if by the end of Hollinghurst's text Will Beckwith's world seems to be collapsing around him, and he may be at the beginning of a voyage of self-discovery that involves Oedipalization and so shame, the final lines of the text should put beyond doubt any uncertainty that he will in fact be affected by the multiple revelations that have so recently occurred: returning from his traumas to seek solace at the Corry, he finds that "[t]here were several old boys, one or two perhaps even of Charles [Nantwich]'s age, and doubtless with their own story, strange and yet oddly comparable, to tell. And going into the showers I saw a suntanned young lad in pale blue trunks that I rather liked the look of" (336). The queer body, like the raced body, occupies the very center of England; neither is going to disappear.

The history of "post"-colonial theory indicates, from the vantage point of the fin de siècle, a marked tendency to essentialize the categories of "the East" and "the West" in the attempt, by theorists in both "the West" and the Third World, "to constitute an object both for analysis and for resistance" (Young 1995: 165; and see Fanon 1967 and Nkrumah 1965). The consequences of this failure of discrimination have been the creation and reification of this binarism and the homogenization of "the East" or "the Third World" much to the detriment (with some notable exceptions) of analyses of individual and different kinds and degrees of colonization and its effects.

A similar effect of the lesbian and gay political movements of the 1970s and 1980s may be observed: in order to demand equal rights and freedoms, lesbians and gays constituted themselves—with the concurrence of the heteronormative majority—as a minority as essentially different from white heterosexuals as, for example, African-Americans constructed themselves (and were constructed) as distinctly different communities suffering discrete kinds of oppression (D'Emilio 1983, Seidman 1993). As throughout the eighties it became clear that Thatcherism and Reaganism were unresponsive to the rights of minorities, and the sixties Civil Rights movements died, the differences among lesbian- and gay-identified people became more apparent; the inability of the lesbian and gay communities to influence their governments' (non)responses to the HIV/AIDS pandemic exposed differences among lesbian and gay people and led to a radical interrogation of the limits of gay and lesbian essentialism.

The birth of queer politics at the beginning of the 1990s was a direct reaction against lesbian and gay essentialism: its radical interrogation of the life/death, male/female, hetero/homo, lesbian/gay binarisms underpinning heteronormativity is a project that seeks to undermine and destroy essentialist constructions of subjectivity so as to expose the myth of the autonomous subject. The queer project's concern to expose the social constructedness of race, gender, sexuality and sex itself has as its goal the freeing of desire from its Oedipal bases so that individuals are freed to experience varied subjectivities, a multiplicity of pleasures, a plurality of shifting subject positions. Queer speaks as the Other, from the position of the Other, deconstructing all binarisms between self and the self's constructed Other, raced, gendered, sexed, or classed (Duggan 1992, Warner 1993, Martin 1994, Creed 1994).

While queer theory tends to credit Foucault with inspiring its radical agenda, its project bears a startling resemblance to Deleuze and Guattari's rhizomatic theory, and also to their critique of psychoanalysis and capitalism. An engagement with *Capitalism and Schizophrenia* would, we believe, advance the queer and "post"-colonial projects and contribute to their attempts to dissolve those binary categories that underpin patriarchal privilege and white race hegemony. This chapter has been an attempt to initiate such an engagement.

NOTES

1. Our use of "'post'-colonialism" follows the practice best explicated by Joseph Pugliese (1995) to signal our own growing unease that, too frequently, this theoretical paradigm masks the reinstatement, in practice, of a paternalistic view of decolonized or decolonizing powers, and of a participation in the power/knowledge paradigms established by the colonizing power(s).

2. The first name of the text's protagonist may suggest an association with William Shakespeare, especially the sonnets' narrator, the self-nominated "Will" who is the lover of a beautiful youth in the sonnets; and of particular interest here would be the late sonnets, 134 and 135, in which "Will" puns on his name and its signification of sexual desire, and on (both male and female) genitalia. This sense of "will" as the penis and as sexual desire suggests the more colloquial "willy" in common use in the late twentieth century (and used by Will to describe the penis of a Chinese youth) and associates Will Beckwith's forename with his surname: "beck" commonly connotes "a sign or significant gesture, especially one indicating assent or notifying command" (*OED* sb. [2] 1) and hence, "the slightest indication of will or command, and *transf.* absolute order or control" (sb.[2] 2). Will Beckwith's name aptly suggests, then, both the canonical origins of his literary style and inclinations, his sexual object preference, and his assumption of command in the gratification of his sexual appetites and control over the objects of his desire. Of addition relevance here may be the phallic pun implicit in the French *bec* as signifying the physical apparatus through which will is exercised: hence the name would suggest "Will with *bec*." "Beck" as it signifies a brook or stream (*OED* sb.1.1) also suggests the

aquatic environment of the pool that lies at the center of the text and around which so much of its sexual activity circulates, and which gives the text its name, in addition to the fluidity of the prose style of the text; and in its more common literary use to denote "a brook with stony bed, or rugged course," the first syllable with Will's surname may suggest the rocky road of the desires depicted in the textual inscriptions of same-sex alliances ("The course of true love never did run smooth"!). See further, on "will," Eric Partridge ([1947] 1968: 218–19. Partridge observes that "[i]n Shakespeare, the nexus between the sexual act and literary creation is closer, more potent, more subtly psychosomatic than in any other writer, whether of verse or of prose" (219). This nexus is notable in the production of this text and, ironically, this nexus's absence is the cause of Will Beckwith's failure to produce the biographical text Nantwich wishes/wills him to write.

3. Among Aldrich's catalog of British homosexual writers infatuated by "the Mediterranean" were William Beckford (1760–1844, and perhaps another influence on Hollinghurst's choice of name for his protagonist?), Byron, Shelley, Keats, Walter Pater, John Addington Symonds, A. E. Housman, W. J. Cory, John Addington Symonds, Algernon Charles Swinburne, Oscar Wilde, Lord Alfred Douglas, E. M. Forster, Norman Douglas, W. Somerset Maugham, and Compton Mackenzie. See also Jonathan Dollimore's "Wilde and Gide in Algiers" and "Desire and Difference" (1991: 3–18, 329–56) and Joe Orton's *Diaries* (1986) for an analysis and a further example of the influence exercised by "the Mediterranean" over the imagination of British homosexual men during the last two centuries. In his important study of the homoerotics of Orientalism, Joseph A. Boone examines "the sexual politics of colonial narrative so explicitly thematized—in th[e] voyages to the Near East recorded or imagined by Western men" (1995: 89) and adds Robin Maugham, Michael Davidson, Lawrence Durrell and Rupert Croft-Cooke to this catalog of English "literary-artistic vacationers and sojourners" to the Mediterranean Near East in this century.

4. For an astute analysis of Firbank's fascination with people of color, his identification with them, his ostracization from "straight" society, and his depiction of them as erotic types, see William Lane Clark (1993). A first-edition copy of Firbank's *The Flower beneath the Foot* given to Will by Nantwich is crushed into the mud during Will's assault by the skinheads, suggesting a pathetic linking of Will to Firbank and to the flower through Nantwich's agency.

WORKS CITED

Aldrich, Robert. *The Seduction of the Mediterranean: Writing, Art and Homosexual Fantasy.* London: Routledge, 1993.

Bhabha, Homi K. "The Other Question: The Stereotype and Colonial Discourse." In: *The Politics of Theory*, edited by Francis Barker. Colchester: University of Essex. Rpt. *Screen* 24:6 (1983), 18–36.

Boone, Joseph A. "Vacation Cruises; or, The Homoerotics of Orientalism." *PMLA* 110, #1 (1995): 89–107.

Brown, James N., and Patricia M. Sant. "Empire Looks East: Spectatorship and Subjectivity in 'Karain: A Memory'." In: *Joseph Conrad: East-European, Polish and World-wide*, edited by Wieslaw Krajka. *Conrad: Eastern and Western Perspectives*, Vol. 8. New York, Boulder, Lublin: Columbia University Press, 2000.

———. "Settling Identities: Britishness Abroad." In: *Constructing British Identities: Texts, Sub-texts, and Contexts*, edited by Andrew Benjamin, Ban Kah Choon, and Robbie B. H. Goh, 2001.

Clark, William Lane. "Degenerate Personality: Deviant Sexuality and Race in Ronald Firbank's Novels." In: *Camp Grounds: Style and Homosexuality*. Amherst: University of Massachusetts Press, 1993.

Creed, Barbara. "Queer Theory and Its Discontents: Queer Desires, Queer Cinema." In: *Australian Women: Contemporary Feminist Thought*, edited by Norma Grieve and Ailsa Burns. Melbourne: Oxford University Press, 1994. 151–64.

Deleuze, Gilles, and Félix Guattari. *Anti-Oedipus. Vol. 1 of Capitalism and Schizophrenia* [1972], translated by Robert Hurley, Mark Seem, and Helen R. Lane. Minneapolis: University of Minnesota Press, 1983.

———. *A Thousand Plateaus. Vol. 2 of Capitalism and Schizophrenia* [1980], translated by Brian Massumi. Minneapolis: University of Minnesota Press, 1987.

D'Emilio, John. "Capitalism and Gay Identity" [1983]. In: *The Lesbian and Gay Studies Reader*, edited by Henry Abelove, Michèle Aina Barale, and David M. Halperin. London: Routledge, 1993. 467–76.

Dollimore, Jonathan. *Sexual Dissidence: Augustine to Wilde, Freud to Foucault*. Oxford: Clarendon Press, 1991.

Duggan, Lisa. "Making It Perfectly Queer." *Socialist Review* 22, #1 (1992): 11–31.

Edelman, Lee. "The Plague of Discourse: Politics, Literary Theory, and 'AIDS'." *Homographesis: Essays in Gay Literary and Cultural Theory*. London: Routledge, 1994. 79–92.

Fanon, Frantz. *The Wretched of the Earth* [1961], translated by Constance Farrington. Harmondsworth: Penguin, 1967.

———. *Toward the African Revolution: Political Essays* [1964], translated by Haakon Chevalier. Harmondsworth: Penguin, 1970.

Firbank, Ronald. *Prancing Nigger* [1925]. London: Duckworth, 1929.

Foucault, Michel. *The History of Sexuality, Vol. 1: An Introduction* [1976], edited by Robert Hurley. New York: Vintage, 1990.

Hocquenghem, Guy. *Homosexual Desire* [1972], translated by Daniella Dangoor. Series Q. Durham: Duke University Press, 1993.

Hollinghurst, Alan. *The Swimming-Pool Library* [1988]. London: Vintage, 1989.

Lacan, Jacques. *The Four Fundamental Concepts of Psycho-Analysis* [1973], translated by Alan Sheridan. Harmondsworth: Penguin, 1994.

Martin, Biddy. "Sexualities without Genders and Other Queer Utopias." *Diacritics* 24, #2/3 (1994): 104–21.

Nkrumah, Kwame. *Neo-Colonialism: The Last Stage of Imperialism*. London: Heinemann, 1965.

Orton, Joe. *Diaries, including the Correspondence of Edna Welthorpe and others*. Edited by John Lahr. London: Methuen, 1986.

Partridge, Eric. *Shakespeare's Bawdy: A Literary and Psychological Essay and a Compre-*

hensive Glossary [1947], revised and enlarged. London: Routledge and Kegan Paul, 1968.

Pugliese, Joseph. "Parasiting 'Post'-Colonialism: On the (Im)possibility of a Disappropriative Practice." *Southern Review* 28.3 (1995): 345–57.

Said, Edward W. *Culture and Imperialism*. London: Chatto and Windus, 1993.

———. *Orientalism: Western Conceptions of the Orient* [1978]. Harmondsworth: Penguin, 1991.

Seidman, Steven. "Identity and Politics in a 'Postmodern' Gay Culture: Some Historical and Conceptual Notes." In: *Fear of a Queer Planet: Queer Politics and Social Theory*, edited by Michael Warner. Minneapolis: University of Minneapolis Press, 1993. 105–42.

Spivak, Gayatri Chakravorty. "Can the Subaltern Speak?" In: *Marxism and the Interpretation of Culture*, edited by Cary Nelson and Lawrence Grossberg. London: Macmillan, 1988.

Treichler, Paula. "AIDS, Homophobia, and Biomedical Discourse: An Epidemic of Signification." In: *AIDS: Cultural Analysis/Cultural Activism*, edited by Douglas Crimp. October Books 43. Cambridge, Mass.: MIT Press 1987. 31–70.

Warner, Michael. "Introduction." In: *Fear of a Queer Planet: Queer Politics and Social Theory*, edited by Michael Warner. Minneapolis: University of Minneapolis Press, 1993. vii–xxxi.

Watney, Simon. "The Spectacle of AIDS." In: *AIDS: Cultural Analysis/ Cultural Activism*, edited by Douglas Crimp. October Books 43. Cambridge, Mass: MIT Press, 1987. 71–86.

Weeks, Jeffrey. "Post-Modern AIDS?" In: *Ecstatic Antibodies: Resisting the AIDS Mythology*, edited by Tessa Boffin and Sunil Gupta. London: River Oram Press, 1990. 133–41.

———. "Preface to the 1978 Edition." Guy Hocquenghem, *Homosexual Desire* [1972], translated by Daniella Dangoor. Series Q. Durham: Duke University Press, 1993. 23–47.

Young, Robert J. C. "Anti-Oedipus: The Geopolitics of Capitalism." In: *Colonial Desire: Hybridity in Theory, Culture and Race*. London: Routledge, 1995. 166–74.

Chapter 8

The United States in South Africa: (Post)Colonial Queer Theory?

Ian Barnard

Race, nation, gender, and sexuality should not be enunciated as separate axes of identity that cross and overlay in particular subject positions, but instead as systems of meaning and understanding that formatively and inherently define one another. In other words, race does not exist independently of sexuality (and vice versa), to become variously sexualized when particular sexual identities are considered in conjunction with specific racial attributes. Rather, race is always already sexualized as sexuality is always already nationalized, and so on. My interest, then, is also in how queer theory and postcolonial theory might interrogate and reconfigure one another, in colonial queer theory, and in the possibility of a queer postcolonial theory, or a postcolonial queer theory.

To exemplify some of these conjunctions and disruptions I'll here discuss two gay male porn videos of South Africa, a discussion that, I hope, will both test queer theory's limits and suggest its possible future interrelations with anti-racist and anticolonial work. Both *The Men of South Africa*, and its sequel, *The Men of South Africa II*, were made in the early 1990s in a South Africa still under formal apartheid, are "all-white" and "all-male," and are distributed by a mail order company in San Francisco specializing in "exotic" gay pornography. My aim is not merely to point to examples of racism in white gay cultural productions, but rather to trace the ways in which sexual, national, and racial identities can define one another in these productions. Such a story tells us as much about the meaning of gayness as the meaning of whiteness. This is not to suggest that either meaning is fixed or that the relationship between these two categories is stable; in fact, here (and always, I suspect) gayness is as slippery as whiteness: neither identity has meaning in and of itself but depends for its various meanings on its interactions with and constitution and construal by other identities and discourses. I do not make claims, then, for all sites of gay culture and identity or for all sites of white gay culture and identity; rather, by delineating one way in which white racism and gayness produce each other I hope to unsettle the conventional wisdom that assumes that racist institutions are also reactionary in the arena of gay rights. Concurrently, and rather than conceding Queer Theory to whiteness, I want to show that by identifying the racist potential of gayness as a category, queer interventions not only make race queer but also constitute integral components of antiracist analysis.

Two prefatory axioms. First, I see this project as a critique of queer theory, but also as very much enabled by and part of the imperative of queer theory. Second, I take it for granted that the specification of whiteness is essential to antiracist work, and that such a specification is not coterminous with a white supremacist celebration of whiteness, or a liberal white insistence on the many ethnicities of whiteness in order to diminish and dilute the naming and analysis of white racism.

Many of the existing attempts to analyze whiteness have noted that the terms of whiteness appear elusive, especially when whiteness is not treated in opposition to nonwhiteness; it seems easier to say what whiteness is not than what it is (the specifics of the content of whiteness seem to elude white people, in particular). But perhaps we can create a new perspective on whiteness by looking at the ways in which gendered race and sexuality construct each other, and at what the resulting substitutions, displacements, and conflations suggest about racial definitions and constructions, about the workings of whiteness, about the disparate uses, denials, and specifications of whiteness.

We can see a specific instance of the conjunction of race, sexuality, and nationality through narrativizing a particular construction of whiteness in the *The Men of South Africa* and *The Men of South Africa II*. Since the means of this narrativization produces South African gay culture for U.S. consumption, my particularity turns on gendered nationalist identifications and relations between the United States and South Africa, various trajectories of U.S. imperialism, and the production of gay identity, and, ultimately, a gay U.S. imperialism. I see these videos as constitutive articulations of a complex relationship not only between race and sexuality but also between the United States and South Africa, and as telling indices of particular cultural conjunctures at this historical moment in the United States and in South Africa, as South Africa itself encapsulates the collision and collapse of "First" and "Third" Worlds. The historical moment in which culture in South Africa is now being produced makes South Africa an especially fertile ground for revealing the interstices and intersections of multiple (subject) positions and identifications, and the processes by which new national and communal identities are formed and figured. Because of the long enforcement of formal apartheid, South Africa is only now seeing a tangible fruition to its own equivalent of the Civil Rights movement that is commonly mythologized to have procured similar results in the United States three decades earlier. Concomitantly, as questions of lesbian and gay rights only have entered the realm of sustained public debate in the United States in the 1990s, South Africa now holds the distinction of being the only country in the world to constitutionally prohibit discrimination based on sexual orientation.

The videos, then, are emblematic of disparate hierarchies and sequences in the attainment of different kinds of civil rights, and of the multilayered imbrication of queer discourses with other structures of power and formations of identity, particularly as the videos trace the racialized construction of white gay male identities. This construction is a product of its particular South African manufacturers and of the demands of its target U.S. consumers, inasmuch as manufacturer and consumer continually construct and reconstruct each other and their product.

The most telling moment in *Men of South Africa II* unexpectedly interpolates the images of black people with wild animals as exoticizing frame for the white sex performers. The video encloses the black crowd within the white narrative: we see a young white man masturbating in a bedroom; then, suddenly, we are treated to a series of exterior shots of elephants and ostriches; these are followed by a lengthier scene in which a naked white man masturbates outdoors; we then move to the (old) South African flag, the (apartheid) State President's office, the crowd of black people walking, and a few springbok and zebra; finally we return to a masturbating white man.

Black South Africans here are treated—like the animals—as props; they are accorded no individuality, agency, subjectivity, or humanity. Black people serve to enrich the locale with extra otherness and at the same time by counterpoint to emphasize the normalcy of the otherwise exoticized white characters. Because the black people in *Men of South Africa II* are scenery, they are not potential voters (as the conventions of gay pornography seldom position anyone as a potential voter); they are not potential sex partners, or sexual subjects either. As in the first video, all the "characters" in *Men of South Africa II* are white (a fact that is perhaps anxiously dramatized by a bleached blond in the first video), but the video's ambiguous discernment of these white characters' relationship to First and Third Worlds, to other South Africans, and to their U.S. viewers marks a cynical logic of neocolonial appropriation: inasmuch as viewers are supposed to desire the exotic but only insofar as it is containable, white people, here, can be much better black people than black people themselves. As we have seen with characters like Song in David Henry Hwang's play *M. Butterfly* and Dill in the film *The Crying Game*, dominant subjects are more willing and able to know and play out their own fantasies of the Other—Woman, in the case of *M. Butterfly* and *The Crying Game*— than the Other is; in so doing they can also hope to annihilate the presence of the Other altogether by incorporating this phantasmatic Other into their own performances.

Because all the white characters in the video are homoerotically coded, the videos present as whitewashed a face of gay South Africa, and I would suggest, of gayness in general, as they do of South Africa in general. At the same time that South Africanness is whitewashed in the videos, then, gayness is racialized as white. This depiction of an all-white gay South Africa in stark contrast to the history of queer organizing in South Africa adds force to the argument that the South Africa of the videos is based on their viewers' (and perhaps producers') fantasy of South Africa rather than on a South African "reality." Evidence of the explicit multiculturalism of South Africa's public queer communities, and of their involvement in apartheid and antiapartheid politics, has multiplied in the nineties:

for instance, in Johannesburg's 1993 lesbian and gay pride parade one very visible male marcher brandished a placard reading "Viva! Democratic Erections" ("Gay"), a punning reference to the imminent end of formal apartheid. Recent gay South Africans' self-representations are diametrically opposed to the logic of the videos, in terms not only of racial diversity but also of political affiliation.

The kind of representation of race in the South African videos impacts the racialized construction of both South African and gay identities, and the cultures and organizations for whose benefit these constructions are deployed: these representations show how sexual fantasies in general are integral to narratives of race, and vice versa; they demonstrate how the marks of gay culture may be interdependently appropriating and appropriated by other regimes of identity and domination (including the trope of travel); they're a fantasy of colonial nostalgia for U.S. viewers; and they create a complicity between the videos and similar characterizations of South Africa by the pre-Mandela apartheid South African government.

Given the usual hostility of right-wing regimes to lesbians and gay men, surely the greatest irony of the videos' intrication with the apartheid state lies in their irretrievable gayness. But this congruency represents more than just another instance of gay white racism, or evidence that an all-white cast can be as racist a porn convention as the one that exoticizes people of color as super sexual objects of the white gaze or perfect sex partners for the white subject. The specific permutations of the race/sexuality conjunction are embodied in the final scene from the first *Men of South Africa* video, where the video's two blondest performers urge viewers, "Come to our country, there are lots of us around, come and see us, we never run out of time." They stand naked, looking directly into the camera, and repeat variations on the invitation to South Africa several times in English and Afrikaans. The scene—and the video—ends with the two performers embracing and kissing each other. Significantly, when the one performer euphemistically refers to "our country," the other assertively interjects "South Africa," as if to emphasize the specificity of their nationalistic appeal, as if to counteract the white South African shame that characterized the export of South African heterosexuality in the waning days of apartheid—even Jamie Uys's blockbuster film *The Gods Must Be Crazy* was screened in the eighties in the United States as an "African" or "Namibian" film, presumably so that producers and distributors could avoid the embarrassment and financial loss concomitant upon promoting a white South African film in the face of boycotts and sanctions against South Africa.

This final scene of the *Men of South Africa* video also points to the complex racial and national potentialities for gay porn conventions (we never tire, we're waiting for you, this is your utopia), and particularly for the conventions of "amateur" or "real-life" pornography that is regaining popularity in the nineties. The "we never run out of time" line plays into anthropological reductions of the Other to eternal savagery, analyzed, by, for instance, Edward Said's *Orientalism*, Johannes Fabian, and Chandra Mohanty. The embrace, unusual in gay porn "solo" videos (that is, videos that otherwise depict only solo masturbation scenes), underscores the illusion that this is a utopian homoerotic space—earlier hints of danger merely enrich this homoerotic experience. A gay agenda, then, becomes paradoxically congruent with the policies of the pre-1994 South African government that not only enforced apartheid, but also prohibited public displays of homosexuality, criminalized private consensual homosexual sodomy, and banned pornography. Of course, the videos make no mention of witchhunts against gay men or bannings of gay publications taking place in South Africa at the very time that they were in production. On the contrary, the coding of almost all the performers in the video as gay reinforces the sense of a safe haven for white gay U.S. Americans and perhaps gay U.S. Americans of color in South Africa.

This delusory construction of gay South Africa is absolutely in sync with the apartheid South African government's constructions of an all-white South Africa, and with tourist propaganda in the eighties that denied the realities of apartheid, of a multicultural society, and of racial conflict in South Africa. Under apartheid black South Africans were both psychically and literally bracketed out of the white South African imaginary of full South African nationality and citizenship: the psychic work revolved around the fiction that South Africa was a European nation, and a democratic country; the material embodiment of this fantasy encompassed government legislation that created "homelands" for black South Africans in order to justify denying them citizenship and thus civil rights in South Africa "proper." The idyllic all-white beach scene in the typical South African tourist postcard of the 1980s gave no indication that 85.2 percent of the population of this country was black, and that this black majority was forcibly excluded from the postcard beach. Official South African tourist propaganda was in the same vein: white South Africans assumed (usually correctly) that white visitors from other countries would want to visit an all-white pseudo-European enclave in darkest Africa; while many white South Africans actually believed that they lived in an all-white country (this much has changed today), most overseas white people suspected better. In fact, the attraction of South Africa as a white tourist destination was precisely the promise of danger lurking just outside the comfort zone—fantasies of animal sexuality to spice up the familiar reality of all-white action; wild animals and black people safely cordoned off from luxurious tourist hotels. The videos are especially significant because they attempt to conjure up this picture of South Africa in the early 1990s, with Nelson Mandela released from prison and the ANC and South African Communist Party unbanned, with white South Africans being forced to confront the reality of their multiracial nation as never before.

Given the desperate importance that the apartheid South African government attached to the task of attracting white tourists to the country in the face of sanctions and boycotts and when apartheid was being most strenuously challenged, the scene at the end of *The Men of South Africa* can almost be seen as a commercial commissioned by the apartheid government itself. Such a collaboration is not as unlikely as it might sound. While, as I have indicated, the apartheid South African government did have a homophobic history, the history of apartheid in South Africa also fundamentally contests received liberal wisdom in the United States that homosexuality is the final taboo in the hierarchy of persecuted identities, and that homophobia necessarily overrides racism among bigoted South

Africans and U.S. Americans. In the early eighties, candidates running for office for the ruling National Party in South Africa had no compunction in appealing specifically to racist white gay voters—vote for us, we'll support gay rights and keep South Africa white. The invitation to visit South Africa at the conclusion of *The Men of South Africa* even suggests that South Africa and the United States might be able to continue their collaborations in white supremacism by tapping into a lucrative gay male tourist market in the United States. This market is already familiar with a host of upscale gay cruises and tours (some specifically to Third World countries to pursue racist sexual fetishes), and will accept the racist recreation of a disappearing South Africa under the aegis of the erotic conventions of middle-class white gay male culture in the United States. In this way gayness—which is always and only white—sustains whiteness, and white supremacy.

The collusion of gayness with racist whiteness alerts us to yet another problem with identity politics to add to those already elaborated by feminist and queer theorists wary of the essentializing and homogenizing potentialities in the identity politics traditions in the United States. This collusion might also point us away from gayness and in the direction of "queer" as a political category.

By arguing that gayness in this instance enables racism, I am insisting that we once and for all abandon not only the notion that gayness can be "apolitical," but also the idealistic and complacent hope that gayness inevitably represents some kind of oppositional political position. In their work on literary and cinematic representations of race and sexuality, Christopher Lane has explained how racial Others can be deflected or displaced representations of white gay male sensibilities, relationships, and desires, and Richard Dyer has traced racial whiteness's enunciation in terms of order and rationality, and, specifically, its colonization of normative (patriarchal) heterosexuality. In the *Men of South Africa* videos, however, substitution has the opposite trajectory from what we might expect, one that is perhaps not as compatible with conventional political formulations of gay sexuality as only oppressed or as automatically subversive of hegemonic institutions. Whereas in Lane's argument there is a correlation between gayness and coloredness, suggesting an undisciplined or transgressive or taboo quality to both, and for Dyer heterosexuality and whiteness describe and circumscribe each other, again situating homosexuality in the realm of nonwhiteness or marginality, in the South African videos gay maleness comes to stand for white maleness, and vice versa.

This congruency and conflation is partly due to the difficulty, on the part of white people, of specifying the content of whiteness per se (thus whiteness is delineated in terms of something else—gayness—or against something else—blackness), but surely is also a response to the increasing social unacceptability of a discourse of white separatism and a concomitant fashionable legitimacy in depicting gay identity, which is putatively white and all-male. Gay is the code for white. This coding is much more than merely an instance of a metonymic fetishization that caters to the specialized tastes of a particular subculture, because it demonstrates not only the centrality of gayness to other forms of identification and to culture in general, but also the dominant's resilience and resistance to real change or loss of power—the ways in which historically dominant configurations of power, and privileged individuals and institutions can reinvent themselves as they continually constitute, incorporate, and transform new social subjects and cultural formations. Dyer points out that whiteness needs to demonstrate its virtues to justify continued domination. In the videos we see whiteness seeking to justify itself via gayness. One of the few ways to construct a white South Africa without immediately provoking antiracist outrage is to use these codes of gay maleness: a gay discourse (both in the United States and in South Africa) can appear to be progressive while in fact entrenching racist domination and recruiting new converts to this racist agenda.

Ironically, this white supremacist substitution colludes with the arguments of some black nationalist organizations and individuals, both in the United States and in South Africa, that homosexuality is foreign to black people, and that black queers have been contaminated and co-opted by imperialist white cultures. Contrarily, this unholy alliance between homophobic black nationalism and homophilic white supremacy could provide one of the best counterattacks against that black nationalist position, showing how it undergirds homosocial white domination. The interdependency of whiteness and gayness here also undercuts primitivist stereotypes of the precolonial Third World as blissfully nonhomophobic that are now popular among many liberal gay scholars in the West.

Finally, the interdependent substitution of whiteness for gayness suggests one possible understanding of the absence of—indeed, the impossibility of—an official discourse of colored queerness in the United States. Together with the trendy litany of minoritized identities that divides people into discrete categories of race, gender, and sexuality, and that thus cannot conceptualize queers of color, or white female queers, this conflation of gayness and whiteness erases the existence of queers of color in the United States, and in South Africa, where an imperialist U.S. gay teleology is already imposing its own models of identity, of queerness, and of queer progress onto the South African scene.

My own concerns are cross-cultural, not in the sense of the coverage model of western academic and pedagogical multiculturalism that seeks to articulate a comprehensive (and imperialistic) universalism, but in my attempts to bring into strategic juxtaposition certain historical moments of cultural visibility, intervention, and transcendence of raced sexual subjectivity precisely in order to trace the shape of such imperialisms as they generate and are themselves transformed by discourses of deviant sexuality. Much commendable work by social scientists has already been undertaken in the empirical elaboration of geographically diverse queernesses, as has a greater quantity of less careful work in which, typically, a white westerner uses the trope and privilege of travel and the sanctioned promise of investigating difference to recapitulate a putatively universal and ahistorically transcendent gay identity, and to interpolate the metropolitan traveler as the arbiter and omniscient cataloger of the queer world (in the form of the scientist, historian, storyteller). The production of otherworldly gaynesses becomes an opportunity only to enrich and expand the reach of hegemonic positionalities, much as the discourse of multiculturalism has emphasized the enrichment potential of cultural diversity for a still centralized white subject by avoiding confrontation with racist power relations and institutions. Similarly, literary and historical projects that attempt to locate and claim a lesbian or gay past, or lesbian and gay "foremothers" and "forefathers" in order to inscribe them into a linear and unified gay tradition, necessarily impose a specifically western and modern teleology of identity, sexuality, and liberation onto historically and culturally diverse (and often alien) subjects, and thus reinforce the imperialist relations that are already inherent in such a project's almost inevitable origin in the white western academy. Knowledge is never benign, and, certainly, apparatuses and institutions of knowledge production will always contextualize any "knowledge" thus produced, as will the situation of the investigator of knowledge as someone with the privilege, resources— and historically enabling legacy of economic and military imperialism—to travel, write, and acquire.

The elite institutions from which queer theory advances have their counterpart in the paternalistic activist wisdom of lesbian and gay organizers in the United States who judge the level of "progress" another country is making in the arena of lesbian and gay rights by the uniquely U.S. trajectories of Stonewall, coming out, and identity-based civil rights. Of course, it is always the U.S. standard that these other countries must live up to, and, naturally, the United States is always the leader in this race for gay utopia.

The United States, then, is marked by a colonizing gay identity that erases global cultural difference and imperial power relations. Books and articles about "The Global Village of Gay/Lesbian Rights" (Clark) are flourishing. I receive an e-mail about a new book series from the University of Chicago Press: Worlds of Desire. In 1994, the twenty-fifth anniversary of Stonewall, pride parades around the United States were organized around the theme "A Global Celebration of Pride and Protest." The theme of San Francisco's 1995 Lesbian, Gay, Bisexual, and Transgender Pride Celebration Parade and Festival was "A World without Borders." In a San Diego gay newspaper in June 1995, a picture from the recent pride parade in neighboring Tijuana, Mexico, was captioned "Reminiscent of the first San Diego Pride Parade in 1975, approximately 150 people gathered for the first ever Tijuana Gay Pride Parade on Saturday, June 15" ("Mexico"). Clearly, the United States is the only model for anyone else to follow. In 1996, the theme of the Los Angeles Gay and Lesbian Pride Celebration was "Pride without Borders." And U.S. gay tourists and gay do-gooders, and, increasingly now, but still in smaller numbers, lesbian tourists and do-gooders from the United States, travel in record numbers to Third World countries to sightsee and to "help" establish gay organizations in those countries. Mexico continues to receive huge loans from the United States. This gay and U.S. imperialism was recently made quite explicit in the United Kingdom via a December 1995 capsule article in a Southern California gay newspaper entitled "British Gays to Colonize Island." Apparently, gay activists planned to protest Britain's restrictive immigration laws by occupying the island of Lundy, erecting a gay flag, printing gay money, and issuing gay marriage licenses (Wockner).

The far reach of United States (and, in turn, other western) gay imperialism is evident even in the recently published book *Defiant Desire: Gay and Lesbian Lives in South Africa*, where the white South African editors make an unprecedented effort to treat the diversity of South Africa's queer cultures, but still fall into the trap of internalizing U.S. models of gay progress and thus reproducing U.S. imperialism, too. For instance, in his chapter in the volume on the history of lesbian and gay organizing in South Africa, Mark Gevisser, one of the book's editors, concludes, "Only in the 1980s did black men and women begin to play an active role in gay politics" (29), apparently oblivious to the ways in which his uncritical deployment of the category "gay" and his assumptions of what constitutes "gay politics" a priori exclude many uniquely black and uniquely South African queer identities and formations from his purview.

The particular cultural texts that I have examined have been produced by, in, and for an intermittently and dialectized English-speaking questionably metropolitan West, and as such make the extension of queer theory's racial content to the politics of (post)colonial internationalism coterminous with queer theory's own constitution in the sites of knowledge that have informed and exposed that imperialist advance. In *Culture and Imperialism*, Edward Said points out that in the late twentieth century the United States has become the preeminent imperial power; the subjects of my own study, centered in the United States, necessarily speak of the imperialist projection in queer theory, even as this theory critiques an apparently heterosexual and sometimes homoerotic western colonialism.

This personal/political analogous/conflictive collusion has been exemplified in the timely tabloid queer-trashing of Manuel Noriega and Saddam Hussein (each "exposed" as a transvestite who has sex with boys or men) soon after the United States attacked their countries, and in gay male desire for Jeffrey Dahmer and O. J. Simpson. These two kinds of queer reading—queerness as demonization, queer desire for demons—come together as "terrorism" irrupts in the domestic sphere: a May 1995 *Globe* report "revealed" suspected Oklahoma City bomber Timothy McVeigh's "kinky obsession" with fellow suspect Terry Nichols ("Mad") at the same time that some gay men were infatuated by the white, boyish, crew-cut McVeigh's TV images, an infatuation that had subversive potential in the context of the mainstream media's racist and imperialist first assumption that the bombing had been the work of "Middle-Eastern terrorists."

That the 1995 O. J. Simpson criminal trial should not only have generated worldwide interest, but that U.S. news stations should laud this interest, is indicative of the ways in which cultural imperialism undergirds the production of calculated knowledge bases that, in turn, shape political aspirations and formations. Given the work of queer theory in rereading popular culture (that is, the very antiseparatist ideology that distinguishes queer theory from some other paradigms of sexuality), and my own suggestion of the cross-categorical relevance of anomalous axes of power, oppression, and resistance, queer reading must be understood, in addition to and by way of its other effects, as in some way underscoring a colonizing imperative.

ACKNOWLEDGMENTS

I thank Roxana M. Dapper, Maggie Sale, Judith Halberstam, and Bruce M. Abrams for assisting me with this chapter.

WORKS CITED

Clark, Keith. "The Global Village of Gay/Lesbian Rights." *Gay & Lesbian Times* (San Diego) (15 June 1995): 38–39.

Dyer, Richard. "White." *Screen* 29.4 (1988): 44–65.

Fabian, Johannes. *Time and the Other: How Anthropology Makes Its Object.* New York: Columbia University Press, 1983.

"Gay Abandon." *Weekly Mail* (South Africa) (15–21 Oct. 1993): 4.

Gevisser, Mark. "A Different Fight for Freedom: A History of South African Lesbian and Gay Organisation—the 1950s to the 1990s." In: *Defiant Desire: Gay and Lesbian Lives in South Africa,* edited by Mark Gevisser and Edwin Cameron. Johannesburg: Ravan, 1994. 14–86.

Hwang, David Henry. *M. Butterfly.* New York: Plume-Penguin, 1989.

Lane, Christopher. *The Ruling Passion: British Colonial Allegory and the Paradox of Homosexual Desire.* Durham: Duke University Press, 1995.

"Mad Bombers' Kinky Secret." *Globe* (30 May 1995): 6–7.

The Men of South Africa. Video. Trekker Productions-International Wavelength. 1991.

The Men of South Africa II: Boereseuns/Boer Boys. Video. Voortrekker Productions-International Wavelength. 1992.

"Mexico Celebrates Pride." *Update* (San Diego) (21 June 1995): 1.

Mohanty, Chandra Talpade. "Under Western Eyes: Feminist Scholarship and Colonial Discourse." *boundary 2* 12.3–13.1 (1984): 333–58.

"Saddam's a Sex Pervert." *National Examiner* (12 March 1991): 4–5.

Said, Edward W. *Culture and Imperialism.* New York: Knopf, 1993.

———. *Orientalism.* 1978. New York: Vintage-Random, 1979.

Wockner, Rex. "British Gays to Colonize Island." *Gay & Lesbian Times* (San Diego) (7 Dec. 1995): 30.

Chapter 9

Other and Difference in Richard Rodriguez's *Hunger of Memory*

David William Foster

> I felt such contrary feelings.
> —Rodriguez, *Hunger of Memory* 53

> Writing these pages, admitting my embarrassment or my guilt, admitting my sexual anxieties and my physical insecurity, I have not been able to forget that I am not being *formal*.
> —Rodriguez, *Hunger of Memory* 130

> I am writing about those very things my mother has asked me not to reveal.
> —Rodriguez, *Hunger of Memory* 176

It is not my intent, nor my interest, to engage in a gay reading of Richard Rodriguez's *Hunger of Memory* (1982). It is not that such a reading would be inappropriate or impossible, and I am not referring simply to the fact that one can engage in a revisionist reading of Rodriguez's text, written before his public acknowledgment of being gay, in order, therefore, to discover ways in which his text might provide glimpses of such an identity, such that that identity would now be evident on the basis of an informed rereading. Such a rereading is certainly eminently legitimate: texts are read and reread in an accumulative process of interpretation that allows us to see them in new lights on the basis of myriads forms of new knowledge: the possible Jewish roots, for example, of many Spanish authors, an identity made possible by the return to an open culture in Spain since the death of Franco, have made possible reinterpretations of key works, such as Francisco de Rojas's *La Celestina*. It has been important to understand how text signed by her husband or by both of them, but in all likelihood written exclusively by her allows for feminist readings of the plays of María Martínez de Sierra. The homoerotic facts of Lorca's life—indeed, the possibility that his execution may have been related to a case of gay revenge or to a plan to execute him for being so openly gay—now allows for a gay reading of his entire oeuvre, despite the serious misgivings of a critical legacy that would prefer to discredit the validity, and in some cases even the truth, of such an attribution (Gibson; Sahuquillo).

Moreover, the creation of a Chicano cultural consciousness allows for a re-reading of innumerable work written before the Chicano Movement that can now be claimed to be foreshadowings, harbingers, pretexts of a properly speaking Chicano literary tradition: knowledge (and ideology) at a particular point in time creates the conditions for the rereading of a cultural production prior to that time. On this basis alone, it would not be improper nor a violation of scholarly ethics (as though charting a gay identity were somehow a violation of scholarly ethics, of the same order as discovering a criminal past) to wish to discover in *Hunger of Memory* an anticipation of the conditions that will latter allow Rodriguez to lay public claim to his identity as a gay man (Stavans; Rodriguez, "Late Victorians"; Postel and Gillespie).

By suggesting that, under the circumstances of Rodriguez's public persona, a gay reading would not be improper, one does not mean, of course, that there is a formula to be applied to a text that will either discover in the text, in the fashion of a chemical test, something like a gay message or a gay subtext. Nor does one mean that the text somehow becomes more meaningful, more eloquent, more verisimilar because the "truth" of the author's sexuality has been laid bare, as though the truth of one's sexuality were determinant of his entire character. Indeed, precisely because homophobia makes one's alleged "deviant" sexuality so overwhelmingly meaningful for understanding his whole social and psychological makeup, it becomes necessary to resist such grandiloquent claims for the importance of the sexuality of an individual—or, in this case, of an author. The degree to which sexuality is important for a text, the degree to which there is a semiotics of sexuality underlying the text as cultural discourse is a function of the critical enterprise, but not an a priori condition, cause, or premise of the latter. Such a premise is described by Lee Edelman under the rubric of "homographesis":

Like writing, then, homographesis would name a double operation: one serving the ideological labor of disciplinary inscription, and the other resistant to that categorization, intent on *de*-scribing the identities that order has so oppressively inscribed. . . . In the first sense, homographesis would refer to the cultural mechanism by which writing is brought into relation to the question of sexual difference in order to conceive the gay body as text, thereby affecting far-reaching intervention in the political regulation of social identities. The process that constructs homosexuality as a subject of discourse, as a cultural category about which one can think or speak or write, coincides, in this logic of homographesis, with the process whereby the homosexual subject is represented as being, even more than inhabiting, a body that always demands to be read, a body on which his "sexuality" is always already inscribed. (10)

On this basis, a gay reading of *Hunger of Memory* would necessarily explore how it *might* be considered in view of the author's subsequent public declaration of a gay identity, but it would have to take up the question of what is understood by a gay identity, how Rodriguez might understand it, and how he has situated himself in his writing and public discourse since such an acknowledgment. Furthermore, it would have to consider the general question of what a gay identity means in any sense for a literary text (it certainly must mean something: only a homophobic position could argue categorically that it means nothing, since every fact of textual production is liable to the process of interpretation, which is, after all, the source of meaning). And too, it would have to offer, as any critical act must do, a persuasive calculus for determining the importance of textual elements within the framework of whatever might be called a "gay" interpretation. To the extent that it is customary to require overdetermined meanings for those textual elements that a particular ideological stance (in this case, homophobia) would choose to deny as either existing or as relevant, it would, finally, be necessary to make allowances for a circumstance of critical blindness. To be sure, the critic might choose not to meet the burden of overdetermined proof out of a refusal to collaborate with the dynamics of homophobia (homologous with those of racism, sexism, and other symptoms of the denial of the Other), but this would be to run the risk of an accusation of intellectual insubstantiality.

There is a further observation necessary here, and that is why or at what point it would be proper to engage in a gay reading of Richard Rodriguez's text. I cannot answer this question in any satisfactory way. In one sense, subsequent writing signed by him deals with gay topics and subtexts in such a way that it becomes reasonable to engage in a rereading of earlier works—much as John Rechy's interest in Chicano themes at a certain point in his career makes it profitable to examine all of his writing as a Chicano oeuvre (something that critics had been reluctant to do on the basis of his early novels, where gay thematics involved characters who were alleged to be only nominally Chicano.) Alternatively, a critic who has a particular point to make through a gay reading—not just a general characterization, but an interpretation that might tie in with other issues, say, to the effect that the argument in *Hunger of Memory* for the need for the Chicano to create a public identity (which Rodriguez argues bilingual education to hinder) is related to the way in which the concept of "gay identity," in terms of modern American politics, is always part of a public person—will legitimate the interpretive practice through the characterization of the importance of that point. Thus, one cannot, in principle, find anything wrong with a gay reading of *Hunger of Memory*, as fraught as it may be with critical difficulties. But, then, one always assumes texts never to say directly what it is that requires critical exposition.

My interest, rather, is with a more properly queer reading of *Hunger of Memory*, queer in the sense of that which disrupts the binary imperative, the norm of compulsory heterosexuality, and the negation of identity difference, sexual or otherwise (Jagose). *Hunger* is a landmark text of Chicano writing, especially autobiographical writing (Flores; Marquez, "Richard Rodriguez's *Hunger of Memory* and the Poetics of Experience"; Marquez, "Richard Rodriguez's *Hunger of Memory* and New Perspectives on Ethnic Autobiography"; Villanueva-Collado; Saldívar;

Rose; McKenna 50–70), as much for the complex argument that Rodriguez develops concerning the role of the Spanish language and Hispanic culture in the Chicano community (Shuter), as for the ways in which that argument confronts usually unquestioned axioms of bilingual education and the Chicano movement (unquestioned, at least, in the early 1980s). Rodriguez argues for the need to construct a public persona in English (the achievement of which is marked in his case both by the use of the first name Richard and by the writing of Rodriguez without an accent mark) and to compete in American society without defensive reference to the otherness (as either a victimization or a privileged endowment) of Aztlán, such that he has ended up with one of the most extensive bibliographies of critical commentaries on his work of almost any other Chicano writer, a bibliography that refers little to the literary or cultural issues of his writing and more to the political ideologies with which it intersects in the often raucous debate over bilingual education.

The view of Rodriguez's *Hunger of Memory* as essentially a queer text means to sidestep the by now abundantly rehearsed arguments about its relationship to the bilingual education debate and whether it constitutes a legitimate view within the debate and whether or not it constitutes a sellout to certain right-wing ideologues who, incorrectly, satisfy themselves that Rodriguez is arguing for underdifferentiated assimilation into a dominant and hegemonic English world in which Hispanic culture survives only as a misguided resistance to assimilation and, indeed, as a social problem ("Rodriguez . . . rapidly becomes—at a very early age to be sure and whether he admits it or not—a spokesperson for the right wing of this country" [Flores 85]; surely this is a fine example of the function of the critic to speak to/for the author a dirty secret that the latter may not be able to admit to openly; Alarcón, on the other hand, speaks unmincingly of Rodriguez's "'bad faith'" [150]—as though the scare quotes mitigated the attribution; Hogue speaks confidently of what *Hunger* "shows unconsciously" [58] and of the "impasse" of the book's meaning [60]; Rodriguez, "Richard Rodriguez's *Hunger of Memory* and New Perspectives on Ethnic Autobiography," surveys other pertinent opinions). A close reading of Rodriguez's text does not support the comfortable conclusion that it is a right-wing fantasy of assimilation; quite the contrary, as it is a subtle meditation on the pathos of maintaining a life aligned with both cultures and the complex process by which a coming to terms with how such an alignment may be constructed.

An integral part of this complex process is the perception and analysis of differences, and it is a process that belies the antibilingualism/antibiculturalism proposition that the Hispanic must necessarily be submerged in the Anglo if the individual is to succeed in a world of which the latter is the unimpeachable master (Sánchez is the only other critic to focus specifically on Rodriguez's concepts of difference in a discussion of *Days of Obligation*, although without an interest in the relationship between difference and queering social categories; she does, however, make passing references to his gay identity). Rodriguez's personal memoir is all about difference, and on this basis alone it is difficult to understand how anyone could attribute to the text and defense of a uniform Anglo sameness that will significantly diminish the role of the Hispanic. Rodriguez's interest in difference is what, after all, I would now begin to argue is fundamentally queer about *Hunger of Memory*. Making and marking differences is what queer theory is all about. Accordingly to Alexander Doty:

Queer positions, queer readings, and queer pleasures [contra-straight, rather than the strictly antistraight]—are part of a reception space that stands simultaneously beside and with that created by heterosexual and straight positions. These positions, readings, and pleasures also suggest that what happens in cultural reception goes beyond the traditional opposition of homo and hetero, as queer reception is often a place beyond the audience's conscious "real-life" definition of their sexual identities and cultural positions—often, but not always, beyond such sexual identities and identity politics, that is. (15)

To be sure, we understand that the dominant difference has to do with sexual desire, and sexual desire is only randomly mentioned in Rodriguez's text and never in any way that would give the impression that such desire is homoerotic or that there is a homoerotic dimension to the issues of personal identity the author describes himself as working through. This is, certainly, of significant importance for understanding *Hunger of Memory* and is what, as I have argued above, subtracts it from the realm of gay writing. But regarding the cruciality of difference and the way in which differences along multiple axes are overdeterminations of one another, in the sense that any one difference is a synecdoche of overarching structures of difference, one can propose for purposes of discussion that difference in certain highlighted areas points toward difference in other areas that are not explicitly dealt with. Surely differences are not to be taken here as deterministic from one category to another, nor is there anything categorical about their assessment. Rather, the point is in the reasonableness of opening an inquiry into the potential homologies from one category to another, particularly when the categories that one is allowed to be spoken of opening, such as language preference and difference, exist alongside categories that one cannot undertake so easily, such as sexual preference and difference.

Queer can best be understood, not as a synonym for "lesbigay," but for a position that questions the ideologies of social construction in the first place, those constructions that enable and oblige us to speak of male versus female or, in certain limited reconfigurations, of lesbian, gay, and other alternative categories that may or may not adhere to the female/male binarism. Queer, in such a view, becomes a deconstructive reading of the overdetermined systems of, in a first instance, sexual difference and particularly of views of such difference as being intrinsically universal and natural (i.e., not constructed by social ideologies). Certainly, queer need not refer only to sexual issues, and an adequate inquiry to why the sexual is such a dominant, and domineering, social discourse (i.e., not why it is so important to human existence, but why it is so crucial to the discourse of social regulation) would focus at some point on how a queer sexuality is both part of a larger agenda of queerness and one of a number of queer subscriptions.

When seen in this fashion, queer not only refers to other ways of social being, but it also enables the examination of other ways of social being as impinging on the specifically sexual. It thus becomes possible to engage in an examination of the ideologies of the cultural construction of such difference in terms of what the agents, motives, and practices are of such constructions, toward perceiving how discussions of the cultural (including, therefore, the sexual) can, therefore, involve, if only implicitly and unconsciously, a question of those constructions.

For example, when Rodriguez undertakes, in the chapter titled "Credo," to describe his relationship with Catholicism, there is a queering of meaning, first, by virtue of his understanding that religiosity works in concert with the social text (that is, it is not a privileged otherworldly domain separate from the social), and, second, as a consequence of understanding how religion serves as one way of constructing the other, with other understood either as oneself vis-à-vis society at large or as the difference between social subjects within society, as in the case of those individuals we sense to be different from ourselves within the social body.

Rodriguez dwells at length on his separateness from society at large, perhaps one of the most crucial in the book from the point of view of the role of education and the minority student, titled, rather intriguingly, "The Achievement of Desire." Basing himself on the British scholar Richard Hoggart's *The Uses of Literacy* (1957), Rodriguez describes himself as an exemplar of Hoggart's paradigm of the "scholarship boy." This student, in the process of obtaining an education, necessarily grows distant from his family: the child from a disadvantaged social background acquires the academic skills to aspire to a social position that raises him (due note is taken of the sexism of Hoggart's analysis) above that of his parents, and he ends up alienated from them, no matter how much they may continue to attempt to maintain a familial relationship with him. The result is often a sense of loss on the part of the parents and a sense of anxiety provoked by shame over the "ignorance" of the parents and then shame over that shame, with frustration, anger, and recriminations often occurring on both sides.

Rodriguez is careful to point out that he was lucky always to receive the admiring support of his parents, even when his father may have in passing questioned the need for formal education, and in this Rodriguez was more fortunate than many scholarship boys, who may have to face outright hostility from family members over their scholarly attainments and further ambitions. Rodriguez will go on in subsequent chapters of his memoir to describe how he reconciles his education with his parents' backgrounds, a reconciliation that has to do with his perception of the relationship between the Anglo public realm and the Hispanic private one, but not all scholarship boys are able to achieve such a reconciliation. Indeed, Rodriguez's whole play of public versus private in the opening chapter, titled "Aria," is devoted to maintaining this fundamental difference in view of how, from the ethnic minority student's point of view, the public is dedicated to the destruction of the private (and, moreover, from Rodriguez's point of view, bilingualism is an ineffectual antidote to this pattern of destruction).

In the process of thinking through the relationship between the public and the private, between English and Spanish, and between formal education and homely culture, Rodriguez constructs a complex understanding of those forces that other the individual within his society. What is engaging about Rodriguez's discussion on this point is the extent to which he describes a process that alienates rather than homogenizes (the myth of universal public education in America) and how that process brings a questioning of authority and a realignment of allegiances. It is, consequently, a process that is far from "natural," and there is no mistaking in Rodriguez's rhetoric the same wrenching separateness in his view of the career of the scholarship boy that we have come to associate with the drama of coming out sexually within the family circle (48).

In a further passage, Rodriguez speaks of the transference of authority from one father figure to another as part of the development of the scholarship boy. In so doing, he chooses not to mention the Socratic formula and its sexual dimensions (various scholars have noted this relationship; see Case 43–44 in particular). True, as a scholarship boy, Rodriguez's first authority figures are those patriarchal stand-ins of Catholicism, demanding nuns, and one must always recall that, in its original Athenian version, the Socratic formula always involved a continuity between father figures rather than the rupture Rodriguez describes (Halperin passim). But the formula remains the same as regards the way in which the authority of education involves an intimate relationship (whether or not sexual or sexualized) between student and teacher (49).

"The Achievement of Desire" is peppered with passing comments and focused commentaries on how the process of education creates an othering of the scholarship boy, reinforcing a difference from his roots; the process is even more pronounced, of course, in the case of the transition from home Spanish to school English, even when his parents decide to speak English at home in order to reinforce the need for their children to acquire that language. The result becomes what the child perceives as a jarring contrast between his formal school English and their "broken" versions of it. One of the consequences is that one withholds from the parents "any mention of what most mattered to me: the extraordinary experience of first-learning" (51). The idea that the child has now a secret life, one that cannot be revealed, one that is felt to be singularly different from that of his parents and their household are all very strong propositions regarding something, elementary education, that is usually considered essentially innocuous. Not that elementary education does not have its problems, the issues, some of them quite heated, associated with bilingualism being among them (see Romero; Torres, for discussions of issues of bilingualism in Rodriguez's writing). But the idea that elementary education, especially at the hands of reverent and dedicated nuns, can produce such an acute separation from the family is cast in rhetorical terms one usually sees for political convictions that get one thrown out of the father's house or sexual preferences that may provoke a similar reaction.

Again, I certainly do not mean to be insinuating that Rodriguez is here using such a highly charged description of the disruption in family allegiances produced by elementary education as a cover for describing the anxiety, not of the scholarship boy, but of the gay child. Maybe he is, but this cannot be ascertained in any critically acceptable fashion. What can be ascertained is the level of eloquent rhetoric with which the author works here and the echoes it has with other discourses of social difference. Because the main point here is the need to confirm a major structure of difference, one that significantly challenges, on the one hand, the image of children's comfortable assimilation into an elementary education that is meant to be of a whole with their home life and their place in society. Of course, it is well known that this does not happen easily and, often, does not happen at all, but the causes are commonly held to be for reasons far removed from the ones that Rodriguez enumerates from the perspective of the scholarship boy.

On the other hand, from the point of view of the ideology of bilingual education to which Rodriguez has opposed himself, in ways that have branded him essentially as a traitor to Chicano/Latino culture (Marquez and Saldívar are particularly energetic in their rhetoric in this regard), there is nothing in the career of the scholarship boy that can be satisfied by the majority of the programs identified as "bilingual," since it is rare that they aspire to the level of intellectual needs (as much as one might wish they did) that Rodriguez sees the scholarship boy demanding or growing to demand. Part of Rodriguez's opposition to bilingualism takes the following form:

Supporters of bilingual education thus want it both ways. They propose bilingual school as a way of helping students acquire the skills of the classroom crucial for public success. But they likewise insist that bilingual instruction will give students a sense of their identity apart from the public. (34)

Clearly, the scholarship boy ends up with an identity that may not be the conventional public one (because of his inordinate drive to acquire learning), but it is hardly akin to the private one, as the alienation from the family he describes takes place. By the same token, as stated, bilingual education, if only for lack of personnel, will never satisfy the needs of the scholarship boy. To be sure, one might argue that, precisely, bilingual education will keep the scholarship boy from ever emerging, and therefore impede the development of anxiety, alienation, rejection of familial authority, the "betrayal by learning English" (30). But it does so at the expense of denying difference, not the difference between English and Spanish, but the difference between the private and the public, and it is precisely this crucial difference around which Rodriguez constructs his personal identity.

This queering of both the private text (the rejection of the sameness of the home in Spanish and the school place in Spanish) and the public text (the rejection of the sameness of the individual and society under the aegis of the public discourse promoted by schooling in English) leaves the scholarship boy caught in the highly charged complications of identity that Rodriguez describes. But it also gives him the markedly differentiated identity, that of one rescued from overdetermined indifference, that generates a text like *Hunger of Memory* (I use deliberately the archaic meaning of "indifference"—a lack of difference or distinction—as a variant of underdifferentiation in order to underscore how the ignorance, the ignoring, of difference brings with it a lack of interest in what the unrecognized difference might mean for unquestioned social ideologies).

In the case of religion, the discovery of the other lies elsewhere other than the difference between the individual and society. Rather, it turns on processes by which individuals are differentiated from one another, but again always in terms of an analysis that repudiates the indifference of a social text driven by the imperative of uniform sameness. Rodriguez was raised a Catholic—he cleverly states that he "was *un católico* before I was a Catholic" (81)—before Vatican II, and he recalls vividly the Baroque pageantry of the Church, which has become considerably diminished since Vatican II, especially with the disappearance of the mass in Latin and the participation in English of the mass-goers in the responses to the ritual enacted by the priest, who now faces the public rather than the tabernacle (Rodriguez has insisted repeatedly that his *Days of Obligation* is about being a Catholic, not about being Hispanic or being Chicano, although it has been consistently reviewed as though it were only the latter; Postel and Gillespie 41).

Rodriguez makes much of these changes. Often, those trained in languages and literature (Rodriguez did doctoral studies in English at the University of California at Berkeley, as well as studying at Stanford and Columbia) miss the Latin mass because of its extensive linguistic and cultural echoes. Unquestionably, the changes dictated by Vatican II altered substantively the relationship between priest and mass-goer, especially the latter's relationship to the sacrifice of the mass, with the removal of the altar boy, who responded in a Latin he often did not understand, as a stand-in for the faithful. In this sense, Rodriguez charts a subsidiary structure of the othering, that which takes place between a before and an after of the traditional Latin mass, between those who identified with the former and those who prefer the mass in English.

But the question of difference between two versions of the Catholic mass is only secondary to the major issue of difference Rodriguez charts in the chapter titled "Credo," that of the issue between Catholics and non-Catholics. Both the cultural institutions of religion in the United States prior to the 1960s and the internal ideology of the Catholic Church (often driven in the early mid-century by a siege mentality because of the cultural institutions of religion dominant in the United States at the time) favored practices of separation that were frequently taught in stark forms by elementary-school nuns. These images underlie much of what Rodriguez has to say about his formation first as a *católico* (and, certainly, non-Anglo Catholics must have felt even more separateness than Anglo ones did) and then, in Catholic grade school, as a Catholic (78). His difference, of course, is not neutral: one's own identity is always the marked or privileged one, and the Other's is conceived only as *not* what one's own is. The disjunction, thus, is not between Catholics and Protestants, between one group of Christians and another one, but between Catholics and non-Catholics, with Protestants being only one subset of the latter. Ecumenism encourages a continuity of understanding between Christian sects and between all religious systems, but this does not counter the way in which individuals may always view themselves, in religion as in all cultural matters, in marked and unmarked terms, as the privileged We versus the incidental, excluded, legitimately discriminated Other.

From such a point of view, one's own identity is imbued with profound symbolic resonances, and in the case of Catholicism, for many the changes of the sixties have the principal defect of attenuating the resonances on which a powerful sense of identity functioned. Indeed, Rodriguez calls himself a "ghetto Catholic" (79), a term that expresses the radical separation from the non-Catholic. The degree to which this Catholic identity of difference is determinant for the autobiographical narrator of *Hunger of Memory* is evidenced by the profound emotionalism with which he characterizes, not his religiosity as such, but his relationship to pre-Vatican II Catholicism. For example, and quite surprisingly, Rodriguez provides the following meditation on Catholicism and sexuality:

The Church, in fact, excited more sexual wonderment than it repressed. I regarded with awe the 'wedding ring' on a nun's finger, her black 'wedding veil'—symbols of marriage to God. I would study pictures of martyrs—white-robed virgins fallen in death and the young, almost smiling, St. Sebastian, transfigured in pain. At Easter high mass I was dizzied by the mucous perfume of white flowers at the celebration of rebirth. At such moments, the Church touched alive some very private sexual excitement; it pronounced my sexuality important. (84)

Rodriguez does not specify what the parameters were of his sexuality that the Church pronounced as important; however, as a child or young man, there is reason to believe it to be essentially free-floating and unformed. Rodriguez uses such highly rhetorically charged terms here with reference to emotional and explicitly sexual responses to the trappings of Catholicism as he does elsewhere in his memoir with regard to other cultural matters, terms such as "awe," "excitement," "wonderment," and "dizzied." There has long been a camp homoerotic response to the pageant of Catholicism, whether it be on the level of the emotional energy that is an integral part of traditional Catholicism, the otherworldly transcendence the pageantry intends to provoke, or a reading of the disjunction between this pageantry and everyday life or between this pageantry and secular forms of pageantry as the complex sense of kitsch often alleged to be central to the gay sensibility. The only thing specifically homoerotic about Rodriguez's account is the reference to St. Sebastian, who is a widely recognized "gay patron saint" (he adorns the cover of Kaja Silverman's *Male Subjectivity at the Margins* and innumerable gay-marked publications). Such an association comes from both the way in which, like all martyrs, he was one quintessential outsider (cf. the gay director Darek Jarman's *Sebastiane* [1976]) and the allusions to sadomasochism in his particular form of martyrdom: the arrows with which he is killed are as much instruments that leave him "transfigured with pain" (note Rodriguez's use of the semireligious word "transfigured," although "transported" might have been even more explicit) as they are symbols of the suffering of unrequited love: in Jarman's film, St. Sebastian is executed by his military captain, Severus, not because he refuses to renounce his Christianity, but because he spurns the latter's sexual advances.

Again, I am not attempting to read homoeroticism into Rodriguez's words, which, it must be noted, begin by dealing with the way the Church handles sexuality, to then move on to one child's high-pitched erotic reaction to ritualized Catholicism. Of note is the fact that Rodriguez notes the irony of the use of near-naked figures of Christ in the Church, while at the same time its priests and nuns preach the renunciation of the body. But what is significant here is the way in which that renunciation is juxtaposed to the emotional and sensual, explicitly identified as sexual, provocation that the ecclesiastical drama "touches alive." Sexual arousal is not, one assumes, an inherent goal of the Church's pageantry (although it may well be a calculatedly subliminal force), and one could expect few Catholics to be as willing to be as dithyrambic as Rodriguez.

However one calculates the specific sexuality of Rodriguez's description and what it may mean with reference to what he calls "my sexuality," the important point to be made is that this passage is the basis for an analysis of difference: the feelings aroused by Catholicism, particularly in its pre-Vatican II version, as opposed to the sensory deprivation to be found in non-Catholicism, in the world of individuals whose lives were not based on Catholic ritual. He speaks of "two wheels of time" (95), the ordinary one of secular holidays, seasons, the first day of school, and Church time, the calendar in which every day has some liturgical meaning that relates back to ritual and pageantry.

Rodriguez marks other differences that are equally rhetorically charged for him, such as the role of Latin, also presented in terms of difference. I have already spoken of how Latin is crucial to the transformation of the Church by Vatican II. Significantly, Rodriguez, while mentioning the standard arguments for retaining Latin, especially its link to tradition, underscores another dimension of difference that is characterized in less than conventionally religious terms. By contrast to the Vatican II argument that Latin alienated the faithful from the mass by using a language few understood (and medieval ecclesiastical Latin can hardly be said to be particularly difficult linguistically or stylistically), Rodriguez argues for the way in which Latin allowed the individual to retreat into a private world of reflection, to tune out of the everyday world. This structure of difference, which returns to one of the overarching themes of *Hunger of Memory*, that of the private versus public and the error of underdifferentiating them in favor of the latter, is one that promotes the sense of difference that is to be found in something like Latin-induced reveries. The same difference applies to the young Rodriguez's work as an altar boy. After assisting at a funeral, he says, "And then I would return. To class or to summer. Resume my life as a boy of thirteen" (99). This difference, ecclesiastically inspired, especially to the degree that it is related to a sense of the difference from the world of the individual, takes its place with the inventory of emotional differences described in these pages.

Any close reading of *Hunger of Memory* must reveal that the right, whether religious, educational, or social, can take little consolation in Rodriguez's charting of the differences between a Hispanic private world and an Anglo public one. And there is certainly cold comfort to be derived from his reservations about bilingual education. For there is no repudiation of Hispanic culture in Rodriguez's text, but rather a careful charting of differences between the Hispanic and the Anglo, an understanding that one is not the other, that the former is not to be submerged in the latter, and that each has its own specific symbolic power in the complex identity of Chicano subjectivity. By queering both the right's commitment to indifference through the loss of the Hispanic and the commitment of the ideology of bilingualism to the underdifferentiated conversion of the private into public, Rodriguez charts differences on many levels: the linguistic, cultural, religious in explicit language, and the sexual and erotic by synecdochal and metonymic implication. His highly charged and delightfully fruity rhetoric has nothing to do with the flat periods of the assimilationist ideologues, as it has little to do with the strident charges of Aztlán separatism. By engaging in a subtle analysis of cultural difference, Rodriguez opens up spaces for unconventional, nonstraight identities. This is much more the basis of the controversies it has provoked than the really very minor way in which it addresses bilingual education. The queer principles explored by *Hunger of Memory* are as threatening to the right-wing ideologues as they are to the aggressive heterosexist standard-bearers of Chicano movement politics such as the Corky Gonzales of *Yo soy Joaquin*: it is in terms of the challenges to closed ideologies of either stripe that Rodriguez's book can most profitably be read.

Rodriguez takes up again the issues of underdifferentiation in his chapter on "Profession," in which he describes the painful process that leads him to abandon completion of his doctoral dissertation and to refuse offers of appointments as a professor of English at prestigious universities. Renewing the analysis of guilt that plagues the scholarship boy, the minority doctoral student, as much as he may defend civil rights and questions regarding access by minorities to the educational system, sees himself as having profited from an unfair disadvantage: the true minority students are those individuals of the working class, both Anglo and non-Anglo, who have been deprived of adequate primary and secondary education in a way he has not because of "the foolish logic of this program of social reform" (151). Decrying the absence of a proper class analysis of the issue of educational discrimination, Rodriguez develops his opinion that minority placement programs end up favoring individuals like himself who have little need for them and who can only end up mortified at having taken advantage of them: "I felt self-disgust" (170).

I cannot analyze here the legitimacy of Rodriguez's analysis, since this would require a bibliography in sociology that is not pertinent to this study. Rather, my goal is to demonstrate how Rodriguez again deploys the question of indifference to the designation of minority status. Here the logic of indifference obliges the individual to assume an identity that becomes problematical not because it has little to do with him, but because it underestimates other differences that have been involved in his construction of identity. Thus, the individual is obliged to wear the precious mask of the assigned identity, while at the same time realizing that it does not correspond to his sense of personal and social self:

I was a minority. I believed it. For the first several years, I accepted the label. I certainly supported the racial civil rights movement; supported the goal of broadening access to high education. But there was a problem: One day I listened approvingly to a government official defend affirmative action; the next day *I* realized the benefits of the program. I was the minority student the political activists shouted about at noontime rallies. Against their rhetoric, I stood out in relief, unrelieved. *Knowing:* I was not really more socially disadvantaged than the white graduate students in my classes [at Berkeley]. *Knowing:* I was not disadvantaged like many of the new nonwhite students who were entering college, lacking in good early schooling. . . . Slowly, slowly, the term *minority* became a source of unease. (146–47)

The perception of a separation from the imposition of a constructed discourse provides the dislocation of the "unrelieved" narrator, whose disagreement leads him once again to queer the social text he inhabits, with the result that one of his professors ends up shouting at him over the telephone whether he had "decided to fail" (167). This radical separation from the received social text, this retreat into "Romantic exile" (171), marks the narrator with the stigma of Otherness he keeps renewing in his successive encounters with processes of underdifferentiation that leave him living a lie.

The final chapter of *Hunger of Memory* is titled "Mr. Secrets," the name his mother and family give him for the way in which he withholds from them the different sense of self that emerges from the encounters with social underdifferentiation. Rodriguez strives never to become alienated from his family in the sense of the violent confrontations born of frustration, incomprehension, and resentment that are often the lot of the scholarship boy, and he is determined to retain a place within a circle whose intimacy is now nuanced by the careers of his brother and sisters, their spouses and children. With regard to the latter, there is a very perceptive discussion of how the sharp disjunction between his mother's private voice, formerly used within the confines of the hearth, and her public voice, formerly used for strangers, yields to her use of her public voice with the strangers who have now come into the family and who have never known Spanish, including her grandchildren.

But for all his efforts to retain family ties, the Otherness of the scholarship boy becomes also the alienation of the adult and the separation from the father, identification (irrespective of love) with whom is considered by our society (no matter what they know about Freud and Lacan) to be crucial for the confirmation of social identity and an acceptable masculinity. Foreshadowing his later book, *Days of Obligation; An Argument with My Mexican Father* (1992), Rodriguez closes with a scene of leave-taking from his father:

I take [the coat] to my father and place it on him. In that instant I feel the thinness of his arms. He turns. He asks if I am going home now too. It is, I realize, the only thing he has said to me all evening. (195)

Significantly, the father's simple question is not quoted directly, and not even those words are his. Although there is never any sign of a loss of affection for the family—indeed, Rodriguez never seems to lose his concern that the difference acquired by first the scholarship boy and then the minority student will produce a damaging alienation—the accumulated burden of difference creates the Mr. Secrets and brings with it communicational silence. It is true, of course, that the process of differentiation that Rodriguez describes in *Hunger of Memory* cuts in all directions, not just in terms of those produced around intellectual/professional children vis-à-vis their working-class families, and the consequences of this fact create the complex texture of social juxtapositions that make up Rodriguez's memoir. If difference properly defined does undoubtedly affect the relationship between individuals and their families, Rodriguez shows how in his case it turns around varieties of language, multiple versions of religion, and unhomologizable social processes (whether because of their "foolish logic" or other causes). In all of these cases, however, what is involved, and what the narrator pursues with the dogged intention of carrying out his "act of contrition" (153), is the forging of a discourse of othered difference via a privileged act of writing and involving the rhetorically charged expression of "things too personal to be shared with intimates" that will, with the definitiveness of the published book, cut him off forever from the comforting sea of social indifference.

WORKS CITED

Alarcón, Norma. "Tropology of Hunger: The 'Miseducation' of Richard Rodriguez." In: *The Ethnic Canon; Histories, Institutions, and Interventions,* edited by David Palumbo-Liu. Minneapolis: University of Minnesota Press, 1995. 140–52.

Case, Sue-Ellen. "The Student and the Strap: Authority and Seduction in the Class(room)." In: *Professions of Desire: Lesbian and Gay Studies in Literature,* edited by George E. Haggerty and Bonnie Zimmerman. New York: Modern Language Association of America, 1995. 38–46.

Doty, Alexander. *Making Things Perfectly Queer; Interpreting Mass Culture.* Minneapolis: University of Minnesota Press, 1993.

Edelman, Lee. *Homographesis; Essays in Gay Literary and Cultural Theory.* New York: Routledge, 1994.

Flores, Lauro. "Chicano Autobiography: Culture, Ideology and the Self." *The Americas Review* 18.2 (Summer 1990): 80–91

Gibson, Ian. *Granada en 1936 y el asesinato de Federico García Lorca.* Barcelona: Crítica, 1979.

Halperin, David M. *One Hundred Years of Homosexuality and Other Essays on Greek Love.* New York: Routledge, 1990.

Hogue, W. Lawrence. "An Unresolved Modern Experience: Richard Rodriguez's *Hunger of Memory." The Americas Review* 20.1 (Spring 1992): 52–64.

Jagose, Annamarie. *Queer Theory; An Introduction.* New York: New York University Press, 1996.

Marquez, Antonio C. "Richard Rodriguez's *Hunger of Memory* and New Perspectives on Ethnic Autobiography." In: *Teaching American Ethnic Literatures; Nineteen Essays,* edited by John R. Maitino and David R. Peck. Albuquerque: University of New Mexico Press, 1996. 237–54.

———. "Richard Rodriguez's *Hunger of Memory* and the Poetics of Experience." *Arizona Quarterly* 40.2 (Summer 1984): 130–41.

McKenna, Teresa. *Migrant Song; Politics and Process in Contemporary Chicano Literature*. Austin: University of Texas Press, 1997.

Postel, Virginia I., and Nick Gillespie. "The New, New World: An Interview with Richard Rodriguez." *Reason* 26.4 (August 1, 1994): 35–41.

Rodriguez, Richard. *An Autobiography: Hunger of Memory; The Education of Richard Rodriguez*. New York: Bantam Books, 1983, c1982.

———. *Days of Obligation; An Argument with My Mexican Father*. New York: Penguin Books, 1993, c1992.

———. "Late Victorians: San Francisco, AIDS, and the Homosexual Stereotype." *Harper's* 281.1685 (October 1, 1990): 57–66. Chapter Two of his *Days of Obligation*.

Romero, Rolando J. "Spanish and English: The Question of Literacy in *Hunger of Memory*." *Confluencia; revista hispánica de cultura y literatura* 6.2 (Spring 1991): 89–100.

Rose, Shirley K. "Metaphors of Myths of Cross-Cultural Literacy: Autobiographical Narratives by Maxine Hong Kingston, Richard Rodriguez, and Malcolm X." *Melus* 14.12 (Spring 1987): 3–15.

Sahuquillo, Angel. *Federico Garcia Lorca y la cultura de la homosexualidad masculina: Lorca, Dali, Cernuda, Gil-Albert, Prados y la voz silenciada del amor homosexual*. Alicante: Instituto de Cultura "Juan Gil-Albert," Diputación de Alicante, 1991.

Saldívar, Ramón. "Ideologies of the Self: Chicano Autobiography." *Diacritics* 15.3 (Fall 1985): 25–34.

Sánchez, Rosaura. "Calculated Musings: Richard Rodriguez's Metaphysics of Difference." In: *The Ethnic Canon; Histories, Institutions, and Interventions*, edited by David Palumbo-Liu. Minneapolis: University of Minnesota Press, 1995. 153–73.

Shuter, Bill. "The Confessions of Richard Rodriguez." *Cross-Currents* 45.1 (1995): 95–105.

Silverman, Kaja. *Male Subjectivity at the Margins*. New York: Routledge, 1992.

Stavans, Ilan. "The Journey of Richard Rodriguez." *Commonweal* 120.6 (26 March 1993): 20–22.

Torres, Lourdes. "Spanish in the United States: The Struggle for Legitimacy." In: *Spanish in the United States: Sociolinguistic Issues*, edited by John J. Bergen. Washington, D.C.: Georgetown University Press, 1990. 142–51.

Villanueva-Collado, Alfredo. "Growing Up Hispanic: Discourse and Ideology in *Hunger of Memory* and *Family Installments*." *The Americas Review* 16.3–4 (Fall-Winter 1988): 75–90.

Chapter 10

In Search of a Lost Body with Organs: Reclaiming Postcolonial Gay Interiority after Bersani's Reading of Gide

Christian Gundermann

Attacking what is put as a "rage for respectability . . . in gay life today" (*Homos* 113), Leo Bersani's essay "The Gay Outlaw" offers a reading of various French modernist texts, including André Gide's primitivist novel *L'Immoraliste*. Bersani draws on Gide's text to conceptualize a gay "outlaw" subjectivity that is meant not only to challenge the U.S.-American focus on gay civil rights by abolishing the citizen as such, but also to contribute to anticolonialist politics. Bersani argues that the narcissism of Gide's "Immoraliste" jettisons notions of self and relationality altogether, and thus transcends power in general, and in particular the power-ridden colonial relation.

In this chapter, I wish to engage critically with theories of gay subjectivity that, like Bersani's, seek to diffuse or undo the effects of power and hierarchy on sexual relations by abandoning the concept of self and relationality *tout court.* Earl Jackson's *Strategies of Deviance* formulates in a more sustained theoretical manner the paradigms we find in Bersani's writings. Although I do not deny the importance of a critique of the self-possessed, white, humanist, indicatively male heterosexual subject and its projective and sacrificial relations with the external world, I question the lack of conceptual differentiation in Bersani's and Jackson's categorical rejection of selfhood, relationality, and interiority. Bersani and Jackson rightfully argue against philosophical traditions that oppose subjects and objects starkly. Yet the primitivist gay foreclosure of interiority as such in the wake of Gide risks a politically retrograde flatness, an immunity to anticolonialist and antihomophobic critique rather than the progressive politics toward which Bersani gestures.[1]

Through readings of postcolonial texts by the West German writer and ethnographer Hubert Fichte, whose oeuvre is informed by the French primitivist tradition that Bersani cites but transcends it in crucial ways, I propose to render problematic the prominent notion of gay subjectivity as antirelational and ex-timate, that is, immune to the "trappings" of intimacy. Fichte was born in 1935. The half-Jewish author established himself with four experimental autobiographical novels in the late 1960s and then produced ethnographic sketches of New-World African and African cultures, which he published in journals and as radio plays. Simultaneously, Fichte worked on over twenty volumes of autobiographical ethnographies titled *Geschichte der Empfindlichkeit* (*The History of Sensibility*) between 1968 and 1986, in which he attempted to forge a gay aesthetics. These volumes were mostly published after he died from AIDS in 1986. My readings focus on two of Fichte's texts: the 1981 novel *Platz der Gehenkten* (*Execution Square*), set in Morocco, and the ethnographic novel *Explosion,* set in Brazil and published after Fichte's death in 1986.

THE END OF PSYCHOANALYSIS, INTERIORITY, AND GOOD CITIZENSHIP IN *HOMOS*: BERSANI'S TRANSGRESSIVELY INDIFFERENT GAY SUBJECT

In the chapter "The Gay Outlaw" of his 1995 book *Homos,* Bersani reads Gide's North African primitivism as a "potentially revolutionary eroticism" (122), as a liberation from relationality, and therefore also as an end to colonial relations: "By abandoning himself to the appearances of sexual colonialism Gide was able to free himself from the European version of relationships that supported the colonialism" (122). The break with the relational paradigm itself becomes possible through "a profound indifference to . . . otherness" (123), through a form of sex that has eliminated from itself the "necessity of any relation whatsoever" (122), and through the notion of a self that is fundamentally empty and without depth. Although Bersani knows that this indifferent relation, or nonrelation, to the (colonial) other is enabled by a colonialist paradigm in which the "natives" simply do not qualify as worthy of any sustained interest on the part of the European traveler (such as Gide), Bersani nevertheless stipulates this form of (non)relationality as a model for a revolutionary, narcissistic ethics that could avoid the power and hierarchy endemic to any form of relation of a self to an other:

Michel's [the protagonist's] pederasty is the model of intimacies without intimacy. It proposes that we move irresponsibly among other bodies, somewhat indifferent to them, demanding nothing more than that they be as available to contact as we are, and that, no longer owned by others, they also renounce self-ownership and agree to that loss of boundaries which will allow them to be, with us, shifting points of rest in a universal and mobile communication of being. (128)

In a pastiche on Christian ethics, Bersani insists on Michel's "loving the other as the same, in homo-ness" (128). Michel's "lawless pederasty" creates a "community in which the other, no longer respected or violated as a person, would merely be cruised as another opportunity, at once insignificant and precious, for narcissistic pleasures" (129).

My main objection to Bersani's vision of homosexuality as homo-ness is that, no matter how appealing it may appear for its eschewal of violence, power, and hierarchy, it ultimately avoids and obscures the *question* of power and leaves power itself untouched. Asking this question becomes all the more pressing because Bersani's pastoralism is not innocent. Bersani brings up the topic that the indifference he valorizes is foremost an indifference directed against "Africans from whom they [Europeans like Gide] bought cheap and, to their minds, exotic sex" (122). But Bersani chooses to disregard this question just as quickly, to make himself indifferent to it, so to speak. His pastoralism constructs an ethics of the present moment without wanting to account for all that enables this present moment.[2] The question is not only whether an empty self might theoretically contribute to a more appealing ethics than notions of self predicated on difference and otherness. The question is: who can afford such a shattering moment or moment of self-less indifference, and at whose expense? We may discover that the Gidean primitivist (non)self as Bersani understands it, though potentially a conceptual challenge to colonialist objectification, is only a fleeting moment, one stage in a cycle that, as a whole, confirms the colonial paradigm rather than challenges it.

The selfless and otherless sexuality that constitutes the driving, pastoral moment of Bersani's theorizing (and that resembles Gide's primitivist utopia) relies not only on a disavowal of the dependence of this (potentially) anticolonialist construct on real colonialism, but also on a notion of the body as separate from self (the self being riddled with the traps of interiority and therefore power), on a body as pure surface.

The protagonist of Gide's *Immoraliste,* Michel, is a man whose "pederasty" is a "sexual preference without sex" (*Homos* 118), Bersani insists, because the radicality of his particular form of sexuality, "intimacies without intimacy" (128) with Arab boys, is that it "eliminates from 'sex' *the necessity of any relation whatsoever*" (122, Bersani's emphasis). This form of sexuality is predicated on a particular kind of physicality, on becoming "a *desiring skin*" (119, Bersani's emphasis). By means of a paradoxical move simultaneously inward and outward, Michel denudes himself of any profundity, peeling away, in Bersani's reading, layers of "inauthentic" deep self to arrive at the "surface that is hidden; the authentic [that] is the superficial" (120). "The narcissistic expansion of a desiring skin," Bersani argues, " is also the renunciation of narcissistic self-containment" (120). This unbounded "naked flesh . . . extends itself into the world, abolishing the space between it and the soil, the grass and the air" (120); it "can *touch* everywhere" (120, Bersani's emphasis). The sun, so Gide's text wants to make us believe, burns out all the internal spaces of Michel's body: "the sun was burning. I offered my body to its flames . . . my entire being shifted toward my skin" (*L'Immoraliste* 67).[3]   Desire, in such a model of nonrelation of self to other, is reduced to "formal affinities that diagram our extensions" (*Homos* 121). Bersani uses this model of radical ex-timacy to arrive at an ethics of the present moment, repudiating "intersubjectivity as we have come to prize it in western culture, with all its intensely satisfying drama of personal anguish and unfulfilled demands" (124) because it is a "reining in, a sequestering, of our energies" (124). The psychoanalytic subject of the unconscious is ostensibly left behind in Bersani's reading of Gide as a waste of energy: "And if, as I have argued, psychoanalysis undermines its own claims to the control of personal identity, it also immobilizes the human subject in its persuasive demonstration of an irreducible, politically unfixable antagonism between external reality and the structures of desire" (124).

My claim is simply that the unmediated Gidean body as Bersani constructs it cannot exist; that Gide's and Bersani's (fetishistic) belief in this uncoloniz/ed/ing body is purchased at the cost of perpetuating a very real colonial relation; that the increased political efficacy that Bersani claims for this account of subjectivity over against the "inescapably conservative implications of any discipline [i.e., psychoanalysis] that traces for us the intractability of human desire" (124) is efficacious only abstractly, that is, within the confines of a system of "formal affinities" that leaves any real bodies behind, yet depends on these real bodies while disavowing that it does. In the Gidean scenario, these real bodies are the Arab boys. The relation to the Arab boys, a "strangely undemanding" homosexuality in Bersani's reading, is nevertheless tainted by a strangely oblique remark concerning the economic aspect of Michel's "revolutionary" form of (non)relation. After a description of the profound effect the African climate has on the narrator's translucent consumptive constitution, a few puzzling lines point to an altogether different form of consumption:

Ashour and Moktir initially kept us company; I still enjoyed their light friendship which only cost half a franc a day; but before too long, bored by them, not feeling as weak anymore as to be in need of their exemplary health, no longer finding in their games the nourishment that I required for my amusement, I returned to Marceline. (57)

Michel's "mov[ing] irresponsibly among other bodies" (*Homos* 128) is accompanied by a reference to money: the boys' friendship is so light, it costs less than half a franc a day. I propose to scrutinize the trace of interiority as I read this reference to the economic aspect of Michel's colonial relation to the boys. In order to do so I propose to take a longer detour through Hubert Fichte's postcolonial writings. Gide's North African "lightness," his "formal affinities" are taken up in Fichte, developed systematically as a gay aesthetics, and transformed in ways that may help recover the residue of Michel's body behind his sunburned skin. Fichte's transformations will also assist in asking certain pressing political questions that Bersani's Gide eschews.

THE SPLIT GAY SUBJECT AND FICHTE'S AUTOBIOGRAPHICAL MODEL

Fichte scholars have repeatedly stressed the importance of the concept of "inter-ness," "trans-ness," or "between-ness" for Fichte's autobiographical structure without, however, adequately describing the interface of primitivism and gay aesthetics as they dissolve traditional autobiographical notions of identity in

Fichte's oeuvre. Leo Kreuzer sees in Fichte the proponent of a "polychronous asynchronicity of the human psyche" (*Literatur und Entwicklung* 89). This *asynchronicity* is, according to Kreuzer, structurally analogous to the syncretism of Afro-American religions, Fichte's main object of study, which assemble disparate, historically heterogeneous material and thus resist developmental streamlining as Fichte's model of autobiography does. Kreuzer argues that a narrative "I" comes into existence in Fichte's writing only as an "I" in quotation marks so as to guarantee a construction that avoids the subsumption of earlier, more archaic layers under a putative developmental synthesis. Kreuzer also draws attention to the aesthetic and mimetic affinity between Fichte's primitivist autobiographical structure and the structure of the black syncretistic cultures of the Americas.

What is at stake in Fichte's ironic doubling of the "I" where a first person narrator says "I, say I, would never write a book in the first person singular" (36), and subsequently decides to put himself in quotation marks in order to pry open a space of nonidentity within identity: "Put your I in quotation marks. / Call yourself 'novel'" (37)?[4] In other words, how important is it that Fichte and his literary *double* are not only non-self-identical but also self-identical? Gay identity, Fichte suggests, can only survive as an infidelity to the maturational concept of self, as prior to, outside of, or against, the self. Yet how are we to understand the paradox of the "I" in quotation marks? The structure of Fichte's autobiographical project, whether articulated as the metonymic displacement between Jäcki and Fichte or the dynamics of an "I" within and outside of quotation marks, consists of a paradoxical claim to, and rejection of, identity; in fact, the two moves, which seem to be mutually exclusive, constitute each other as a specific form of gay subjectivity.

A recurring motif in Fichte's oeuvre is the following metaphor of the subject as specular device: "I am a drop, mirroring the universe—not consciously, but rather optically? (*Versuch* 38). It becomes a *Leitmotif* in the novel *Platz der Gehenkten* (*Execution Square*), one of Fichte's last works, which is set in Morocco. Thorsten Teichert argues that, due to its rigorous formal conception, *Platz* turns most consistently against "the prevalent assumption in classical psychology of a rigid opposition between consciousness and external reality" (277). Fichte critics seem to agree that the aesthetic conception of *Platz,* as Böhme puts it, develops most congruously the notion of "language as pure surface" (*Hubert Fichte* 394), arriving at a form of subjectivity that knows neither property nor boundaries and self. Unmistakably, Fichte's Morocco novel replays the primitivism of Gide's *Immoraliste.*

By way of sketching the "plot" of *Platz,* one should note that the first-person narrator of *Platz* and his partner Irma are repeating a trip to Morocco that they had taken over fifteen years prior to the time of narration. With *Platz* the narrator attempts to "stage" (*Platz* 109) in 1985 the traumatic event of a plane crash off the coast of Morocco (near Agadir) in 1970 in which Jäcki believed Irma had died. Irma and Jäcki had separated on their trip through Morocco in 1970 and Irma was to take the plane that crashed. For several hours after receiving the news about the crash, Jäcki did not know that Irma had missed the plane, that she was, in fact, safe.

Repeating and staging is to be understood literally here; that is, in 1985 the narrator and Irma travel to the same places together, separate at the same point as they had in 1970, and attempt to repeat every move from fifteen years before, including the trip that the traumatized Jäcki took to Agadir to find out about Irma's fate—the trip the novel refers to cryptically as "the nocturnal journey" (215). A public square in Marrakech whose Arabic name, *Djemma el-Fna,* Fichte translates as "square of the hung," "square of the dead," or "reunion of the people who are afraid" (108) is the kind of allegorical, ritualistic space that structures many of Fichte's novels. As the central and eponymous space in the novel, we need to examine the phenomenon of *Platz der Gehenkten* in two respects:

First, *Platz der Gehenkten* as novel is the space of a doubled doubling: the narrator repeats a previous, traumatic trip, and "nonfictive" like all of Fichte's texts, the novel "repeats," or duplicates textually, this actual repetition. The text is thus already the *mise-en-abîme,* or mirroring of the mirroring, it performs a short-circuiting of reality, which is the most striking aesthetic quality of the novel on the macro- and microstructural levels. The novel, further, must be read as an explicit thematization of the gap between Fichte's autobiographical personae (here primarily the Jäcki of 1970, and the "I" of 1985) and the literary attempt at closing it. What needs to be understood are the aesthetic means by which Fichte's novel envisions a closing of this gap, and further, how this closing is related to queer sexuality—the novel calls it "bi."

Second, the actual square "Platz der Gehenkten," or *Djemma el-Fna*, is also a space of doubling or mirroring; in fact, it is the writing process itself that is symbolized by the figures of the Moroccan scribes who work at the "Platz der Gehenkten." The narrator finds in these scribes the symbolic (and material) representation of the duplication process that he himself is staging. The dew drop motif also resurfaces in this passage in relation to the writing process:

The scribe is bi.
Between customer and paper.
Between writing tool and Execution Square.
The scribe draws a grid onto the sheet.
Into this grid he fills his letters of conjuration.
A mirror image [*Spiegelbildlich*]—according to the laws of symmetry.
Where am I?
Doubled or in two halves? [*Doppelt oder zweimal halb?*]
Can I exist only within a split?
Between dream and dream?
Dew drops mirror the oasis.
Am I one of Irma's photographs? (107)

The passage opens with the line "The scribe is bi," and elaborates this notion, which is in all of Fichte's texts the prime marker of Fichte/Jäcki's own queer subjectivity,[5] as a functional and spatial "between-ness" in the two subsequent lines that both start with "between." The text then moves onto the split that subtends the autobiographical edifice of Fichte's oeuvre: "Where am I?/ Doubled or in two halves?" By way of the analogy with the scribe and his activity, this split (like its magical closing) is articulated as specular [*spiegelbildlich*], and with reference to

Irma's photography in the last line as visual.[6]

Note the link this passage establishes between writing, visuality, and sexuality. The metaphor of the scribe articulates an impossible, catachrestic subject position because it stands for two mutually exclusive moments. On the one hand, the scribe produces a text from which he is removed: the text is not his own; he merely acts as an intermediary, as tool "between customer and paper." On the other hand, the specularity of the scribe's activity symbolizes the mimetic and magical potential of the writing process ("letters of conjuration") in a book that itself attempts the literal, ecstatic, mimetic, and unmediated transcription of external form (or world) onto paper. The activity of the "primitive" scribe promises a form of plenitude and control that appears to contradict his own subject position as mere tool in a process he cannot control.

Fichte's text also imitates the oral literary traditions of Morocco, the figure of the story tellers who "turns into the king, the mother, . . . the ostrich" (175) and thus "reproduces the story a second time" (175). Like the story teller's histrionic body, Fichte's text itself wants to become the ecstatic medium, the paper the excited skin of the narrator's body being touched by the lover:[7] "To reproduce touch, smell . . . with scribbles on paper?" (181). In fact, the narrator himself turns into paper:

I.
Jäcki.
Turns into letters.
Charred wool.
Scraped ink paste.
The Djemma el Fna passes through me. (85)

The text abounds with scenes of a sexual nature, which ricochet back to reflections on the narrative process and its temporality:

The three fat thumbs of the sausage vendor busying themselves with my key tag which is as thick as a thumb, and behind the creases of his Djellabah he hides his Coca Cola bottle. It takes as long as I take to tell it. (155)

The ostensible congruousness of the temporality of the process of narration with the temporality of the symbolic sexual act alludes to Fichte's attempt at collapsing the subjects of enunciation and utterance. The text attempts to capture the moment of enunciation itself into the text. This moment is the magical moment where the difference between the two separate temporalities breaks down—magical because "in reality" the separation between the two temporalities constitutes the very possibility of the writing process and of subjectivity itself. In the following passage, the narrator tries, and naturally fails, to close the gap between the subjects of enunciation and utterance:

Is eternity really long enough for this moment in which I miswrite the letter T of the word

moment—in reality I miswrite the letter W of the *word word*—, the screeching of the swallows, just before that the barking of the dogs, . . . to have repeated itself innumerable times.
Dew drops mirror dew drops in the universe [All]—Nothing. (215, my emphasis)

The passage tries to close the gap, and it necessarily fails because, if it succeeded, it would undercut its own precondition. Writing as magical "conjuration" attempts that which is shown as impossible in the passage above. This attempt of the writer's to catch up with the fleeting moment of enunciation, to represent the present as present, to stop the passing of time, is an allegory of Fichte's attempt to catch up with Jäcki—the hope to be able to affirm wholeness.[8]

The narrator, however, knows that his text can only exist "within a split," that the "scribe" needs to remain "bi," that is, spliced into an absent space "between," neither inside nor outside, and at the same time both, in order to perform the magical ritual or "conjuration" that enables his text to come alive, to produce the only kind of plenitude that Fichte's decidedly antiessentialist, antioriginary aesthetics allow:

Where am I located when I write?
Here or there or in between or nowhere?
Yes, then, after all: Life a dream?
The nocturnal journey?
Circular dream?
To castrate oneself with the shards of a mirror.
The hermaphrodite.
To project outward with mirrors [*Wegspiegeln*].
To turn into a fatamorgana during the journey.
Between dream and dream.
The Indian dew drop that mirrors the universe [*All*]. (215)

Plenitude as an optical trick that follows the laws of symmetry. The passage where the narrator attempts to catch up with the passing of time articulates the magical, utopian moment where the two separate and irreconcilable temporalities finally appear to congeal into wholeness through a specular technique. Fichte's text itself becomes visual, nontextual: the ekphrastic doubling of the word "word" (as in "of the word word") in Fichte's text inscribes the moment of the shortcircuit, the mirroring axis along which a moment of seeming stasis and plenitude can occur.

The take offers the "hope" for an intersecting of the irreconcilably split halves of the self between the author Fichte and the protagonist Jäcki, or the I and the "I" ("doubled or in two halves?" [107]). This intersecting promises to happen in the endless oscillation of mirrorings (as "fatamorgana" [215]), in the magical *mise-en-abîme* of self-images where the subject would represent himself as whole by representing his own vanishing point in the space of a hypothetical eternity. The utopian possibility of such a specular "healing" is linked with visual technology in the passage on the scribe, notably both with the scribe's symmetrical technique and with Irma's photography–the imaginary photograph (in Lacan's sense) as the image of a whole self: "Am I one of Irma's photographs?" whereby the verb "to be" is to be understood as denoting plenitude. Yet "being" as a possibility only in the realm of optical projection: "to project outward with mirrors" (215) in order for that projected image to form a wholeness elsewhere, the wholeness of the "fatamorgana." Yet this is not an essential possibility, merely the vanishing point that is a position "between dream and dream" (215); in other words, a form of (visual, optical) being that is predicated on the nonbeing or absence of the subject—therefore, the enigmatic reference to a Lacanian specular castration that the narrator inflicts upon himself. Being is enabled as the short-circuiting of the constitutive narrative split; the text calls this short circuit "circular dream" (215)—the very "circular dream" that the novel *Platz* itself attempts to be.

In order to examine the sexual specificity of the visual and specular (self)-castration that enables Fichte's "circular dream" or fiction as *mise-en-abîme* of the self, I will turn to Earl Jackson's theory of gay subjectivity as specular fragmentation. Jackson's readings of gay cinema (films by Derek Jarman and Pedro Almodóvar) and gay pornography describe a narrative and specular structure that explains the structure of Fichte's autobiography as a postmodern, specifically queer mode of representation.

According to Jackson, within a confessional, autobiographical mode, the gay pornography under scrutiny (which is, for him, indicative of a larger trend in postmodern gay culture) articulates a play with the representational split between the subject of enunciation and the subject of utterance. While a traditional autobiographical text is predicated on bridging the gap between the narrating voice and the narrated personae of the text under the assumption of a basic identity of the narrating voice with its subject of the utterance, the gay pornography that Jackson analyzes does not naturalize this split by suturing the two subjects.

In Jackson's example, the video *The Boys of Venice,* the character of the scene is called "Scott Taylor" and his name coincides with the pseudonym of the actor Scott Taylor. The intradiegetic character "Scott Taylor" masturbates to a set of intradiegetic cameras, and the scene thus mirrors the extradiegetic situation in which the professional porn model Scott Taylor "really" masturbates to the "real" extradiegetic camera. According to Jackson, this *mise-en-abîme* produces a "nonidentical subject whose intra- and extradiegetic 'identities' are asymptotically inscribed across the representational topography of the film" (148). The effect of the mirroring produces a difference between the two subjects, as the acts of the intradiegetic "Taylor" produce a metadiegetic comment on the extradiegetic ("real") posing of the porn model. More importantly, the cause-effect relation is reversed: rather than representing himself in the porn film, the extradiegetic Taylor comes into existence only as a retroactive effect of the intradiegetic/metadiegetic commentary by "Scott Taylor." In his Lacanian construction, Jackson assumes a fundamental "priority of representation over the subject that representation makes possible" (145). However, Jackson argues that there is not only a split or difference between the two subjects, but also a congealing—the equivalence of identity: the "pornographic genre . . . elides this difference (Taylor is 'really doing it')" (148). It is this elision that allows for the formation of identity. "The profilmic image of

[Taylor] embodies and enfigures the decussation of these ontologically irreconcilable 'subjects,' instantiating the co-incidence of both [Scott Taylor] as a catachresis—a represented subject that is conceivable only as a (metadiscursively) contradicted representation" (149). [Taylor] (in brackets) designates the catachrestic intersection of Taylor and "Taylor," the pornographic gay subject, and is putatively different from the (heterosexual) ideological subject as self-identical, which traditional cinema produces by means of suture, because it—[Taylor], the intersection that enables gay subjectivity—is held together by an "act [that] is real, and is far more important than the identity of its agents, and the coincidence of act and image that pornography requires ruptures the isomorphism of any naturalistic fictional film in which it occurs" (171). The gay subject as pornography constructs it, in other words, fades behind the act that is represented, and thus reflects that "gay men identify with the dissolution of their 'selves'" (141) and "transform the two Lacanian castrations of self-objectification and aphanitic self-exposition into representations of negating affirmations of the gay male subject" (143).

Jackson arrives at an understanding of gay subjectivity as catachresis ("negating affirmation") whose terms elucidate the construction of Fichte's autobiographical edifice. Fichte's text constructs the gay subject—in Jackson's terms we would have to write [Fichte] or [I]—as "Fatamorgana" enabled by a Lacanian specular and narrative castration. [Fichte] as the catachrestic congealing of Fichte and Jäcki is that which comes into being as a vanishing. The narrative frame of *Platz* represents this vanishing; it inscribes the novel as a dream within a dream in which the narrator's awakening is, or, better, might be, nothing but another dream about the awakening. Any secure ground from which to assess reality as real is pulled out underneath the "reader's feet"; that is, there is no last or originary narrative position that would anchor the other ones. The novel's main narrative plane itself is punctured three times by the narrative frame of the "circular dream" in the form of a stanza of five lines:

Waking up.
Between dream and dream
The voice of the singer on the tower.
The word of god.
Sour. (12, 45, 206)

With these lines, the text of the novel is declared a "dream text" in which the narrator uses his (specular) position strategically, as the scribes use the laws of symmetry (107) to produce a textual plenitude from the uncontrollable text of the primary process. The activity of the scribes as well evokes this plenitude in the use of the verb "fill" (107). In other words, Fichte's text implies the possibility of utopian wholeness, yet as "fatamorgana," as a vanishing. The narrator himself is a "nothing," an empty, optical device, located in a transitory "between," a "dewdrop," which has no consciousness of its own.

Like the magical coalescing of the temporalities of enunciation and narrated text, engendered between the apparent binary "eternity"—"moment" as the symmetry of the repeated word(s) "word word" (215), the plenitude of Fichte's textual identity, implied in the German word "*All*" (215) for "universe," is predicated on an oscillation with its binary opposite "nothing," the vanishing of the self in the mirror. In order to be "*All*," in other words, the "I" needs to be "nothing." The final variation on the motif of the specular self as dewdrop inscribes this formal, optical construct: "Dew drops mirror dew drops in the universe [*All*]—nothing" (215). The dash in this line represents the mirror axis, the specular device that keeps "*All*" and "nothing" from collapsing into each other, upholds the constitutive split that enables the oscillation, the most fundamental structure of Fichte's autobiography. By upholding the split, in other words, it enables the *vision* of its "healing." Note the curious play with sameness that the opposition "*All*—nothing" carries and engenders in this sentence, "dew drops mirror dew drops," a narcissistic mutual recognition that is homosexual if one concedes, as Jackson explicitly does, to the (psychoanalytic) equivalence of narcissism and male homosexuality.[9]

For Jackson, gay sexuality is a "circulatory system of expenditure and absorption" (33) and represents a "culturally vital countersubjective possibility" (23) to the murder of the heterosexualizing Oedipal plot (168) because it implies a "pleasure-inflected ethics" (38) predicated on a "reciprocal and mobile sexuality" (10) with objects that are "indifferent" (39). Jackson elaborates this "ethical indifference" in such a way that

[g]ay male lovemaking is a pulsation of inter-ruptions of subjectivity, of inter-ruptions into the subject's somatic extension of his imaginary selfhood by the subject whose object he has ec-statically become. Subjectivity within male coupling is episodic, cognized and re-cognized as stroboscopic fluctuations of intense (yet dislocated, asymmetrical, decentered) awareness of self-as-other, self-for-other. (33)

This fantasy is often called "embracing the world" [*Weltenumarmung*], and reappears in *Platz's* last take as a permutation of the "circular dream"— "The ancient dream: / To unite/copulate with all" (217). Fichte's "gay lovemaking" is thus predicated on the oscillatory and ecstatic conflation of world and self to which Jackson alludes ("self-as-other"). It is also predicated on a notion of the body "without organs," to borrow Deleuze and Guattari's term, on an "ex-timate" body that Fichte captures in the dewdrop motif. The gay subject as dewdrop is an empty optical device. This subject identifies with the vantage point of the camera itself. In Jackson's words, "for the narcissistic subject, the same [loss of a sense of self] can mean freedom of vantage point" (158) because such a subject ostensibly no longer attempts to achieve a sense of control or self.[10] Turning to Fichte's Brazil novel *Explosion,* I will trace the entrails of this body, the constitutive disavowal of interiority. Jackson's and Bersani's idea that "gay men identify with the dissolution of their selves" (*Strategies of Deviance* 141) relies on the disavowal of a messy, unruly physicality that reemerges in Fichte's text.

THE RETURN TO THE SELF THROUGH TRACES OF SHIT, OR: IS BERSANI'S RECTUM REAL?

Recall that Gide's protagonist Michel appreciates the lightness of his "formal affinities" with North African boys because they cost only "half a franc a day." There are similar references to money in Fichte's novels. For less than twenty cruzeiros, we learn in *Explosion,* one can "meet with one's dream" in Bahia, Brazil (337). Gide's half-franc is a feeble trace of an element that becomes more obsessive and disruptive, and that becomes the object of Jäcki's theories, in Fichte's text: a plague that restores Jäcki's body as "drag," weight, interiority, and potential attachment in ways that cross his scheme of being a "dewdrop."

What interests me in particular in the scene from *Explosion* where Jäcki attempts to construct such pure ex-timacy is the trace of such a repressed interiority. The utopian "embrace of the world" enabled by Jäcki's construction of a hypermobile, transitory homosexuality would certainly qualify Jäcki as Bersanian "gay outlaw." But the Jäcki of *Explosion* returns to a self in ways that Gide's Michel eschews, at least in Bersani's reading.

The attraction to one of Jäcki's transitory dreams in the shape of a "trick" in Bahia becomes "dangerous" because it threatens him with attachment. Jäcki pulls back:

Jäcki swore to himself:
Never again.
Love no more.
Pure sex.
Embrace of the world.
Either fulfillment or dream.
Jäcki got used to living between them.
Between images and mud.
Like fish in brackish water.
Bi. (336)

The lure of fusion with the object, which becomes an acute "danger" because the object "was completely there" and "stayed there" (335), has to be mobilized and liquefied through cuts that the text, like Jackson's pornographic apparatus, performs on the syntactic and ekphrastic levels, and that Jäcki eventually performs with the gesture of paying the hustler money for sex:

Therefore Jäcki paid him.
To have the dream of getting the man whom he would never have gotten with love and longing.
At train stations and near the elevator one can have a date with one's dream for twenty cruzeiros
That was Jäcki's utopia.
And so he paid, even though the "Michelangelo" didn't want money.
So that he wouldn't be bludgeoned by his dream, as by a falling statue. (337)

The gesture of paying safeguards that sex becomes or remains "pure sex," guarantees the "characteristic" gay male lack of attachment to sexual objects that Fichte himself has discussed.[11] The act of paying confirms on the social level what Jäcki affirms as the aesthetic and political program of his life: "love no more"—aesthetic and political because this lack of attachment produces the aesthetics and politics of hybridity that he sums up under the label "bi."

The social corollary of Fichte's "anarchically polysemic" syntax that cuts up and reconfigures according to the "pleasure principle," to engage Jackson's terms, is the act of paying the hustler. That hustlers cost only "twenty cruzeiros" in Bahia is determined by an economic structure that must, by all means, be considered less "anarchically polysemic" for the hustler in this scene than for Jäcki. The fear of fusion, which leads to a lack of attachment, grounds Jäcki's postcolonial and queer hybrid notion of "bi" as bisexuality and bicontinentality. But as the scene from *Explosion* ironically intimates, this lack of attachment, this utopian queer fluidity is also linked to monetary liquidity. Jäcki, a First World citizen, can afford to be so "fluid" because he is "liquid." Jackson refers to this link (between fluidity and liquidity) in passing, almost by way of a slip, when he delivers evidence of the prevalence of these (utopian, truly queer) forms of fluid desires and identification within gay culture:

These principles are exploited and disseminated in the gay-oriented marketing practices in *GQ, International Male*, etc., and more explicitly represented in the flyers and videos in which porn stars demonstrate (for sale) penis extension pumps and other sexually enhancing paraphernalia. The gymnast, model, or porn star becomes both the object of desire and the ego ideal for the gay consumer. (132)

What Jackson's theory does not allow us to address (and Fichte addresses it only ironically in this scene) is that Jäcki's desublimated, fluid pleasure principle cannot operate on the same level as the one of the black "trick." Concerning the economic level, in other words, the egalitarian construction of Jäcki's queer fluidity acts as an obfuscation of a strict hierarchy that it reinscribes, in fact, must reinscribe. That Jäcki relegates the black man to the position of hustler is a prerequisite for Jäcki's egalitarian lack of attachment, for what Jackson calls "politics of jouissance" (34) and "pleasure-inflected ethics in gay male cultural interventions" (38). These ethics are predicated on a certain "indifferen[ce] to the reality of the object" (39).

Yet in different terms, Jäcki may be able to afford fluidity because of his monetary liquidity, the black "trick" does not, and Jackson's "pleasure-inflected ethics" would by definition imply that Jäcki cannot care because of his necessary indifference to the reality of the object. Indifference here denotes both a lack of empathy, but most of all literally *in-difference*, which is to say a lack of difference. But this indifference is obviously *in-different* only in the abstract, and predicated on a factual difference. Fichte's text does make explicit this hierarchy and inequality, but the ironic mode in which this is done may be too glib to be called critical. How does this queer, primitivist fluidity not only disavow its (post)colonial contradiction, but also an internal failure? And how does this internal failure surface in Fichte's text?

Fichte's *Explosion* constructs a "return to self" that is far more than Bersani's "precondition for registration and service as a citizen" (125), where "citizen" is necessarily and only the "good citizen," the cop-out to the system. The return to self might enable the gay subject to take responsibility for the disavowal that lies at the core of the utopian present moment or "embrace of the world"—to take responsibility for himself and the "intractability of [his] desire."

Bersani's "Is the Rectum a Grave?" is perhaps his most influential essay within the field of Queer Studies. The essay's final sentence succinctly formulates the hope that anal intercourse between men may put an end to relations of power between self and other: "Male homosexuality advertises the risk of the sexual itself as the risk of self-dismissal, of *losing sight* of the self, and in so doing proposes and dangerously represents *jouissance* as a mode of ascesis" (222, Bersani's emphasis). To read the essay's title in this light, "the" gay male rectum not only threatens to be a grave, as it does in so much homophobic and AIDS-phobic discourse, it also promises to be the grave of the power-ridden masculine self. It ostensibly offers itself as the escape route from possession and power by burying selfhood.

The scene of Jäcki's encounter with the ideal black man in *Explosion* repeats, as we have seen, many of Bersani's gestures toward a utopian "ethics of the present moment." Even more strikingly, *Platz der Gehenkten* construes the gay subject as identification with the "dissolution of self" (*Strategies* 141), to paraphrase Jackson in his most explicitly Bersanian moment, as nothing but the plain surface of paper and the letters of language. The exchange of money between Jäcki and his lover is central for the construction of Jäcki's unattached queer utopia; this inequitable exchange constitutes the precondition for Jäcki's fantasy of equality as fluidity. The affect that underlies this exchange, however, appears massive, and curiously exaggerated: "Jäcki was struck by the fear . . . of being bludgeoned by his dream" (337). This affect is as different from Gide's and Bersani's lighthearted indifference as are some of the images in the texts. While Gide's and Bersani's Michel enjoys the "pleasures of nude sunbathing" (*Homos* 119), exposes himself to the "breath of air" (119), and is enveloped by "a delicious radiance" (119), Fichte's Jäcki remembers in the sex scene with the black "trick" that he lives "between images and mud. / Like fish in brackish water" (336). While Michel seems to have left behind "mud" in favor of a world of luminous images, Jäcki's "images" (of which the black "trick" is the most radiant one) remain irrevocably attached to "mud."

With Freudian symbolism in mind, should "mud" not be read in connection with money, and, further, with feces as the abject detritus of a body that Fichte's formal scheme attempts to grind to powder and reconstitute as paper and ink in *Platz,* yet that imposes itself massively in *Explosion*? Jäcki's massively messy body in *Explosion* vitiates the "poetic axioms" (*Herzschlag* 276) that allow *Platz* to emerge as the more "beautiful," yet not necessarily the more interesting text.

The exchange of money for sex is a pervasive, almost obsessive topic in *Explosion*. Beyond Jäcki/Fichte's insistence on constructing a realm of unattached "pure sex" (336), the exchange of money for sex is linked with particular sex acts, notably anal penetrations, more specifically, being penetrated. The text points out that money is literally, and almost by way of a spoof on Freudian symbolism, equivalent to the anal:

Every cab driver in Bahia de Todos os Santos could be seduced.
And since they felt normal, they even let themselves be fucked.
For money.
Money meant: I let myself be fucked. (177)

As Jäcki's wish to write a "new ethnology" (177) about Bahian cabdrivers and their sexual habits on the same page intimates, the line "Money meant: I let myself be fucked" is the ethnological formulation of a gift economy à la Marcel Mauss or Claude Lévi-Strauss. Money is given in exchange for the gift the "cab driver" makes with his anus. The ex-timacy of the relations—or shall we say, with Bersani, "formal affinities"—allows the exchange to remain strictly symbolic. Just as money "doesn't stink," the anus given remains abstract in all of Jäcki's encounters that follow the "pure sex" formula.

The most extensive passage in *Explosion* in which Jäcki's principle of "love no more" (336) threatens to erode is the Michael Chisholm episode. Chisholm is, to my knowledge, the only black man who becomes Jäcki's sex partner and yet breaks with the scheme to which the black "trick" succumbs despite his initial refusal to take money for anal sex. Like the black "trick," the New York painter and intellectual Chisholm is "Jäcki's dream man" (629); as in the other scenario, Jäcki's maddening desire for Chisholm leads him to conclude that "Jäcki didn't want to. Love no more" (629), because it threatens to undo his unattached position between the woman Irma and innumerable, exchangeable male bodies, the entire libidinal structure that subtends the narrative edifice of this oeuvre: "That would finish with Michael. / That would have been one whole thing" (631). Chisholm, "one of the great loves of his life" (633), threatens to become the "dream" come true, the dream that was about to "bludgeon" (337) Jäcki in the "trick" scenario before money liquefies the relation and disperses it into the realm of unattached "transitoriness."

Money as solvent is out of the question in the relation with Michael. Michael's economic status as middle-class intellectual of the first world precludes this possibility. The following passage formulates the ultimate stumbling block for the intimate relationship between Michael and Jäcki, a relationship Jäcki desires in Bersani's "unrevolutionary" sense as "intensely satisfying drama of personal anguish and unfulfilled demands" (*Homos* 124). Jäcki escapes from this relationship in order to preserve a Bersanian outlaw existence, for the intimacy with Michael restores an interiority to the body which is troubling and unpleasant:

And then you go to bed with such a sensitive person
And then you give yourself to him
And suddenly it smells like shit.
No, I don't think I could cope with that in the long run.
How would the young African-American, who was so straightforward with his tongue
while kissing, react to Jäcki's shit. (637f)

The money returned in exchange for the anal gift in the abstract arrangement of the outlaw paradigm allows the receiver of the anal gift to reciprocate the gift, but this formalization depends on the relation's ex-timacy. The relation between Jäcki and Michael, on the contrary, is too intimate to enable this neutralization, this leveling or flattening of the body. The intimate body continues to harbor a dark and cavernous secret that keeps secreting unpleasant, even horrifying, substances. The almost absolute abstraction of the body of the narrator, which makes *Platz* Fichte's most "beautiful" and poetically calculated book, also undoes the sensual project—that is, if we understand sensuality as the relation to a body, and between bodies, that are not pure abstraction. The sensuality of *Platz* is a "formal affinity"; its bodies are so abstract that they have jettisoned the sensual, horrifying, messy body.

By way of concluding, against Bersani's celebration of a putatively selfless bodiliness, I argue that the "unclean" or hybrid narrative schemes of Fichte's *Explosion* constitute an important counterpoint. From a postcolonial and queer political perspective, the eruption of the scatological body in Fichte's novels poses the question of power and critique—a question that queer theories of selflessness obfuscate by prematurely declaring it solved. In fact, what gay theories of self-dissolution obfuscate is their own epistemological and political violence.

NOTES

1. Within postcolonial studies, Homi Bhabha has formulated a similar, deconstructive predilection for a notion of a "selfless," antihumanist subjectivity without depth or interiority, as Bersani drawing on the same tradition of twentieth-century French gay writing. Bhabha's essay "Postcolonial Authority and Postmodern Guilt" opens with a passage in which Bhabha cites and elaborates Roland Barthes's notion of an affective syntax, taken from Barthes's Moroccan diaries. Barthes's gay desire here effects a fragmentation of the speaking self, a blurring of self and external world that constitutes the model of Bhabha's postcolonial notion of subjectivity.

2. As Michael Lucey demonstrates compellingly in his 1995 book *Gide's Bent,* a text that predates Bersani's Gide essay but analyzes Bersani's earlier writing on gay subjectivity in connection to Gide's gay primitivism, "Bersani is presenting an ethics of the present moment" (*Gide's Bent* 38). Attempting to "explain ... why [Bersani and Gide] sometimes sound a bit similar" (39), Lucey argues that "[p]rimary sexuality is not (for either Bersani or Gide) a realm in which selves exist coherently. Sexuality is something that has to do with the body, not the self. Sexuality shatters the self, and for Bersani it is when this self that sexuality threatens to destroy nonetheless insists on holding onto its coherence that sexuality falls into power" (39). Leaving behind the relational, however, "holds out the theo-

retical possibility of a sustained, consistently and constantly repeated, present moment in which sex could be just sex, perpetually evading any traps of temporality, any politics of relationality, any social construals" (40).

3. Unless otherwise stated, all translations from the French or German are my own.

4. How significant is it, for example, that Hubert Fichte's middle name is Jakob—the name of which Jäcki, the protagonist of most of Fichte's novels, is the nickname diminutive?

5. "Queer" ("*schwul*") and "bi" are often interchangeable in Fichte's writing.

6. Irma, like her real-life model Fichte's companion Leonore Mau, is a professional photographer.

7. Compare in the context of Fichte's erotic conflation of skin and paper Jackson's argument about the importance of the screen for gay pornography. Jackson lists over ten porn movies that thematize this relation to the visual medium itself: "The movie screen is also eroticized in porn films, in both direct and metaphoric representations" (134). In two of the extensive close readings of porn movies that he provides, Jackson uses the self-reflexive and fetishistic foregrounding of the visual medium (cameras, screens, film, flashlights) as erotic in and of itself to develop larger claims about gay aesthetics from which he then extrapolates to films by Almodóvar and Jarman. In conjunction with the use of visual and filmic techniques in Fichte's writing, I find the parallel between Jackson's analysis of the eroticization of the technology of visual production and Fichte's eroticization of the materiality of the writing process striking.

8. The difficulty in working with an English translation is the untranslatability of some of the turns. "I miswrite," for example, is originally a reflexive verb, "*ich verschreibe mich*," expressing the reflexiveness of the narcissistic construction. "Moment," moreover, is "*Augenblick*" and thus contains a visual and specular aspect (literally "wink of the eye") that is pivotal in Fichte's motif.

9. See the following statements by Jackson: "I will advance definitions of the heterosexual male subject as an 'anaclitic subject' and the gay male as a 'narcissistic subject'" (22). "I use 'narrative' and 'specular' . . . as the specularity of homosexuality and the narrativity of male heterosexuality" (48).

10. This is apparently the difference between the gay narcissistic subject and the imperfect "straight approximation" of gay subjectivity in S/M scenarios (see *Strategies of Deviance* 135), since what the masochistic subject does is eroticize the loss of control, whereas the narcissistic subject simply "enjoys" the complete absence of control as freedom.

11. In his 1976 essay "Jeder kann der nächste sein" on Pasolini's violent death and his film Salò, Fichte writes: "Homosexual behavior is characterized by a frequent, frequently irreversible shift from search for attachment to lack of attachment, from lack of attachment to fetishism and sadism" (HuL1, 135).

WORKS CITED

Bersani, Leo. *Homos.* Cambridge & London: Harvard University Press, 1995.

Bhabha, Homi. "Postcolonial Authority and Postmodern Guilt." In: *Cultural Studies as Critical Theory,* edited by Ben Agger. London: Falmer Press, 1992. 56–66.

Böhme, Hartmut. *Hubert Fichte: Riten des Autos und Leben der Literatur.* Stuttgart: J. B. Metzler, 1992.

Fichte, Hubert. *Explosion. Roman der Ethnologie VII. Die Geschichte der Empfindlichkeit,* edited by Ronald Kay. Frankfurt am Main: S. Fischer, 1993.

———. *Homosexualität und Literatur 1 & 2. Die Geschichte der Empfindlichkeit, Paralipomena 1,* edited by Thorsten Teichert, Gisela Lindemann, and Leonore Mau. Frankfurt am Main: S. Fischer, 1987.

———. *Platz der Gehenkten. Die Geschichte der Empfindlichkeit VI,* edited by Gisela Lindemann and Leonore Mau. Frankfurt am Main: S. Fischer, 1989.

———. *Versuch über die Pubertät.* Frankfurt am Main: S. Fischer, 1982.

Gide, André. *L'immoraliste.* Paris: Mercure de France (Collection Folio), 1902.

Jackson, Earl, Jr. *Strategies of Deviance: Studies in Gay Male Representation.* Bloomington and Indianapolis: Indiana University Press, 1995.

Kreuzer, Leo. *Literatur und Entwicklung: Studien zu einer Literatur der Ungleichzeitigkeit.* Franfurt am Main: Fischer Taschenbuch, 1989.

Lucey, Michael. *Gide's Bent: Sexuality, Politics, Writing.* New York and Oxford: Oxford University Press, 1995.

Chapter 11

Theorizing the "Under-Theorized"

Erich De Wald

Both academics and North American queer communities have taken up the issues of the "transnational" and the "transgender/ed" within the last few years. Institutional scholarship and popular sociologies of contemporary and long-dead "trannies" abound these days in lesbian/gay bookstores and academic journals friendly to such scholarship. Perhaps it is an accomplishment of globalization and "transnational culture" that the categories "transgender/ed," and "queer" more generally, can now include individuals as unalike as Indian Brahmin *hijras*, native North American *berdache*, and American-South working-class drag divas.[2] Presumably this montage is an image of postmodern hybridity—evidence of queer community building and left intellectuals theorizing the "under-theorized."

It's true enough that these individuals have come into contact with one another. It's also obvious enough that this contact involves a translation of sexuality across cultural and national borders. From a western, queer perspective (as if that were a homogeneous point of view), this act of translation "makes sense" of the (transgender/ed) subject by sexing and gendering it. In *Gender Trouble*, Judith Butler provides a groundbreaking analysis of this process that requires every subject to be a gendered subject.

Analyses like those I mentioned above would seem to involve such a translation, such a rendering and gendering. In fact, these analyses seem to involve a process much simpler than the complicated act of "subjection" that Butler conceptualizes. In these studies, the description and translation of "queer subjects" is a single process of finding equivalents and translating gender for gender, word for word. The context of the "other" gender/ed subject, the histories of specific "sex/gender systems," and the process of contact between that "other system" and western epistemologies of gender become ineffective background to the more important work of showing cross-cultural queer community.

This chapter is an attempt to understand this "descriptive" process as an "analytical," epistemological, and often violent one. I'd like to do this by bringing together three texts—Judith Butler's *Gender Trouble*, Leslie Feinberg's *Stone Butch Blues,* and J. K. Gibson-Graham's "Querying Globalization"—that, when read together, complicate the faceless act of "description" and understand it as a moment within a spatial and temporal web of power. By paying close attention to these three texts and especially to their "failures," I want to pinpoint the way that certain privilegings (white, Euro-American, heterosexist) are bound up in theoretical methods, my own included. By reading these texts together, though, I think it becomes possible to see (1) how reading is a process of negotiation, and (2) how the theoretical privilegings that I spoke of work to limit the terrain of that reading-negotiation. This is a theoretical exercise, not a corrective analysis of the search for the transgender/ed Other.

GENDER TROUBLE

The impact of this book on queer theory, but especially on academic theorizations of transgender/ed politics and subjectivities, cannot be ignored. Not only does it problematize transphobic assumptions about the "natural" correspondence between sex and gender. It also responds to and interrogates a crisis in meaning within feminist communities over the category "woman."

This crisis in meaning has "led time and again to a certain sense of trouble" (vii). Of course, "trouble" is an understatement. The "trouble" has often been racialism if not racism, heterosexism if not homophobia, "First World" prejudice if not a process of recolonization. The "crisis" of the "second wave" of white U.S. feminism doesn't just lead to "trouble": it is troubled. White U.S. feminism's strategies for change have often privileged women's oppression over other forms of oppression, understanding oppressions as separate rather than integrally linked. In this move the experiences, positions, and problems of women "other" than white U.S. feminism (women of color, "Third World" women, lesbians, women from working-class backgrounds, transgender/ed women) have been ignored, marginalized, or fetishized. Race, sexuality, class and nation emerge as peripheral interests rather than central problematics.

I want to refuse to cite Butler's text as either a fixative or a preservative of this central problematic of feminism. Instead, I want to read *Gender Trouble* (not as a segment of a philosopher's opus but as a text), and understand the specific movements of race and national identity along the axes of gender and transgender/ism. I am not concerned here with the philosopher's racism (or not). I am more interested in the way that certain discursive privileges (white, U.S.) work by generalizing away from racial and national difference. In the preface, Butler figures the ensuing discussion of the problematic of the "universal woman" in very particular terms. Butler asks,

[T]o what extent does the effort to locate a common identity as the foundation for a feminist politics preclude a radical inquiry into the political construction and regulation of identity itself? What new shape of politics emerges when identity as a common ground no longer constrains the discourse on feminist politics? (ix).

While these questions push feminism to rethink itself and to revitalize its message(s), the method of that message, "radical inquiry," and the substance within the "shape of politics" is either the same or only *generally* different. It is crucial to come to terms with the moments where specific differences and a more universal difference are elided and confounded. These moments are some of the limits and openings of Butler's text.

Gender Trouble's problematic begins with a revaluation of "trouble." Simply put, instead of thinking of "feminism" as outside of "trouble," feminist subjects needs to renegotiate strategies for representing "woman" and try to get "*in* trouble" instead of staying "*out* of trouble" (vii; emphases mine). Staying "out of trouble" implies some sort of safety or protection from the reach of the law that is always already gender/ed and masculinist. Getting "in trouble" seems to accept the "reality" that both foundations and the meanings of those foundations are contingent. Feminist subjects exist *inside* of trouble, understood here as hegemonic[3] culture.

Butler displays the transformative power that feminist strategies might have if they enact and engage with gender/ed behaviors without basing these enactments on foundational myths and inherited but unexamined discourses. These myths and discourses divide nature and culture as "feminine" and "masculine" while at the same time producing gender as the effect of an essential sex. At the heart here, for Butler, is a powerful and violent metalepsis, an effect (mis)represented as a cause. Feminist strategies that make use of the category "woman" without thinking through the production of gender-as-sex end up repeating and recuperating, in the most disastrous way, the very discourses they resist.

There is no "prior to" of patriarchy. The law (understood here as the category "man" reproducing the category "woman") dictates to and dominates feminist "subjects" whose work must be understood and reimagined within a historical narrative that is scrupulously antifoundational; feminist identities, in this project, continuously reconsider the very behaviors, resources, and ideas that make them feminist. In this way, feminism can get "in trouble."

Feminism "in trouble," then, "moves the conception of gender off the ground of a substantial model of identity to one that requires a conception of gender as a constituted *social temporality*" (140–41; Butler's emphasis). Gender *happens* over time in a cultural and discursive domain. A specific gender identity cannot be said to exist prior to the moment of performance or prohibition. Likewise, a gender identity comes about when "the action of gender [as performance] is *repeated*" (140; Butler's emphasis). A heterosexual woman who cooks breakfast and dinner and does the wash over the course of a marriage becomes a woman/wife doing what a woman/wife does. If gender/ed styles like this one "are not expressive [of a gender/ed core] but performative, then these attributes effectively constitute the identity they are said to express or reveal" (141). From this perspective, [gender/ed] identity doesn't entirely take place in the past, beyond the control of the historical agent. Instead, this agent is always engaging in activities that *will have been* gender/ed by a heteronormative discourse that disciplines the body. These combined gender activities become gender/ed identities.

Feminism gets "in trouble" by construing these [gender/ed] identities as historically contingent and malleable. Butler's suggestion is crucial: feminists ought to use notions of gender-as-sex to debunk and rework the system that privileges that notion. In a sense, feminists need to get dirty; feminists need to get "in trouble" instead of opting for a somehow pure, woman-centered politics that refuses patriarchy while comfortably accepting "woman" vis-à-vis "man." Feminists have to put their bodies on the line, understanding the body as "a variable boundary, a surface whose permeability is politically regulated, a signifying practice within a cultural field of gender hierarchy and compulsory heterosexuality" (139).

The body becomes the battleground where an embattled "subject" (a term very much *under erasure* at this point in *Gender Trouble*[4]) takes on the discourse of gender-as-sex and performs these discourses. Instead of insisting on the "truth" of gender, the feminist gender terrorist uses gender/ed norms to show the "truth" of sex as an "effect" of a heteronormative discourse. "Gender ought not to be construed as a stable identity or locus of agency from which various acts follow; rather, gender is an identity tenuously constituted in time, instituted in an exterior space through a *stylized repetition of acts*" (140).

In this passage, there is a tension between the interior and the exterior. This tension consistently surfaces throughout *Gender Trouble*. Recall the question about the substance within "the shape of politics." For Butler, gender, as an identity, operates "in an exterior space." The body, apparently, is "the shape of politics." Gender is a "subjection" of the body. The effects of this gendering on the "subject" can only ever be known in a social space, through language. An individual's gender, then, is only ever the play of forces and the movements of discourses. Difference is regulated in an external space and repeatedly disciplined *on* the body. The internal is precisely off limits; identity cannot be substantial.

It is important to ask what bodies might be refused "subjectivity" in this formulation. And why. Naming the internal "identity" and the external "social location," Paula Moya critiques this

disavowal of the link between identity (with its experiential and cognitive components) and social location (the particular nexus of gender, race, class, and sexuality in which a given individual exists in the world). . . . Butler err[s] in the assumption that because there is no *one-to-one* correspondence between social location and identity or knowledge, there is simply *no* connection between [them] (135; Moya's italics).

Disagreeing somewhat with Moya, I think Butler's disavowal isn't a complete one; it cautions more than it disallows. Butler asks the reader to question "from what strategic position...the disjunctive binary of inner/outer has taken hold" (134), and this is where her book and presumably her own theorization come to a close.

Rather than conceive of this moment as the place where theory ends and application/practice begins, I want to engage this apparent *terminus* of identity claims. Butler certainly agrees that the relation between the "interior" and the "exterior" isn't a simple one. And, as Butler points out, the hegemonic "strategic position" is certainly interested in this "disjunctive binary." [Transgender/ed] people, as Moya asserts, identify with their locations in the "exterior" of "culture" and locate their "interior" identities within that "external" cultural fabric. In one passage, Butler calls these identifications and the processes of identification "styles" and insists that "these [transgender/ed] styles [are] never fully self-styled, for styles have a history, and those histories condition and limit the possibilities" (139). It would appear that history sets the bounds for the game of "subjectivity." In this moment, history as a concept "solves" the problem of "style" and the "disjunctive binary of inner and outer." History would appear to be the space just outside any cultural fabric, the limit that bounds culture and orders it. History limits by defining what cannot be, and orders culture with that denial.

But I don't think Butler would agree with this formulation of history. In critiquing Michel Foucault, she offers a picture of what history is not. She says Foucault mistakenly reads the battle waged on the surfaces of bodies *as* history (130). Butler says, in effect, that Foucault assumes there is a substance prior to discourse, and discourse describes rather than prescribes this body/substance. But Foucault might be read differently, against the grain, to suggest an intense and irreducible simultaneity of differentially situated discourses that are not singular in their location or materiality. These discourses—and their confrontations—have histories. Foucault says: "The body—and everything that touches it: diet, climate, and soil—is the domain of the *Herkunft* [historical]. The body manifests the stigmata of past experiences and also gives rise to desires, failings, and errors" ("Nietzsche" 83).[5] While refusing to entertain the question of the body's priorness, the body's *priority* is significant. Theorizing the body is more than a question of discourses. Foucault implies, with perfectly Foucauldian persistence, that discourses are not equally riddled with power. Diet, climate, and soil—not to mention race, gender, class and nation—politically regulate the surface of the body *as much as* they are regulated.

"History" is assuredly a discourse. But it is not one discourse. In Butler's emphasis on getting "in" trouble, she only makes use of one sense that the word-pair "in"/"out" has. These two words are prepositions that indicate both relations of time ("out of time," "just in the nick of time") and relations of space ("in the house," "out of the country"). How do the spatial possibilities of Butler's word choice open her argument to different historical valences? Butler is right to caution the historian about a foundational myth of the body's materiality. But isn't it possible that the body can be invested with other signifying practices, be on the frontier between different times and different histories, so that "the body is the inscribed surface of events (traced by language and dissolved by ideas), the locus of a dissociated self (adopting the illusion of a substantial unity), and a volume in perpetual disintegration" (Foucault, "Nietzsche" 83) and neither fully "here" nor fully "there"? Can the body be a "zone of contest"[6] where times, spaces, and cultures encounter each other and themselves? Do the "selves" of these "bodies" *necessarily* experience their locations as dissociations?

MORE THAN *GENDER* [IS] *TROUBLE*

The proximity of "selves" and "bodies" is not just coincidental. The intimacy of bodies and psyches requires a scrupulous critical attention to their contingency–critical attention to the body as well as the psyche, critical attention to the forces that inscribe the body and form the "subject." These forces are involved in the process of criticism. These forces are historical forces: the relationship between analyst and analysand, the power of the critic's knowledge. The issue here is simple and crucial: How does the critic—Butler *as* critic—know anything of these bodies, psyches, locations? She certainly understands specific marginalizations (as feminist scholar, as woman), but do these experiences equal the ones that Butler analyzes?

There is no getting around the critic, as if that would even be desirable. But an analysis that assumes a critical clearness of vision comes dangerously close to a panopticism.[7] As if the critic can fully understand the *other*['s] position any more than the other[s] can! Sagri Dhairyam contends that Butler deploys this panoptic politic in her analysis of drag:

Thus Butler, as white and academic philosopher-theorist who is produced by the very discourses of academia, may tell us about stone-butches and powerful femmes and, indeed, produce a discourse of drag that feeds back into the authority of a critical intellectualism capable of provoking yet legislating what is dangerous in philosophical thought. (29)

What is more, "the critic-philosopher's own performance as product-of-systems-of-power is rendered invisible as the intellect evaluates sexuality and the body" (30). This body as object has been e-raced and dehistoricized by the same processes that allow the critic to paint herself transparent.

Margaret Homans discusses this transparency and the political process undercutting it. She starts by looking at Butler's reading of the Aretha Franklin song "You Make Me Feel Like a Natural Woman." In *Gender Trouble*, the song has been so decontextualized that its meaning has been shifted. The fragmented identity Butler finds in "Natural Woman" *might* well be a product of Butler's suspicious process of (mis)translation. In making an R&B song performed by a black woman into a theoreticopolitical argument (constructed by a white woman), Butler doesn't account for the variety of different meanings that the song has; these meanings are as significant to a gender/ed reading of the song as the one line Butler appropriates. "Franklin's refrain coincides with a pro-identity position (the naïve feminists' refrain) as much as it does with her [Butler's] own anti-identity position" (82). The implication here is that Butler's method may well impose a fragmented "subjectivity" on a "subject-effect" that otherwise suggests a negotiation of a woman's ambivalence outside of the fragmented/unified binary. This is not to say that fragmentation or something similar to it doesn't happen for the "subject" of Franklin's song. It's even difficult to imagine a "subject" that doesn't negotiate with h/er surroundings (context) to become an agent. The trouble with "fragmentation" and "ambivalence," though, is that the critic often arrives on the scene, finds complicated-ness, renders/labels it "ambivalent," and then departs the scene of the criticism without complicating the ambivalence and coming to an understanding of how "subjects" act through this complicated-ness. The "subject" of Franklin's song might not describe herself as "fragmented" or "ambivalent." How might she narrate herself, and what might that self-criticism say about "subjectivity" and the politics of negotiated (rather than fragmented) identities? Should the critic listen for signs of this articulation?

Paula Moya criticizes not only Butler but "postmodern feminist theorists" in general for their static disregard toward this articulation. Moya observes the way Butler attempts to forge a subversive feminist agenda that is built on "abstractions" and "experiences" removed from their specific locations in the world. This is the way that "postmodern theory" tends to address "difference": by disavowing "the link between identity (with its experiential and cognitive components) and social location (the particular nexus of gender, race, class, and sexuality in which a given individual exists in the world)" (135). Moya responds to this increasingly "exclusionary" and "totalizing" trend in feminist scholarship by imagining a theoretical framework grounded in the work of Cherríe Moraga.[8] "Unlike postmodernist feminists who understand the concept of 'identity' as inherently and perniciously 'foundational,' Moraga understands 'identities' as relational and grounded in the historically produced social facts which constitute social locations" (127). That there is anything like a "social fact," no matter its production, is obviously a contested point. But this is precisely the point where Moya criticizes Butler for not mapping power in its specificity and responding to historical inequalities and hierarchies of domination. "Power is not amorphous because oppression is systematic and structural" (135). Where are *Gender Trouble* and its gender/ed "subjects" on the map of power that Moya's analysis implies? It is precisely this cartography that remains essential for a feminist practice if it is to negotiate difference and practice theory without concomitantly writing feminist whiteness over raced feminism.[9]

This reading of *Gender Trouble* thus far suggests that "postmodern" theory needs to understand its own embeddedness within specific histories of gender/ed oppression; it also questions whether the history of patriarchy alone determines specific gender/ed configurations. Don't histories of white supremacy and imperialism construct gender/ed bodies and selves? And what are the positions of (white) western gender studies within these histories? What are the histories of certain forms of theory? It is crucial to think about how methods for theorizing have come about through historical processes.

In his study of the formation of the (white) American working class, David

Roediger concludes that class and race identities in the United States are inextricably bound up in one another. Not only did the American racial system—which is both total and dispersed—and the organization of the American working class happen at the same time; it was because of a marking off of white workers against workers of color and slave laborers that a discourse of class identities took hold and gave rise to organized labor. Similarly, feminist consciousness and movement must not be mapped with antiracist movements, nationalist movements, and/or queer movements mapped beside it, at the side, peripherally. These movements compose one another. Cora Kaplan has said,

Class and race meanings are not metaphors for the sexual, or vice versa. It is better, though not exact, to see them as reciprocally constituting each other through a kind of narrative invocation, a set of associative terms in a chain of meaning. To understand how gender and class—to take two categories only—are articulated together transforms our analysis of each of them. (Quoted in Michie 1)

In other words, feminism negotiates its political interests and organizes upon a cultural and political playing field that is constitutively racialized, nationalized, and sexualized. These *other* categories compose feminist "subjects" and the category "woman." Without race, nation and sexuality, "woman" wouldn't exist.

GENDER/ED LOCATIONS

In *Gender Trouble*, Butler makes an intervention into the biographical history of Herculine Barbin, an intersex/ed person living in France in the middle of the nineteenth century. Butler's intervention explores Barbin's life and body as they are represented in Barbin's journals and criticizes Foucault's reading of those journals.

Both Butler and Foucault have responded to the journals written between 1863 and 1868, several years after Barbin had h/er gender legally reassigned. Foucault, who edited and oversaw the publication of the journals in 1980, writes: "Brought up as a poor and deserving girl in a milieu that was almost exclusively feminine and strongly religious, Herculine Barbin . . . was finally recognized as being 'truly' a young man [in 1860]" (*Herculine* xi). After reassignment Barbin was unable to continue h/er relationship with the women s/he had grown up with in the convent at La Rochelle. "He [sic] was incapable of adapting himself to a new identity and ultimately committed suicide" (xi).[10] The memoirs were found with Barbin's body, became part of the psychiatric corpus and then lost currency until Foucault "rediscovered" them and had them published in France in 1978.

For Foucault, it is important that Barbin wrote h/er journals after h/er "'true' and 'definitive' identity" had been "discovered and established" (xiii). It is this new sexual "truth" or determinacy that changes Barbin's life. In h/er memoirs "what she evokes in her past is the happy limbo of a non-identity" (xiii) that was h/

er upbringing in the convent where the feminine was the universal. S/he was and was not this femininity. S/he both possessed and didn't possess it. Before reassignment, specific sexual acts were not necessarily aligned with specific gender/ed identities. After reassignment, identities impinged on pleasures.

For Butler, these pleasures cannot have existed outside of a "dominant culture" (77) that would have forced Barbin to confront identities before sex reassignment. In other words, Barbin was not simply "inside" or "outside" the law.

In effect, s/he embodies the law, not as an entitled subject, but as an enacted testimony to the law's uncanny capacity to produce only those rebellions that it can guarantee will—out of fidelity—defeat themselves and those subjects who, utterly subjected, have no choice but to reiterate the law of their genesis. (106)

Instead of founding an analysis on bodily pleasure, Butler wonders how this pleasure itself is prefigured by the law. Any possible sexual articulation available to Barbin is already produced by the "dominant culture." This culture assumes a "strategic position" and holds Herculine Barbin up as a model of both transgression and recuperation–proliferation and prohibition at once.

These power-moves take a toll on Barbin. S/he herself [sic] presumes at various points that h/er body is the *cause* of h/er gender confusion and h/er transgressive pleasures, as if they were both result and manifestation of an essence which somehow falls outside the natural/metaphysical order of things. (99)

The discourse produces Barbin's body works by dividing the sexes. Anyone "trapped" in the interstice between "man" and "woman" functions as an example of the law's prohibition.

[Herculine's] sexuality is not outside the law, but is the ambivalent production of the law, one in which the very notion of *prohibition* spans the psychoanalytic and institutional terrains. H/er confessions, as well as h/er desires, are subjection and defiance at once. (105; Butler's emphasis)

The law doesn't just coerce Barbin into taking up a gender/ed position. Even Barbin's "choice" to become a man is limited by the boundaries of heteronormative discourse. The "choice" and the choices have been produced. Mechanisms of domination have become processes of normalization, so much so that the "psychoanalytic and institutional terrains" function together. Neither the "body" nor the "psyche" can be said to be the site of resistance to the law. Both locations are part of a legislative procedure. "Discipline 'makes' individuals" (Foucault, *Discipline* 170).

Butler's argument here relies upon Foucault's history of the "functional changes" (Spivak, "Subaltern" 197) in systems of punishment in western Europe at precisely the same time that Barbin lived. For Foucault, this new discourse of normalization "colonized the legal institution" (*Discipline* 231) and made every-one a possible "delinquent." In Butler's argument, this "colonization" has been so effective that the "disjunctive binary of inner/outer" is maintained entirely with*in* the "law."

Foucault's use of the word "colonization," though, suggests a more nuanced discursive terrain.[11] "Colonization" implies an inequality of power, and it is pre-cisely this power that makes the inner/outer binary a useful one. The relative omnipotence of the institutional over the psychic doesn't eliminate the latter; it makes a history of their relationship—and their relationality—all the more neces-sary.[12]

First, the institutional. If the "subject" is "subjection and defiance at once"—centrally ambivalent—then specific institutions would teach "subjection and de-fiance at once." Institutional pedagogy would always be "a frightened repetition of the already said" (Foucault, "Truth and Power" 110), and the subject would always be either the affirmation or the negation of that repetitive articulation. But the convent, as Barbin recollects, does more than either support h/er gender/ed "subjectivity" or punish h/er for it. It is the power of gender, gender/ed power, that "produces things, it induces pleasures, forms knowledge, produces discourse" (119). While this same power marks off the possible from the impossible for Barbin, it also—within the convent and within Barbin's memory of the convent—produces a space not quite heterogender/ed. The history of this space and this empowered production is not a dialectical one of repression and liberation.

Yet in judging Foucault's analysis as "sentimental indulgence" (96) and then moving on, Butler imposes a repression/production that is no more than the syn-thetic resolution of a dialectic. Without wishing power away, it's important to understand the specific and nuanced managerial methods to be found in Barbin's recollections of the convent. While Barbin was eventually expelled from the con-vent by its gender/ed rules, s/he was also able to survive there for quite some time. This survival means something. It suggests that there is a difference between what was produced and what was prohibited. The institution ultimately prohib-ited Barbin and certainly had a hand in producing h/er. But the prohibition and the production were not historically simultaneous. There is a gap here, a time differen-tial, during which an institutional and biographical counter-history takes place. This counterhistory would necessarily understand its relation to a disciplinary mechanism where "all behaviour falls in the field between good and bad marks, good and bad points"(*Discipline* 180), "male" and "female" enactments. These gender/ed limits and the possible perversions of them are never fully calculated by the disciplinary schema that produces to prohibit. This is clearly the problematic of the panopticon. Barbin's biography and the counterhistory I'm proposing move to understand [transgender/ed] history as something other than the transi-tional moment between one moment in the disciplining of the transgender "sub-ject" and the "next" moment. Since the panopticon has "failed" to exert total control, there are cultures of the convent that escape the move of gender normativity from one historical triumph to the next. This counterhistory understands "that the moment(s) of change [must] be pluralized and plotted as confrontations rather than transition[s]" (Spivak, "Subaltern" 197) within a complete and completing narrative of compulsory heterosexuality.

There is a striking similarity between the method of producing Barbin's "subjectivity" and similar methods used by European colonial powers at that time to manage colonial "subjects" and consolidate the domain of empire into one historical narrative. In *Race and the Education of Desire* Ann Laura Stoler suggests that "Europe's eighteenth- and nineteenth-century discourses on sexuality, like other cultural, political, or economic assertions, cannot be charted in Europe alone" (7). Stoler asserts that the colonial state may well have practiced its theories of governance in the colony and then brought those "tested" methods from the laboratory/periphery "back home" to the metropole. This traffic in "subjection" was two-way. Differential, for sure, but two-way. Colonial practices didn't happen exclusively outside Europe. A calculated ambivalence produced by this "dominant culture" doesn't happen within a monolithic institution or under a law without revision. This ambivalence, as well, has (a) history that takes place within a domain that works *at least* two sets of political practices: one peripheral, one metropolitan. It is, of course, no coincidence that the sexual pervert in the West connotes "dirtiness" and "baseness" within the same signifying economy that sees people of color and indigenous peoples as "base" and "sexually lascivious."[13] The "institution" is heterogeneous rather than either centrally ambivalent or irresolutely multiplicitous. This heterogeneity works racializing discourse and heterosexualizing discourse against, with, and through each other while at the same time maintaining these discourses as separate.

Barbin's position *within* metropolitan French society appears far removed from the colonial ventures of the French empire. But the colonial imaginary might simultaneously represent individuals "at home" as though these individuals were colonial "natives" within an expansive colonial regime of discipline. The transgender/ed who has effectively become perverted has also become unclean and therefore native. Herculine could well be part of a signifying chain that goes something like this: pervert-unclean-dirty-dark-native. This chain might well provide a simultaneous support for the maintenance of colonial practices and the growth of heteronormative institutions.

Mechanisms of sexual normalization are bound up in colonial structures of meaning. The institutional life of Barbin is a moment in the long history of the marriage of colonial and heteronormative power. (It seems like a never-ending ceremony.) But while reproducing mechanisms of power, it seems heterocolonial power might well have given birth to something else. The location of this something else in Barbin's life has the utmost importance. Foucault called it "the happy limbo of a non-identity." Butler calls it Barbin's "ambivalence." I think it has something to do with the undecideability of the transgender/ed body.

The body and "ambivalence" are associated terms in Butler's analysis.

[R]ather than understand h/er anomalous body as the cause of h/er desire, h/er trouble, h/er affairs and confession, we might read this body, *here fully textualized*, as a sign of an irresolvable ambivalence produced by the juridical discourse on univocal sex. (99; emphasis mine)

The psychic and the institutional have merged; discourses produce psychic phenomena. The space inside that was previously unknowable is caught in the effects of discourse that are institutional. What was inside is now open for analysis, perhaps because it is a gender/ed event.

This event is one in which the "subject" is "caught between" woman and man. This ambivalence is represented by Butler in the "fully textualized" [!] body of Barbin. This moment of the totally readable body functions as an unexpected hinge where the psychic gets transferred onto the surface of the body. Barbin's desperation and inner turmoil become the mechanism of h/er control and h/er final submission to the material: the corpse.

It remains to be seen exactly how the body has been rendered "fully" textual. Presumably Butler means that the "subject" only has knowledge of h/er body through discourse. The critic can only approach the body (of the "subject"/object) through discourse. For Butler, this is a full textuality. Butler's caution is astute: the critic must not assume a "body" *before* discourse. This doesn't mean, however, that the body doesn't *exceed* discourse. The difference is crucial: a "fully textualized" body is not the same as a body that is always already discursivized. Several questions appear on the horizon of Butler's assertion of full textualization. How can the body and the "subject" be documented and analyzed fully textually in ways that are impossible when the body remains irreducible to but engaged with discourse? What are the responsibilities of the critic to the infinite limit of the [transgender/ed] body and the discourses that it (dis)enables? Freudianism and gay liberationism are two opposing examples of these discourses. Butler's work as critic maintains and might well encourage a reading of the [transgender/ed] body as the seat of excess. Rather than read the [transgender/ed] body as "delinquent" (the word is Foucault's), uncontrolled and uncontrollable, I'd like to shift the critic's view of the [transgender/ed] landscape as Spivak suggests and plot discursive moments (such as Barbin's gender reassignment) "as confrontations rather than transition[s]." Barbin's body does not reside entirely outside of discourse: it is not the un-tamed other. Instead, her body marks the confrontation of heterogeneous discourses, any one of which hasn't "fully textualized" h/er body, despite their aims at doing exactly that. Neither the "other world" of the convent or h/er confrontation with authority during her gender reassignment in 1860 is Barbin. Similarly, h/er agency, however limited by death and h/er corpse, moves across the horizon of the convent, psychoanalysis and discipline. The history of legal gender reassignments, the subaltern history of the sisterhood of the convent—these institutional histories are not Barbin's psychoanalytical history. And a narrative of the moments of crisis and resolution between these different discourses would not be a total history. Nor would the sum of everything that exceeds be the total biography of Barbin.

(While Butler herself did not set out on an ethnography, she ends up attempting a comment on the psychobiography of an individual based on Foucault's reading of Herculine Barbin's journal and on the journal itself. This necessitates an ethnographic method: a theoretical practice of "subject"/object relations that has learned from its own critique. Necessary questions: What is the effect of attempting to render an oppressed body "fully textual"? There is an immense need in Butler's text to make the body transparent to/for the gaze. What is this thing, the body, that it needs to be made into something entirely textual? And, what is the difference between this [transgender/ed] body and the desire of the critic? The body has to be critically approached through but never reduced to discourse.)[14]

Barbin's ambivalence looks different now.

As does the suicide that it produced. According to Butler, Barbin's ambivalence was "a fatal ambivalence" (99). A centrally produced split between "subjection" and "defiance" formulates a "subject" in Barbin who lives to die. Power produces a "failed subject." (Is the "subject" anything else?) While biographizing Barbin requires dealing with the fact of h/er death, it also requires understanding h/er "subject" as something more historical and even substantive than h/er dead corpse. Hetero-juridical discourse can certainly be held responsible for Barbin's death, but the time of h/er life says something. H/er negotiation of sex-as-gender repeats a gender/ed life with difference. This difference has a [transgender/ed] history that marks an agency that is plainly not summed up by a gender/ed analysis of an institution or a psychoanalytical critique of power. The history of one domain contains the history of confrontations with other domains, but is not a precise mapping of any complete space or whole "subject."[15]

The goal is not a library of endlessly pluralized histories. The limits of pluralism are well enough known. Simply affirming a multiplicitous landscape would miss the point of Butler's critique. A brand of relativism is no more nuanced than Butler's all-consuming, ambivalence-breeding discourse. Chris Straayer has said that Butler's method "limits the 'imagination' of her theorization" (155). Butler's "worlding"[16] creates a world contained within one discourse; Straayer imagines not one discourse but many discourses—"Dominant" ones and "formative counterdiscourses" (155) all on a gender/ed terrain similar to the one I've described. Translating these counterdiscourses and creating a discussion between them is a necessary and critical project. In the rest of this chapter, I consider the [transgender/ed] "subject" engaging in the practice of translation. I intend this practice to have learned from history, but also to engage specifically with the boundaries, responsibilities, and "failures" of its and my own "worlding."

BODY FORCES

In her influential 1993 novel *Stone Butch Blues* Leslie Feinberg maps the life of Jess Goldberg. Born after World War II in upstate New York, Jess "didn't want to be different" (13). But early on, Jess figured out that s/he wasn't quite boy or girl. S/he runs away from home as h/er parent's scorn worsens and moves from one group of friends to another. Before venturing outside the authority of h/er parent's home, there is no word to describe how s/he feels, looks, is. Then, Jess discovers the community of the local (pre-Stonewall) gay bar. There s/he discovers the possibility of being a butch and owning h/er butch desire. S/he learns that the outside world will see h/er as "he-she," and those on the "inside" will know h/er as a butch. The plant closings and social changes of the sixties turn Jess's life upside down. S/he can no longer just get a job in a factory with other butches; economics force h/er to try passing. Similarly, the lesbian feminist activism that spreads out from college campuses calls the "patriarchal tendencies" of butch-femme sexuality into question and wrecks havoc on the lifestyle that Jess and h/er lover have. Jess leaves h/er home, h/er lover, and starts taking hormones. "I've seen about it on TV," Jess says. "I don't feel like a man trapped in a woman's body. I just feel trapped" (159). After several months without noticing a difference, one day Jess starts getting smiles from passersby instead of snarls and sneers. S/he is a man for all the world to see. After developing a few friendships with straight men, love relationships with straight women (in one such affair the straight woman never knows that Jess "fucks" her with a dildo instead of a "real dick") and working in factories as a man and not as a "bulldagger," Jess decides to stop taking hormones. Being perceived a man hadn't made h/er feel "real": "And then I knew I wasn't going home, I wasn't traveling backward. I was hurtling forward toward a destination I couldn't see" (223). After a year off hormones, Jess's body starts changing again. H/er hips widen, h/er beard grows "wispy and fine" and h/er face looks "softer." "I remembered what it was like to walk a gauntlet of strangers who stare—their eyes angry, confused, intrigued. Woman or man: they are outraged that I confuse them" (224). Jess then moves to New York City and, after several years of loneliness and hard living, befriends h/er redheaded neighbor Ruth, "who [is] different like me" (248). It is because of Ruth's friendship and the confidence it builds that Jess is able to travel back to Buffalo and reconnect with the past: the butch-femme community s/he had grown up in. When Jess goes to Buffalo, s/he finds out that Butch Al, one of the butches she respected most, has been institutionalized. Jess visits Al and begins to understand how Al had survived "by forgetting, going to sleep, going away! She went underground, hid for safety just as I'd done" (288). When Jess returns to New York, s/he emerges from a subway station and happens upon a rally for queer rights. Jess speaks from the stage and says that s/he has often been the outsider, defending h/erself alone because it's the only way s/he knows how to fight.

There's lots of us who are on the outside and we don't want to be.... We need you—but you need us, too. . . . I don't know what it would take to really change the world. But couldn't we get together and try to figure it out? Couldn't the *we* be bigger? (296)

With that broad, homogenizing stroke, the novel ends. This moment resonates with earlier ones in *Stone*. When Jess went to see an ob-gyn, the receptionist in the office assumed Jess was some freakish man. After Jess saw the doctor, the receptionist said, "You got what you wanted, now leave." "You're wrong," Jess responded. "I got what I needed. You have no idea how much I want" (236). These two moments share a powerful politics of reclamation. The latter is a response to a lifetime of being read the wrong way. The former announces a call for coalition.[17] It is this combination of registering the past and strategizing in the present that announces a new understanding of the relationship between the institutional and the psychic, identity and social location, or the personal and the political.

Both situations mentioned above imply a mathematics of the self that is one of the central problematics of *Stone Butch Blues*. In a fight with an old butch friend, Jess recollects that s/he "wanted butchness to be a quantity, not a quality, so I could out-butch her" (283). Perhaps Jess would like to be able to count the constitutive members of the coalitional "we," the items on the list of h/er wants or the prerequisites of butchness. All the problems in h/er life that come about politically (from interactions with "others") might come to an end if stock is taken and decisions are made. But this accounting consistently comes up short. A straight co-worker tells Jess in the midst of her transition (from perceived female to perceived male): "'You're already a man, you don't have to prove that. You just have to prove what kind of man you want to be'" (185). While this ethical negotiation applies specifically in the text to Jess's sense of h/erself as butch, it also applies to the constitution of the political "we." H/er position along the "man/ woman" continuum will not bring an end to h/er troubles. This positioning is in its turn determined by and determines h/er position along other spectrums–namely, race, nation, class, and sexuality. The "failure" of Jess's [transgender/ed] accounting marks the end of Jess's history. It marks the beginning of another history of another sort of negotiation. A mathematics of gender gives way to a performativity of gender, race, nation and class that forces Jess to continually reexamine h/er own responsibility, h/er own context and h/er own relationship to power in those contexts.[18]

TRANSGENDER/ED, TRANSNATIONAL, TRANSLATIONAL

It is precisely this performativity that Feinberg extends and uses to complicate the picture of transphobic violence. [Transgender/ed] "subjects" need to move outside of their communities and across national borders if coalition building is to be negotiated and worked. There is not one stage, but many.

Thinking Jess Goldberg in a transnational frame involves thinking race and thinking nation. Certainly the two—nation and race—are not synonymous, but the relationships between nations are often cut across by imperial relationships and legacies that have functioned largely through a hierarchization and race-ing of peoples, cultures and ethnicities. Distinct groups called races with distinct political systems called nations have interacted in the international arena. But the bulk of this chapter has so far attempted to consider the particular position of the "subject" who is at once subject to and different from the nation-state, especially the "subject" who defies the gender/ing of the nation. This "subject," then, is not a representative of the nation. The interaction between this "subject," whether s/he be Jess Goldberg or Herculine Barbin, and the "subject" of another nation-state is not an "international" one; it is, more precisely, a "transnational" one. This transnational relationship goes across national borders.

And those borders are often specifically racial. Unlike a lot of 1990's white U.S. queer literature, *Stone Butch Blues* actually takes up the issue of its own position in racial/ized hierarchies. The novel does not provide the perfect ethical moment, but it does provide at least three scenarios that position Jess as specifically white and specifically American gender freak: h/er stays with the immigrant family that lived across from h/er family during h/er childhood (13–15), h/er relationships with the Native American women s/he worked with in a factory during h/er life in the butch-femme community of Buffalo (75–80) and h/er friendship with a black butch—Ed—and their nights out at a black queer bar on "the other side of the tracks" (54–58). In all three scenes, Jess gets invited, in a sense, into specific communities of color because members of each community ask or encourage h/er to participate. In the factory populated largely by Native American women, Jess is asked to start the song that the women sing every morning at the beginning of their shift. At first s/he is unable.

"I can't," I protested. I felt near tears. No one said a word. They just kept working in silence. By lunchtime I realized there would be no songs until I began one. *Why?* I wondered. *Why are the women doing this to me? Are they making fun of me?* I knew it wasn't true. They noticed how quietly I mouthed the words to songs. They were inviting my voice to join theirs. They were honoring me again. (79)

Rather than safely and passively participate in the "native ritual" Jess feels "invited" to join in. Reading against the grain, it seems like Jess is obliged to participate. S/he transitions from passive (white) observer to markedly-different-but-active (white) ritual-member/observer. There is at least a two-way theorization of the "other." While Jess strategizes h/er involvement, the women do as well. After Jess is laid off, the women invite h/er to a party. The relationship between Jess and the native women is not limited entirely to the factory. While the novel never suggests an extended relationship among them after Jess leaves the factory, it remains a possibility.

This scene is not without its limits. Jess, an individual without community, is contrasted with the native women who have plurality and strength in numbers. One wonders what interest the native women have in Jess if they already have so many people around them. By telling the reader about h/er invitation to the party, Jess suggests more than just genuine friendship. Is Jess also the object of sympathy? Or maybe Jess is an object of desire for the women's different desires. Yvonne, the daughter of one of Jess's co-workers, "was the girlfriend of a local organized crime boss. That didn't stop us [Yvonne and Jess] from knowing where each other was in the room during those socials. I think all the women noticed right away" (78). If Yvonne has an individuated relationship with Jess, that means the other women do to. The space of the factory, like that of the gay bar and of the immigrant family's apartment, is one with many different desires. While Jess often re/presents her co-workers as a mass of people, Jess's storytelling also demassifies them and allows the reader the possibility of many desires.

These interactions take place within the geographical United States. But the presence of desires other than Jess's and the movement of intentions (such as those of the women in the factory) that make use of Jess—these conditions complicate the space of the nation. Jess's (white) desire for Yvonne is not alone; Yvonne also desires Jess. Jess wants to belong to a community like the native women's; the women undeniably have numerous reasons for "accepting" Jess. White and of color, straight and transgender/ed—these "subjectivities" are desirous at the same time and in the same place, in a zone of contest.

I think this desiring sphere of contest and identification can be read against a different national/ist conception of identification and contestation. In *Imagined Communities*, Benedict Anderson says that a new temporality—the "meanwhile" (24)—emerges with the nation. This "meanwhile," simply put, narrates an event (here) in nation A. "Meanwhile," another event occurs (there) in nation B. The two events influence each other just as histories of the past and visions of the future do. These other influences are just that: they do not have a hand in determining the distinct events in nations A and B.

Anderson's theory of national temporalities also describes a certain cartography of the nation and its other. On this map, the nation/self and the nation/self's other trade, interact, and fight. These interactions are all extensions of the self. The skin, as it were, of the (every) nation remains intact. The nation seems to learn, to nourish, and to survive through perception rather than absorption or consumption.

While this epistemology of nation, identity, and citizen works throughout *Stone Butch Blues*, there is another movement of identification and citizenship. The "subjects" and citizens of different communities and nations speak to and recognize each other within the boundaries of the *same* space (factory, bar, apartment) that means *differently* for each of them. This space is neither here nor there; nor is it neither. The borderlines that appeared to fully separate each nation one from the other now seem to seep and give way, but they do not disappear.

In her essay "Querying Globalization," J. K. Gibson-Graham[19] analyzes this metaphor of seepage and infection. It is usually used to describe capitalism and transnational corporations (TNCs) as infectious agents and the Third World nations and communities as victims and the infected/afflicted. But Gibson-Graham wonders just why this contagion is almost always represented as one way.

Her argument begins with a look at Sharon Marcus's attempt to rethink the "rape script." For Gibson-Graham, both rape and globalization are wound up in a scripting that is both undeniable and inevitable. She describes a reality in which "'rape has always already occurred and women are always either already raped or already rapable'" (Gibson-Graham 2).[20] Capitalism, like men, has the ability to spread and invade. Capitalism is represented as *inherently spatial* and as naturally stronger than the forms of noncapitalist economy (traditional economies, "Third World" economies, socialist economies, communal experiments) because of its presumed capacity to universalize the market for capitalist commodities (5; emphasis mine).

This script figures everything outside of capitalist economics "as inevitably and only ever sites of potential invasion/envelopment/accumulation" (6).

"One of the powerful things about rape in our culture is that it represents an important *inscription* of female sexual identity" (13; Gibson-Graham's emphasis). But this inscription can be met with other inscriptions that understand the power *and* limits of the globalization script. "The script of globalization need not draw solely upon an image of the body of capitalism as hard, thrusting, and powerful" (17). While it penetrates, invades, and impregnates, it also leaks. Its seed is malleable. It is also subject to infection. Both capitalism and heterosexuality are invested in preserving the script that figures the woman as always already raped.

Challenging this representation might "get globalization to lose its erection" (7). Gibson-Graham proposes two strategies for changing the globalization-as-rape script. One involves correcting the conventional narrative of globalization. The body of the TNC is not impenetrable; it is susceptible to infection. The companies that are globalizing are not as large as they seem. Gibson-Graham uses the term "'multinational' because it suggests that the corporation is subject to the jurisdiction of several nations, whereas 'transnational' implies transcendence of national jurisdiction" (7 n9). These companies are usually only "bi- or at the most quatrinational in their scale of production" (8) and are limited by the policies of the nations in which they operate. There are other nodal points of power that can be used to resist globalization and exploitation. The state, the labor union, communities—these are all examples of institutions that can launch a counternarrative to challenge the globalization script.

By defining the agents of globalization, though, as subject to the power of the nation, Gibson-Graham limits her own argument by describing, on a grand scale, a historical moment in which nations with loyal citizens oppose TNCs. The nation certainly had and often still has a moral and political power to limit the movements of subjects and corporations. By appealing to the nation as an impediment to globalization, though, Gibson-Graham references a "meanwhile." Pushing her argument a bit, it becomes possible to see that the border-crossing and sex-switching "subject" is "subjected" to more than one institution, whether it be the nation, the community, the family, or the union. The agency of this "subject" is determined by and responsive to more than one authority. The border is not so impermeable; the citizen is not so dependent on the nation alone.

S/he moves within a historical time significantly different from the "meanwhile" of nationalism. This leads Gibson-Graham to ask, "Could we not see multinational corporate activity in Third World situations in a slightly different light, as perhaps sometimes unwittingly generative rather than merely destructive?" (10)? Could we not see the citizen as different from and bound to the authority of the institution? S/he is subject to specific communities within and between nations, to corporations, and to epistemologies that are grounded in and make sense of these contexts.

The position of the nation, which has so often been identified as "woman," is no longer subject to the (neo)colonial powers. Nor is it solely the mouthpiece of its supposed husband, the TNC. The dynamic of "advanced country" to "less developed country" (LDC) is no longer a heteronormative couple: man and wife. Nor, heeding Gibson-Graham's call, is the TNC the new bridegroom of the nation. *He* is not all that potent. *She* may not be so womanly, after all. It is in this transnational context that the [transgender/ed] "subject" has been "discovered" by western, queer communities.

How does "gay liberation" signify in this mapping of transnational power? There is certainly no quick and easy political program that arises from the compli-cated relations between queers in the materially flooded first world and "queers" and gender outlaws in a "Third World" that functions alternately as a resource bin and a tourist depot for the West. M. Jacqui Alexander contends that "[t]he [neo-colonial] state actively socializes loyal heterosexual citizens into tourism, its pri-mary strategy of economic modernization by sexualizing them and positioning them as commodities" (69). At the same time, however, advanced-capitalist states such as the U.S. might well rely on this heterosexualization of neocolonial citizens at the same time that it liberalizes its own state practices to accommodate the economic collateral and capital power of middle-class United States (white) gay men. Spivak's statement for England of the nineteenth century translates well to this context: "[I]mperialism, understood as England's social mission, was a crucial part of the cultural representation of England to the English" ("Three Women's Texts" 243). An advanced capitalist state might well use its lesbian and gay tourists/citizens as capitalist missionaries while at the same time allowing the neocolonial state to use this sexual tourism as evidence of the licentiousness of neocolonial citizens.

What are the heterosexist U.S. national interests of contemporary liberal affirmations of "gay marriage," the "gay family," and "'gays' in the military"? With these three assimilationist strategies, advocates say "we" will still be able to "do what we do." The important thing is that "we" get to do "it" anywhere and under any banner or institution. It could be argued that this is an infection like those that Gibson-Graham theorizes, and that accepting marriage, family, and patriotic duty are negotiations at the border between "het" and "homo" culture. In accepting the names/signifiers "marriage" and "family" as the practices/signifies "queer rela-tionships" and "queer bonds and social ties," it could be argued that queers are neologistically changing the modes of sexual reproduction. But, one has to won-der, what is so new?

The missionary position of these three rights-claims—making (queer) babies for the country and the economy—is so transparent. The discourses of "gay marriage," "gay family," and "gays in the military" have this position encoded within them. This intersection between nationalist and liberationist discourses presses the viability of any movement for sexual liberation. Especially if it has any hope of moving across borders.

What remains doubly erased and disciplined here is the sexual autonomy of the transnational citizen. According to Gibson-Graham, resisting this erasure of the possibility of agency involves calling the bluff of the globalization-as-rape script. It also involves telling new stories. These stories make "room for the penetration of globalization/capitalism by the local. Localization, it seems, [has often been figured as] not so much 'other' to globalization as contained within it, brought into being by it, indeed part of globalization itself" (24). But these local resistances needs to be—must be—weaved into a narrative that revises "the concept of location, stressing and stretching the 'original' meaning in working toward more progressive practices of transnational cultural politics" (Kaplan 148). As Caren Kaplan asserts, the local must be retold in the form of a narrative that links locations, shows their embroidery, and refuses to be localized. "Such a revision of critical practice produces the grounds for a rejection of unitary feminism [and queer politics] in favor of solidarity and coalitions that are not based on mystified notions of similarity or difference" (148).

Notice how this narrative doesn't create a chain of equivalents in the form of "straight marriage is queer relationship so queer relationship is straight marriage." Instead of equivalents there are equivalences. The former is resigned to the past where A and B met and became the same thing. The latter is a present-tense gerund. It is a moment of two things coming together and equaling. It doesn't imply a predestined encounter or a necessary future marriage of the two terms. It is a moment of translation where A and B are strategically read as the same by a critical "subject." It is a reading across a border, a *trans*-lation, which does not equal.

Trans- is across national borders, is across epistemologies of gender, and is involved in translating from language to language. It is the movement of ideas, "subjects," and work (both economic and political) across borders that are already gender/ed, racialized, nationalized, and capitalized. Discourses of nationalism have so often been invested in maintaining the purity of "Mother England" or "Mother India" that the [transgender/ed] "subject" has had to resist that puritanical authority along with the rape-scripted violence of the transnational corporation.

Herculine Barbin, in Butler's analysis, falls prey to a central splitting between the two faces of heteronormative authority: the prohibition and production of deviancy. This renders all h/er actions futile. There is no "happy limbo of a non-identity." S/he kills h/erself or is killed by this position between articulations of power. But I have stressed the counterhistory implicit in Barbin's not-necessarily-fatal attempt to make a viable "subject"-position at the border. S/he did not always live in the interstice, the space between. Instead, s/he moved across that space, into production and prohibition. It is a space not unlike the scenarios in *Stone Butch Blues* where desiring and intrusive native American women shift from massified to individuated. These are moments of serious play where different, dare I say new, configurations of subject/other relations negotiate the so-called "public sphere."

Herculine Barbin's last journal entries suggest a person wanting to get on with h/er life as a "man." This life is stopped short by the kindness of people from h/er past, the ignorance of h/er mother and the reminiscences of life as a "woman." H/er past haunts her/m. It holds her/m back; it gives her/m life. It is the history of h/er body, the [gender/ed] memories neither wholly below the skin nor on h/er flesh that fill the final pages of h/er journal. Butler collapses this sentimental rememoration into a spatial "ambivalence." I think we can purposefully see Barbin's "ambivalence" as spatial and temporal. H/er historical identifications and shifting alliances are the "subject" of this [transgender/ed] history and the agenda of this feminist historiography.

NOTES

1. I completed this chapter while studying at the New School for Social Research. I'd like to thank Amitabh S. Rai, Ph.D., for inspiration, criticism, and instruction. I'd like to thank Joby Gelbspan for turning me on to the finer points of nuance, and the Gibson-Graham essay. Finally, I'd like to thank Michael Auerbach just because.

2. See *Gender Reversals and Gender Cultures: Anthropological and Historical Perspectives*, edited by Sabrina Petra Ramet; Serena Nanda's *Neither Man nor Woman: The Hijras of India*; Lady Chablis's *Hiding My Candy: The Autobiography of the Grand Empress of Savannah*; and Leslie Feinberg's *Transgender Warriors: Making History from Joan of Arc to Dennis Rodman.*

3. I use "hegemony" here in the sense that Antonio Gramsci developed. He opposes "hegemony" to "direct domination," the former being exercised by "the dominant group . . . throughout society" and the latter pertaining more to "command exercised through the State." "Hegemony" operates through "consent" given by the "great masses of the population to the general direction imposed on social life by the dominant fundamental group; this consent is historically caused by the prestige (and consequent confidence) which the dominant group enjoys because of its position and function within the world of production" (12).

4. Following Martin Heidegger, Jacques Derrida puts words "under erasure" (*sous rature*) to demonstrate not only "the arbitrariness of the sign" that designates a concept such as "subject," but also the necessity of using the sign ("subject") to discuss the concept's inadequacy (*Of Grammatology* 44–65).

5. Foucault spends the introductory pages of this essay differencing *Herkunft* from *Ursprung*, two words Nietzsche uses in *The Genealogy of Morals. Herkunft* contains the sense of "family" and "descent," "tradition" as well as "irresistability." It is driven, but not quite determined. With this meditation in mind, I translate *Herkunft* as "historical" (83).

6. Myra Jehlen uses this phrase, drawn from "histories of difference," to mean the "territory whose contours are sketched as overlappings rather than boundaries, a terrain of mediations and equally of confrontations" (57). The body, understood in this way, is an object of control. It represents a territory to be conquered, dominated, managed.

7. "The panoptic mechanism arranges spatial utilities that make it possible to see constantly and to recognize immediately" (Foucault, *Discipline* 200). The prisoner in the panopticon, understood here "as a generalizable model of [social] functioning" (205) "is the object of information, never a subject in communication" (200). How can the critic

understand h/erself within this "functioning" while imagining *other* functionings and practicing the difference? Can the critic do so with Butler's theory?

8. Moya's essay responds to both Judith Butler's and Donna Haraway's uses of Cherrìe Moraga in their work and then, most significantly, constructs what Moya calls a "realist" theory of identity. This "realism" that Moya theorizes, I think, is informed by contemporary (postmodern) debates about "reality" and its contingency. Moya's "realist theory" claims the right to decide what is "real."

9. This phrase is borrowed in sense from Sagri Dhairyam's critique of recent queer theory:

"'Queer theory has come increasingly to be reckoned with as a critical discourse, but *concomitantly writes a queer whiteness over raced queerness*; it domesticates race in its elaboration of sexual difference" (26; italics mine).

10. Foucault switches pronouns haphazardly in what I can only assume is a comment on Barbin's "sexual non-identity" (*Herculine* xiv). My pronoun-ciations mark the transgender/ed "subject" consistently as both (genders, sexes) and as neither.

11. Foucault sparingly refers to "colonization" or colonialism in *Discipline and Punish,* or in his work more generally for that matter. See pages 29, 231, 279, and 314n1 of *Discipline.*

12. I am indebted to the work of Ernesto Laclau and Chantal Mouffe for an understanding of the politics of necessity and the structures of fields of discursivity. See *Hegemony and Socialist Strategy,* especially pages 93–148.

13. Diana Fuss brilliantly explores this relatedness in a critique of Freud's homo*phobia* and colonialist sentiments in his *Totem and Taboo* and *Group Psychology and the Analysis of the Ego.* See *Identification Papers,* 32–46.

14. As an aside, Naomi Schor has also been "authorized" ("By whom?" is an exceptional question) to enter Barbin and determine h/er life. In an endnote Schor says that Barbin "did not write her memoirs as a man because she never adjusted to her belated masculine identity" (274–75 n11). Schor goes on to refer to Herculine Barbin (the chosen name of the "subject" of the memoirs) as Herculine-Abel and as "him." It is interesting that these masculinizing and terrorizing moments shift according to Schor's reclamations and disavowals of Barbin as a feminist "subject."

15. A history is domain-bound (if we have learned from Moya's critique); it marks "functional changes in sign-systems" (Spivak, "Subaltern" 197) that occur as moments of contact and destabilization between different domains.

16. The word is Spivak's. I vulgarize it to mean the inscription of meaning "upon what must be assumed to be uninscribed earth." Spivak remarks that her "worlding of the world" is a vulgarization of an idea of Martin Heidegger from "The Origin of the Work of Art" ("Three Women's" 260 n1).

17. It is interesting to ask how this vision of coalition (mis)matches Butler's own vision of coalitional politics. The two might well be read together, forming a theoretical practice: "It would be wrong to assume in advance that there is a category of 'women' that simply needs to be filled in with various components of [difference] in order to become complete" (Butler 15).

18. The butch experience, as Feinberg lays it out, often requires an understanding of the power differentials between men and women, among men and among women. When Jess's friend tells her, "you just have to prove what kind of man you want to be," he also confesses that he was raped in prison. Jess understands h/er own power against his vulnerability. Similarly, a butch having sex with a femme involves a nuanced understanding of vulnerability and power differentials that "natural men" might not have, as Jess's

straight girlfriend points out (192–93). These masculinities would never be appropriate as such in front of "the law."

19. J.K. Gibson-Graham is a pseudonym for two authors: J. Gibson and K. Graham. Since the article uses a singular pronoun to refer to the two authors, I do the same.

20. By inhabiting, altering, and extending Marcus's argument, Gibson-Graham deconstruct—in the best possible way—the globalization and rape scripts alike.

WORKS CITED

Alexander, M. Jacqui. "Erotic Autonomy as a Politics of Decolonization." In: *Feminist Genealogies, Colonial Legacies, Democratic Futures*, edited by M. Jacqui Alexander and Chandra Talpade Mohanty. New York: Routledge, 1997. 63–100.

Anderson, Benedict. *Imagined Communities: Reflections on the Origin and Spread of Nationalism*. London: Verso, 1983.

Butler, Judith. *Bodies that Matter: On the Discursive Limits of "Sex."* New York: Routledge, 1993. ix–xii.

———. *Gender Trouble: Feminism and the Subversion of Identity*. New York: Routledge, 1990.

Derrida, Jacques. *Of Grammatology*, translated by Gayatri Chakravorty Spivak. Baltimore: Johns Hopkins University Press, 1974.

Dhairyam, Sagri. "Racing the Lesbian, Dodging White Critics." In: *The Lesbian Postmodern*, edited by Laura Doan. New York: Columbia University Press, 1994. 25–46.

Feinberg, Leslie. *Stone Butch Blues*. Ithaca: Firebrand, 1993.

———. *Transgender Warriors: Making History from Joan of Arc to Dennis Rodman*. Boston: Beacon Press, 1997.

Foucault, Michel. *Discipline and Punish: The Birth of the Prison*, translated by Alan Sheridan. New York: Vintage, 1995.

———. Introduction. *Herculine Barbin, Being the Recently Discovered Memoirs of a Nineteenth-Century French Hermaphrodite*, translated by Richard McDougall. New York: Pantheon, 1980. vii–xvii.

———. "Nietzsche, Genealogy, History," translated by Donald F. Bouchard and Sherry Simon. In: *The Foucault Reader,* edited by Paul Rabinow. New York: Pantheon, 1984. 76–100.

———. "Truth and Power," translated by Alessandro Fontana and Pasquale Pasquino. In: *Power/Knowledge: Selected Interviews and Other Writings: 1972–1977,* edited by Colin Gordon. New York: Pantheon, 1980. 109–33.

Fuss, Diana. *Identification Papers*. New York: Routledge, 1995.

Gibson-Graham, J. K. "Querying Globalization." *Rethinking Marxism* 9.1 (Spring 1996/ 1997): 1–27.

Gramsci, Antonio. *Selections from the Prison Notebooks*, translated by Quintin Hoare and Geoffrey Nowell Smith. New York: International Publishers, 1995.

Homans, Margaret. "'Women of Color' Writers and Feminist Theory." *New Literary History* 25 (1994): 73–94.

Jehlen, Myra. "Why Did the Europeans Cross the Ocean: A Seventeenth-Century Riddle." In: *Cultures of United States Imperialism,* edited by Amy Kaplan and Donald E. Prose. Durham: Duke University Press, 1993. 41–58.

Kaplan, Caren. "The Politics of Location as Transnational Feminist Critical Practice." In:

Scattered Hegemonies: Postmodernity and Transnational Feminist Practices, edited by Inderpal Grewal and Caren Kaplan. Minneapolis: University of Minnesota Press, 1994. 137–152.

Laclau, Ernesto, and Chantal Mouffe. *Hegemony and Socialist Strategy: Towards a Radical Democratic Politics*. New York: Verso, 1985.

Lady Chablis with Theodore Bouloukos. *Hiding My Candy: The Autobiography of the Grand Empress of Savannah*. New York: Pocket Books, 1996.

Michie, Elsie B. *Outside the Pale: Cultural Exclusion, Gender Difference, and the Victo rian Woman Writer*. Ithaca: Cornell University Press, 1993.

Moya, Paula. "Postmodernism, 'Realism,' and the Politics of Identity: Cherrie Moraga and Chicana Feminism." In: *Feminist Genealogies, Colonial Legacies, Democratic Futures,* edited by M. Jacqui Alexander and Chandra Talpade Mohanty. New York: Routledge, 1997. 125–50.

Nanda, Serena. *Neither Man nor Woman: The Hijras of India*. Belmont, Calif.: Wadsworth, 1990.

Ramet, Sabrina Petra, ed. *Gender Reversals and Gender Cultures: Anthropological and Historical Perspectives*. New York: Routledge, 1996.

Roediger, David. *The Wages of Whiteness: Race and the Making of the American Working Class*. New York: Verso, 1991.

Rubin, Gayle. "The Traffic in Women: Notes on the 'Political Economy' of Sex." In: *The Second Wave: A Reader in Feminist Theory,* edited by Linda Nicholson. New York: Routledge, 1997. 27–62.

Schor, Naomi. "Dreaming Dissymmetry: Barthes, Foucault, and Sexual Difference." In: *Men in Feminism,* edited by Alice Jardine and Paul Smith. New York: Routledge, 1987. 98–110.

Spivak, Gayatri Chakravorty. "Subaltern Studies: Deconstructing Historiography." In: *In Other Worlds: Essays in Cultural Politics*. New York: Routledge, 1987. 197–221.
———. Three Women's Texts and a Critique of Imperialism." *Critical Inquiry* 12 (1985): 243–61.

Stoler, Ann Laura. *Race and the Education of Desire: Foucault's* History of Sexuality *and the Colonial Order of Things*. Durham: Duke University Press, 1995.

Straayer, Chris. "Transgender/ed Mirrors: Queering Sexual Difference." In: *Queer Representations: Reading Lives, Reading Cultures,* edited by Martin Duberman. New York: New York University Press, 1997. 146–61.

Afterword

In the Preface we suggested that our book might point out some of the characteristics of a "postgay" world, by which we meant a world in which the western
notion of fairly strictly binary sexual expression had been called into question.
The subsequent chapters explored related questions and studied social and cultural implications of the ongoing interrogation. The need for such examinations
has become increasingly clear in recent years. Annamarie Jagose, for example,
elsewhere describes the "denaturalisation of gender" as "perhaps the most compelling connection between [gay] liberationist and later queer theories" (43). But
the glue maintaining such a connection remains of dubious value for some. Jagose's
view, after all, is a subtle (and disturbing?) observation that offers a challenge to
"traditional" gays and lesbians. Steven Seidman underscores the attendant controversy in his history of the movement from the *solidarity* of identity (expressed
in gay and lesbian rights groups) to the politics of *difference* (expressed in queer
theory). Seidman describes the challenge to the dominance of the "ethnic" model,
with its emphasis on a "unitary gay identity," as having arisen in three major sites
which he describes as "battles around race, bisexuality, and 'nonconventional
sexualities'" (1997: 121). The impetus this has offered to the emergence of queer
theory becomes clear in his discussion of *Bi Any Other Name: Bisexual People
Speak Out*, in which Lorraine Hutchins and Lani Kaahumanu had "criticize[d] the
gay culture for perpetuating a sexual code that privileges gender preference as
definitive of sexual identity and that assumes individuals neatly fold into heterosexual or homosexual selves" (Seidman 124). Well, don't they?

Queer theory suggests they do not, and this book adds to the mix the issues
arising in postcoloniality as further interrogation of the "essentialist" view of
gender and sexuality. As unsettling as many gays and lesbians find it to be, this
destabilization may also offer a helpful entrée to the "postcolonial" challenge to
western psychology and politics. " 'To queer,' " as Peter Brooker notes, "is to

estrange or defamiliarize identities, texts and attitudes which are taken for granted and assumed to have fixed meanings." By this logic, "queer theory is not therefore a separatist movement claiming an essence of gayness. Rather, it emphasizes the constructedness, plurality and ambivalence of sexual identities" (182). Brooker notes that postcolonial theory similarly offers "a recognition of difference and a common anti-essentialist notion of identity and cultural meaning" and "a shared critique of the cultural hierarchies, universalism and Eurocentrism of Western modernity" (170). Thus, queer theory may productively "defamiliarize" for the West the sexualities of postcolonial countries, as those sexualities may challenge western notions of gay/straight in a number of productive ways.

In short, the advocates of a social constructionist view of sexuality prefer the term "queer" and characterize a more essentialist view of homosexuality as representing an arrest of full sexual expression in its many, and *changing*, forms. Such constructionists can look to the emerging world for evidence (direct or analogical) of their theories. Frank Browning writes, for example, of "the social meanings of sexuality," "the malleability of sexual identities" (vii), and speaks of "enjoying multiple desires in multiple ways" (4). He asks, "Why do we resist the idea that the sexuality we each contain has many forms, the exploration of which can reveal the many faces of our flesh and spirit?" (4). For committed gay and lesbian political activists this may sound a bit like latter-day flower power (be free, free, *free*); conversely, queer radicals criticize older gays for having successfully assimilated into mainstream society and become very much like Ozzie and Harriet—with the few "eccentricities" that did not find a place on *The Truman Show* or the streets of *Pleasantville*. There's still the picket fence. With respect to our book, the real bite of Browning's argument becomes clear when he notes that "the American gay movement is only that—an American movement that owes its form and direction to peculiarly American experience and tradition. . . . [and we have now] come to realize that sexual behavior is not an unvarying force of history, that the way human beings experience one another in the flesh is subject to other forms of economy, social mobility, aesthetic style, spiritual mission, and political generosity" (6). This is an insight that undergirds many of the chapters in this book, expressing itself in the variegation in self-declaration that moves from one writer to the next.

The economic component of sexual identity implied in Browning's remarks may not seem immediately evident, but various writers show the nexus. To this end, Sinfield remarks that urban centers have been crucial in the definition of "the" gay and lesbian identity. In his view "post-Stonewall" gay culture is quite specific to "the metropolitan sex-gender system," tied in very much to "the global centres of capital" (1998: 6), and therefore allows many "gays" and "lesbians" to fall through the cracks in such a narrowly yuppified world. For those without access to capitalistic power, who may in fact be in the United States but be ethnic minorities and/or recent immigrants, "*gay has been a constraint*" rather than a term of liberation (7). Citing Cherríe Moraga and Gloria Anzaldúa as examples, Sinfield argues that for many members of racial minorities a metropolitan gay desire to begin life afresh by breaking away from one's family and traditional religion is really not an attractive (or even culturally possible) option.

At the same time, many within the *queer* movement argue along with Sinfield that essentialist definitions, while politically compelling, lack radical analysis: "By inviting us to perceive ourselves as settled in our sexuality, the ethnicity-and-rights model [propounded by *gay* political activists] releases others ["straights," for example] from the invitation to re-envision theirs." This, so the argument goes, is selling human potential short, since "widening the relevance of dissident sexuality was one goal of 'Queer Nation'" (20). An effect of the queer movement and of the ongoing reflections and self-definitions of such writers as Sinfield and Browning, therefore, is an increasingly multivalent examination of the variegation in sexual expression within any culture, and even, it is suggested, within any individual.

Anthropologist Gilbert Herdt warns western readers against their probable "penchant for dualisms and binary oppositions" (1997: 5), and asks how an observer of other cultures might be expected to "describe the lifeways of people who engage in homoerotic relations in the absence of the very idea of homosexuality" (4). For him,

there is no single word or construct, including the western idea of "homosexuality," that represents them all. . . . [But] their desires and actions make it clear from the perspectives of today that no matter what they have called themselves or the names they have been called, their desiring and loving the same gender are vital parts of their lives. (3, 8)

A modest conclusion, indeed, by western gay political standards. But Herdt also goes on to remark that queer theory argues that "history and culture descriptions are never distinguishable from the authors and assumptions of normality through which subjects or objects are described" (9). Queers, in other words, choose to criticize *any* definition of normalcy; they deconstruct socially constructed sexual norms; they necessarily include among their targets characteristics that writers from the gay and lesbian world espouse as definitive of the "normal" *gay*.

In moving from one chapter to the next, readers will quickly observe that we have approached a variety of topics under this broad theoretical framework but have not always come to the same conclusions. This is a developing and often contentious field of endeavor and its practitioners are in flux; some contributors to the book would not actually consider themselves queer theorists, perhaps not gay or lesbian, but fascinated by the possibilities opened up by the challenges one field offers the other. When this is coupled to postcolonial issues, economics joins hands with psychology and jumps loudly into the middle of the pool. To recap the results:

Dennis Altman's chapter, "Global Gaze / Global Gays," originally appeared in *GLQ* 3 (1997). Noting that western lesbian/gay theorists and activists are beginning to perceive the problems of claiming a universality for an identity that developed out of certain historical specificities, he sets the terms for the questions addressed in subsequent chapters. But Altman argues that American queer theory remains as relentlessly Atlantic-centric in its view of the world as the mainstream culture it critiques. He finds equally intriguing the nonwestern world's apparent lack of interest in queer theory, and the continued usage of the terminology "lesbian" and "gay" by emerging political movements in the Third World. The question, for him, is how to balance the impact of universalizing rhetoric and styles with the continuing existence of cultural and social traditions. He wonders how gay identities will change as Asians recuperate western images and bend them to their own purposes, and he argues that within a given country, whether Indonesia or the United States, Thailand or Italy, the *range* of constructions of homosexuality is growing. Weaving into this tapestry is the fact that in the past two decades there has emerged a definable group who see themselves as part of a global community, whose commonalities override but do not deny those of race and nationality.

The chapters that follow offer site-specific examples of the issues that Altman analyzes from a broadly sociological and political perspective. In "The Perfect Path: Gay Men, Marriage, Indonesia," for example, an article that also appeared in *GLQ* (5.4 [1999]: 475–509), Thomas Boellstorff responds to Altman by using the lesbian, gay, and bisexual movement in Indonesia as a source of theory. With it he develops an "archipelagic" framework for understanding the emergence of lesbian, gay, and bisexual identities in postcolonial societies. From this Indonesian national overview we move to Elizabeth Guzik's intriguing analysis of "another installment in the progression of murderous dyke films," moving the discussion of globalization into the "virtual" world. Guzik's chapter, "The Queer Sort of Fandom for *Heavenly Creatures*': The Closeted Indigene, Lesbian Islands and New Zealand National Cinema," questions the appropriation of national sexual stories (in this case, New Zealand's) by a set of fans connected throughout the world by Internet (but found principally in the United States). The resultant decontextualization is reversed in Guzik's chapter, a postcolonial study of the limitations inherent in global "translations."

The peculiarities of the local amid the global (or the so-called "glocal") manifest themselves in Benzi Zhang's chapter. In Chinese culture the representation of violence is particularly difficult and often characterized by silence, elisions, and ambiguities; rape and homosexuality are part of the "unspeakable" reality that lacks concrete representation in cultural forms. In "Im/De-position of Cultural Violence: Reading Chen Kaige's *Farewell My Concubine*" Zhang analyzes this situation and the dissent it evokes. With reference to Althusser, Bhabha, Craig Owens, and Catherine MacKinnon, he analyzes this breakthrough film as a metaphorical attempt to respond to the Cultural Revolution by portraying homosexuals and victims of rape, excluded from representation by its very structure, returning within it as a figure for—a representation of—the unrepresentable. In so doing, Zhang reminds readers of the great disparity in the "progress" made in sexual rights in various countries in the emerging world. In the process, recent anti-Orientalism and subaltern critiques of colonial, postcolonial, and neocolonial historiography elide the powerful dynamics of interracial desires of same-sex. Liang-Ya Liou's subsequent chapter, "Gender Crossing and Decadence in Taiwanese

Fiction at the Fin de Siecle," demonstrates that there is a markedly more visible treatment of these topics in Taiwan. In her analysis of recent fiction by Li Ang, Chu Tien-Wen, Chiu Miao-jin, and Cheng Ying-Shu she notes the prevalence of sexual topics in works rewarded not only with popularity but also with significant literary awards.

If "nation" provided a common theme for the first chapters, "race"—an increasingly contentious term—forms a nexus for the three that follow. The importance of film and performance studies alluded to by Guzik and Zhang takes center stage in "Racial and Erotic Anxieties: Ambivalent Fetishization, From Fanon to Mercer." Here, Sonia Otalvaro-Hormillosa explores contemporary critical theories on the intersection of race and sexuality that have been inspired by the work of Frantz Fanon. While admiring his work and its influence, however, Otalvaro-Hormillosa notes the lack of an in-depth analysis of the subjectivity of the woman of color in Fanon's work. In her view, this failing is perpetuated in contemporary racialized queer discourse, which is dictated by black-and-white binary systems of thought, such as in the work of authors like Kobena Mercer and Isaac Julien. Her chapter calls for new ways of writing and thinking about racial and sexual fluidity that occurs in the gray areas that have been neglected and overlooked by what she describes as hegemonic discourses on race and sexuality. Where Otalvaro-Hormillosa stresses gender in her discussion of race, James N. Brown and Patricia M. Sant emphasize class distinctions. In their chapter, "Race, Class and the Homoerotics of *The Swimming-Pool Library*," they use the theories of Deleuze and Guattari to demonstrate the interconnectedness of imperialism, capitalism, and class in historical imaginings of "the other" by westerners. In continuing the discussion of race, Ian Barnard emphasizes economics, both testing queer theory's limits and suggesting its possible future interrelations with anticolonial work. He does so by analyzing three social forces: 1) gendered nationalist identifications and relations between the United States and South Africa, 2) the various trajectories of U.S. imperialism, and 3) the production of gay identity through specifically *gay* U.S. imperialism. In "The U.S. in South Africa: (Post)Colonial Queer Theory?" he cites South African gay pornographic videos that narrativize a whitewashed face of gay South Africa (in stark contrast to the history of queer organizing in South Africa) and of gayness in general. The chapter, in sum, critiques paternalistic notions of gay and lesbian "progress."

The next three chapters are intense applications of queer theory to specific texts. David William Foster's "Other and Difference in Richard Rodriguez's *Hunger of Memory*" brings the critique a bit closer to "home." He begins by discriminating between a "gay" reading of a text and a queer reading. The former is here eschewed and the latter embraced as one that disrupts the binary imperative, the norm of compulsory heterosexuality, and the negation of identity difference, sexual or otherwise. What is examined here is the importance of Rodriguez's text in Chicano literature as one that stakes out the enduring importance of difference and the contestation of overdetermined ideologies of social construction—a queering of both the private *and* the public text. Christian Gundermann, in turn, offers a complex criticism of the uses of gay primitivism, noting Gide's appropriation of an exoticized Arabia. In "Reclaiming Postcolonial Gay Interiority After Bersani's Reading of Gide," he reads Bersani's "Gay Outlaw" (which he describes as making a problematic claim to anticolonialist politics) and Earl Jackson's "Strategies of Deviance" with and against the ethnographic writings of the German gay writer Hubert Fichte. Arguing against Jackson's and Bersani's celebration of gay sexuality as the expression of an "ex-timate" subjectivity, and against their "ethics of in-difference" (which Bhabha also finds appealing), the chapter raises the question not so much of a "general" compatibility or incompatibility of postcolonial and queer paradigms, but argues against the construction of a certain "self-less" subject (denying their power and violence?) in the interface of prominent postcolonial and queer theories. We conclude with Erich De Wald's equally difficult "Theorizing the 'Under-Theorized,'" which might be viewed as a further "self"-critique of contemporary queer theory's potentially colonizing impulse. By bringing together three texts by Judith Butler, Leslie Feinberg, and J. K. Gibson-Graham he describes the ways that white, Euro-American, heterosexist privilegings are bound up in theoretical methods that (inaccurately) characterize themselves as objective description. In a complex and suggestive discussion of the life of Herculine Barbin, an intersex/ed person living in France in the middle of the nineteenth century, and of the analysis of her treatment and that of others by queer theorists, De Wald undercuts notions of postmodern hybridity and of theorizing the so-called "under-theorized." In the process, his chapter forms something of an *aria da capo* with Altman's.

We have tried to heed the caution underscored by anthropologists like Gilbert Herdt: constantly contextualize, and recognize one's own context. We cannot have offered a comprehensive view of the issues under discussion; nor, for that matter, do we mean to imply that there is anything but a family resemblance among some of the site-specific examples. Nonetheless, our hope is that we have managed to sample a rich and suggestive body of experience from the viewpoints of compatible disciplines and theoretical approaches. The rich diversity of this collection recalls the complex narrator of Timothy Mo's *The Redundancy of Courage*. Adolph Ng, self-identified as a "Chinese pansy," operates a hotel in a fictionalized version of East Timor. Indonesia is about to invade. "Again," he writes, "I had the sensation of being an invulnerable witness inhabiting a third dimension" (Mo 7). That third dimension in which he hangs suspended is shaped not only by his unacceptable sexuality but also by his own unacceptable (non-Malay) ethnicity. But his life has been rendered *most* bewildering to him by the role the West has played in it. On the one hand, his earlier education in Toronto had suggested the possibility of a life of sexual license that he does not find available to him at home; but on the other hand, he has inescapably seen, as well, that the West supports the extension of Indonesian hegemony—the very power that is crushing his smaller society. In such a world, can the *queer* subaltern speak? Can a Chinese pansy be given a voice? Where do national politics and personal sexuality intersect?

The complex exchange between postcolonial and queer theories has informed the chapters of this book, and has actually had a remarkably enduring, if hidden, history. In what he describes as the recovery of the history of sodomy in the New

World, for example, Jonathan Goldberg discusses at some length a grotesque passage from Peter Martyr's 1516 text, *The Decades of the Newe Worlde or West India*. The incident is reported in the following way:

[Balboa] founde the house of this kynge infected with most abhominable and unnaturall lechery. For he founde the kynges brother and many other younge men in womens apparell, smoth and effeminately decked, which by the report of such as dwelte abowte hym, he abused with preposterous venus. Of these abowte the number of fortie, he commaunded to bee gyven for a pray to his dogges. (Martyr 89v, cited in Goldberg 4)

Martyr goes on to contend that "this stinkynge abhomination hadde not yet entered among the people, but was exercised onely by the noble men and gentelmen. But the people lyftinge up theyr handes and eyes toward heaven, gave tokens that god was grevously offended with such vyle deedes" (90v). In analyzing the motivation for Martyr's positioning of this incident, Goldberg notes the complex portrayal of the slaughter of sodomites as a quasi-democratic device: "Balboa eliminates and supplants the Indian rulers," he writes, "but appears to be acting as the liberator of the oppressed. . . . The Indians who decry sodomy are 'good' Indians . . . [who] have been made the site upon which European values can be foisted, but also an exemplary mirror in which Europeans might find themselves" (5–6).

On one hand, a contemporary reader might ask whether much has changed in the presentation of same-sex activity in the twentieth century. We might note in Rigoberta Menchú's controversial *testimonio*, for example, the following protest, apparently spontaneous:

Our people don't differentiate between people who are homosexual and people who aren't; that only happens when we go out of our community. We don't have the rejection of homosexuality the *ladinos* do; they really cannot stand it. What's good about our way of life is that everything is considered part of nature. So an animal which didn't turn out right is part of nature, so is a harvest that didn't give a good yield. We say you shouldn't ask for more than you can receive. That's what the *ladinos* brought with them. It's a phenomenon which arrived with the foreigners. (Menchú 60)[1]

Menchú's account sounds a good deal like the explanation of the "queer" sexual norms of many of the cultures that have been discussed in this book. But those of us who seek to understand the development of sexual norms in other parts of the world must heed Goldberg's caution: "Without denying the value of affirming solidarity between gay identity and those persecuted for what have been seen as sexual transgressions," he writes, "and certainly with no desire to endorse the misogyny or homophobia that has marked the refusal of such affirmations, it nonetheless has to be recognized that *all* these accounts offer projections upon native bodies" (Goldberg 12). One must maintain a certain humility lest such simplifications continue to misconstrue the world's complexity.

NOTE

1. Gilbert Herdt notes how polyvalent is the apparent native American acceptance of sexual diversity (Herdt, "Representations" 489).

WORKS CITED

Bergman, Emilie L., and Paul Julian Smith, eds. *Entiendes? Queer Readings, Hispanic Writings.* Durham: Duke University Press, 1995.

Bhabha, Homi. "The Third Space: Interview with Homi Bhabha." In: *Identity: Commu nity, Culture, Difference*, edited by Jonathan Rutherford. London: Lawrence and Wishart, 1990. 207–21.

Blackwood, Evelyn, ed. *Anthropology and Homosexual Behavior.* New York and London: Haworth, 1986.

Bleys, Rudi C. *The Geography of Perversion: Male-to-male Sexual Behaviour outside the West and the Ethnographic Imagination, 1750–1918.* New York: New York Univer sity Press, 1995.

Boone, Joseph Allan, Martin Dupuis, Martin Meeker, and Karin Quimby, eds. *Queer Frontiers: Millennial Geographies, Genders and Generations.* Madison, Wisc.: University of Wisconsin Press, 2000.

Brooker, Peter. *A Concise Glossary of Cultural Theory.* London: Arnold, 1999.

Browning, Frank. *A Queer Geography: Journeys toward a Sexual Self*, rev. ed. New York: Noonday, 1998.

Butler, Judith. "Merely Cultural." *Social Text 52/53* 15.3–4 (1997): 265–78.

Campbell, Jan. *Arguing With the Phallus: Feminist, Queer and Postcolonial Theory: A Psychoanalytic Contribution.* London: Zed, 2000.

Caplan, Pat, ed. *The Cultural Construction of Sexuality.* London: Routledge, 1987.

Chan, Jachinson. *Sexual Ambiguities: Representations of Asian Men in American (Popu lar) Culture.* Unpub. Diss. University of California at Santa Cruz, 1993.

Cohen, Lawrence. "Holi in Banaras and the Mahaland of Modernity." *GLQ* 2.4 (1995): 399–424.

Crain, Caleb. "Pleasure Principles: Queer Theorists and Gay Journalists Wrestle over the Politics of Sex." *Lingua franca* (October 1997): 26–37.

Dayal, Samir. "The Subaltern Does Not Speak: Mira Nair's *Salaam Bombay!* as a Postcolonial Text." *Genders* 14 (1992): 16–32.

"Decade/nce: A Tenth Anniversary Special." *Trikone* 11.1 (1996).

Dollimore, Jonathan. *Sexual Dissidence: Augustine to Wilde, Freud to Foucault.* Oxford: Clarendon, 1991.

Duberman, Martin, ed. *A Queer World: The Center for Lesbian and Gay Studies Reader.* New York: New York University Press, 1997.

Duggan, Lisa. "The Discipline Problem: Queer Theory Meets Lesbian and Gay History." *GLQ* 2 (1995): 179–91.

Dynes, Wayne and Stephen Donaldson, eds. *Ethnographic Studies of Homosexuality.* New York and London: Garland, 1992.

Eng, David L. "Out Here and Over There: Queerness and Diaspora in Asian American Studies." *Social Text 52/53* 15.3–4 (1997): 31–52.

Eng, David L., and Alice Y. Hom. *Q & A: Queer in Asian America.* Philadelphia: Temple

University Press, 1998.

"Fair's Fair." *The Economist*. 344. 8025 (12 July 1997): 50.

Foster, David William. *Gay and Lesbian Themes in Latin American Writing*. Austin: University of Texas Press, 1991.

Foster, Thomas, Carol Siegel, and Ellen Berry, eds. *Sex Positives? The Cultural Politics of Dissident Sexualities (Genders 25)*. New York: New York University Press, 1997.

Fraser, Nancy. "Heterosexism, Misrecognition, and Capitalism: A Response to Judith Butler." *Social Text 52/53* 15.3–4 (1997): 279–89.

Gamson, Joshua. "Must Identity Movements Self-Destruct? A Queer Dilemma." *Social Problems* 42.3 (1995): 390–407.

Gokul, Ram. "Understanding Our Gay and Lesbian Children." *Trikone* 12.3 (1997): 8–9.

Goldberg, Jonathan. "Sodomy in the New World: Anthropologies Old and New." In: *Fear of a Queer Planet: Queer Politics and Social Theory*, edited by Michael Warner. Minneapolis: University of Minnesota Press, 1993. 3–18.

Goldie, Terry. "Introduction: Queerly Postcolonial." *ARIEL* 30.2 (1999): 9–28.

Greene, Beverly, ed. *Ethnic and Cultural Diversity among Lesbians and Gay Men*. Thousand Oaks, Calif. and London: Sage, 1997.

Hall, Stuart. "Cultural Identity and Diaspora." In: *Identity: Community, Culture, Differ ence*, edited by Jonathan Rutherford. London: Lawrence and Wishart, 1990. 222–37.

Harper, Phillip Brian. "Gay Male Identities, Personal Privacy, and Relations of Public Exchange: Notes on Directions for Queer Critique." *Social Text 52/53* 15.3–4 (1997): 5–29.

Harris, Daniel. *The Rise and Fall of Gay Culture*. New York: Hyperion, 1997.

Harry, Joseph, and Man Singh Das. *Homosexuality in International Perspective*. New Delhi: Vikas, 1980.

Hayes, Jarrod. *Queer Nations: Marginal Sexualities in the Maghreb*. Chicago: University of Chicago Press, 2000.

Hennessy, Rosemary. "Ambivalence as Alibi: On the Historical Materiality of Late Capitalist Myth in *The Crying Game* and Cultural Theory." In: *On Your Left: Historical Materialism in the 1990s (Genders 24)*, edited by Ann Kibbey, Thomas Foster, Carol Siegel, and Ellen Berry. New York: New York University Press, 1996. 1 34.

Herdt, Gilbert. "Representations of Homosexuality: An Essay on Cultural Ontology and Historical Comparison, Part I." *Journal of the History of Sexuality* 1 (1991): 481–504.

———. *Same Sex, Different Cultures: Exploring Gay and Lesbian Lives*. Boulder, Colo.: Westview, 1997.

———, ed. *Third Sex, Third Genders*. New York: Zone, 1994.

Holmes, Rachel. "Queer Comrades: Winnie Mandela and the Moffies." *Social Text 52/53* 15.3–4 (1997): 161–80.

Huo, T.C. *A Thousand Wings*. New York: Dutton, 1998.

Hwang, David H. *M. Butterfly*. New York: New American Library, 1989.

Ibarra, Eulalio Yerro. "Potato Eater." In: *On a Bed of Rice: An Asian American Erotic Feast*, edited by Geraldine Kudaka. New York: Anchor Doubleday, 1995. 314–25.

Jagose, Annamarie. *Queer Theory: An Introduction*. New York: New York University, 1996.

Joseph, Betty. "Mutations of the Imperial Contract." In: *On Your Left: Historical Materialism in the 1990s (Genders 24)*, edited by Ann Kibbey, Thomas Foster, Carol Siegel, and Ellen Berry. New York: New York University Press, 1996. 35–68.

Kamani, Ginu. *Junglee Girl*. San Francisco: Aunt Lute, 1995.

Khan, Badruddin. *Sex Longing and Not Belonging: A Gay Muslim's Quest for Love and*

Meaning. Oakland, Calif.: Floating Lotus, 1997.

Kibbey, Ann, Thomas Foster, Carol Siegel, and Ellen Berry, eds. *On Your Left: Historical Materialism in the 1990s (Genders 24)*. New York: New York University Press, 1996.

Kudaka, Geraldine, ed. *On a Bed of Rice: An Asian American Erotic Feast*. New York: Anchor Doubleday, 1995.

Kulick, Don. "A Man in the House: The Boyfriends of Brazilian *Travesti*." *Social Text 52/53* 15.3–4 (1997): 133–60.

Lancaster, Roger N. and Micaela di Leonardo, eds. *The Gender/Sexuality Reader: Culture, History, Political Economy*. New York and London: Routledge, 1997.

Lane, Christopher. *The Ruling Passion: British Colonial Allegory and the Paradox of Homosexual Desire*. Durham: Duke University Press, 1995.

Leyland, Winston, ed. *Queer Dharma: Voices of Gay Buddhists*. San Francisco: Gay Sunshine, 1998.

Luke, Allan. "Representing and Reconstructing Asian Masculinities: This Is Not a Movie Review." *Social Alternatives* 16.3 (1997): 32–34.

Manalansan IV, Martin F. "In the Shadows of Stonewall: Examining Gay Transnational Politics and the Diasporic Dilemma." *GLQ* 2.4 (1995): 425–38.

Manderson, Lenore, and Margaret Jolly, eds. *Sites of Desire / Economies of Pleasure: Sexualities in Asia and the Pacific*. Chicago: University of Chicago Press, 1997.

Manrique, Jaime. *My Night with Federico Garcia Lorca*, translated by Edith Grossman and Eugene Richie. New York: Painted Leaf, 1997.

———. *Twilight at the Equator*. New York: Faber, 1997.

Martyr, Peter. *The Decades of the Newe Worlde or West India*. March of America Facsimile series, no. 4. Ann Arbor, Mich.: University Microfilms, 1966.

McClintock, Anne, Aamir Mufti and Ella Shohat, eds. *Dangerous Liaisons: Gender, Nation, and Postcolonial Perspectives*. Minneapolis: University of Minnesota Press, 1997.

Melhuus, Marit, and Kristi Anne Stølen, eds. *Machos, Mistresses, Madonnas: Contesting the Power of Latin American Gender Imagery*. New York: Verso, 1996.

Menchú, Rigoberta. *I, Rigoberta Menchú: An Indian Woman in Guatemala*, edited by Elisabeth Burgos-Debray, translated by Ann Wright. London: Verso, 1984.

Mercer, Kobena. "Welcome to the Jungle: Identity and Diversity in Postmodern Politics." In: *Identity: Community, Culture, Difference*, edited by Jonathan Rutherford. London: Lawrence and Wishart, 1990. 43–71.

Mo, Timothy. *The Redundancy of Courage*. London: Vintage, 1991.

Moore-Gilbert, Bart. *Postcolonial Theory: Contexts, Practices, Politics*. London: Verso, 1997.

Moraga, Cherríe. *Loving in the War Years*. Boston: South End Press, 1983.

Morris, Rosalind C. "Educating Desire: Thailand, Transnationalism, and Transgression." *Social Text 52/53* 15.3–4 (1997): 53–79.

Morton, Donald. "The Politics of Queer Theory in the (Post)Modern Movement." *Genders* 17 (1993): 121–50.

Muñoz, José Esteban. "'The White to be Angry': Vaginal Davis's Terrorist Drag." *Social Text 52/53* 15.3–4 (1997): 80–103.

Murray, Stephen O. "Heteronormative Cuban Sexual Policies and Resistance to Them." *GLQ* 2.4 (1995): 473–77.

———. *Social Theory, Homosexual Realities*. New York: Scholarship Committee, Gay Academic Union, 1984.

Murray, Stephen O., and Will Roscoe, eds. *Boy-Wives and Female Husbands: Studies of African Homosexualities*. New York: St. Martin's Press, 1998.

Nguyen, Viet Thanh. "The Postcolonial State of Desire: Homosexuality and Transvestitism in Ninotchka Rosca's *State of War*." *Critical Mass: A Journal of Asian American Cultural Criticism* 2.2 (1995): 67–93.

Nordquist, Joan. *Queer Theory: A Bibliography*. Santa Cruz, Calif.: Reference and Research Services, 1997.

"Now for a queer question about gay culture." *The Economist* 344. 8025 (12 July 1997): 75–76.

Parker, Andrew, Mary Russo, Doris Sommer, and Patricia Yeager, eds. *Nationalisms and Sexuality*. New York: Routledge, 1992.

Parker, Richard. *Beneath the Equator: Cultures of Desire, Male Homosexuality, and Emerging Gay Communities in Brazil*. New York and London: Routledge, 1999.

Parker, Richard G., and John H. Gagnon, eds. *Conceiving Sexuality: Approaches to Sex Research in a Postmodern World*. New York and London: Routledge, 1995.

Patton, Cindy. "Embodying Subaltern Memory: Kinesthesia and the Problematics of Gender and Race." In: *The Madonna Connection: Representational Politics, Subcultural Identites, and Cultural Theory*, edited by Cathy Schwichtenberg. Boulder, CO: Westview, 1993. Schwichtenberg: 81–106.

Prieur, Annick. "Domination and Desire: Male Homosexuality and the Construction of Masculinity in Mexico." In: *Machos, Mistresses, Madonnas: Contesting the Power of Latin American Gender Imagery*, edited by Marit Melhuus and Kristi Anne Stølen. New York: Verso, 1996. 83–107.

———. *Mema's House, Mexico City: On Transvestites, Queens, and Machos*. Chicago: University of Chicago Press, 1998.

Rashkin, Elissa J. "Historic Image/Self Image: Re-Viewing *Chicana*." In: *Sex Positives? The Cultural Politics of Dissident Sexualities (Genders 25)*, edited by Thomas Foster, Carol Siegel, and Ellen Berry. New York: New York University Press, 1997. 97–119.

Ratti, Rakesh, ed. *A Lotus of Another Color: An Unfolding of the South Asian Gay and Lesbian Experience*. Boston: Alyson, 1993.

Roscoe, Will. *Changing Ones: Third and Fourth Genders in Native North America*. New York: St. Martin's Press, 1998.

Rutherford, Jonathan, ed. *Identity: Community, Culture, Difference*. London: Lawrence and Wishart, 1990.

Schmitt, Arno and Jehoeda Sofer, eds. *Sexuality and Eroticism among Males in Moslem Societies*. New York: Harrington Park Press, 1992.

Schwartzwald, Robert. "'Symbolic' Homosexuality, 'False Feminine,' and the Problematics of Identity in Québec." In: *Fear of a Queer Planet: Queer Politics and Social Theory*, edited by Michael Warner. Minneapolis: University of Minnesota Press, 1993. 264–99.

Schwichtenberg, Cathy, ed. *The Madonna Connection: Representational Politics, Subcultural Identites, and Cultural Theory*. Boulder, Colo.: Westview, 1993.

Seabrook, Jeremy. *Love in a Different Climate: Men Who Have Sex with Men in India*. London and New York: Verso, 1999.

Sedgwick, Eve Kosofsky. *Epistemology of the Closet*. Berkeley: University of California Press, 1990.

Seidman, Steven. *Difference Troubles: Queering Social Theory and Sexual Politics*. Cambridge: Cambridge University Press, 1997.

———, ed. *Queer Theory/Sociology*. Cambridge, Mass.: Blackwell, 1996.

Selvadurai, Shyam. *Funny Boy*. London: Vintage, 1995.

Shepherd, Gill. "Rank, gender, and homosexuality: Mombasa as a key to understanding sexual options." In: *The Cultural Construction of Sexuality*, edited by Pat Caplan. London: Routledge, 1987. 240–70.

Sinfield, Alan. *Cultural Politics/Queer Reading*. Philadelphia: University of Pennsylvania Press, 1994.

———. *Gay and After*. London: Serpent's Tail, 1998.

Smalls, James. "Public Face, Private Thoughts: Fetish, Interracialism, and the Homoerotic in Some Photographs by Carl Van Vechten." In: *Sex Positives? The Cultural Politics of Dissident Sexualities (Genders 25)*, edited by Thomas Foster, Carol Siegel, and Ellen Berry. New York: New York University Press, 1997. 144–93.

Stychin, Carl F., and Shane Phelan, eds. *A Nation by Rights: National Cultures, Sexual Identity Politics, and the Discourse of Rights*. Philadelphia: Temple University Press, 1998.

Sullivan, Gerard, and Peter A. Jackson, eds. *Multicultural Queer: Australian Narratives*. Binghamton, N.Y.: Haworth, 1998.

Truong, Thanh-Dam. *Sex, Money, and Morality: Sex Tourism in Southeast Asia*. London: Zed, 1993.

Wald, Priscilla. "Cultures and Carriers: 'Typhoid Mary' and the Science of Social Control." *Social Text 52/53* 15.3–4 (1997): 181–214.

Warner, Michael, ed. *Fear of a Queer Planet: Queer Politics and Social Theory*. Minneapolis: University of Minnesota Press, 1993.

———. *The Trouble with Normal: Sex, Politics, and the Ethics of Queer Life*. New York: Free Press, 1999.

Waters, Malcolm. *Globalization*. London: Routledge, 1995.

Weeks, Jeffrey. "The Value of Difference." In: *Identity: Community, Culture, Difference*, edited by Jonathan Rutherford. London: Lawrence and Wishart, 1990. 88–100.

Weston, Kath. *Long Slow Burn: Sexuality and Social Science*. New York: Routledge, 1998.

Whisman, Vera. *Queer By Choice: Lesbians, Gay Men, and the Politics of Identity*. New York: Routledge, 1996.

Williams, Walter L. *The Spirit and the Flesh: Sexual Diversity in American Indian Culture*. Boston: Beacon, 1992.

Wright, J. W. and Everett K. Rowson. *Homoeroticism in Classical Arabic Literature*. New York: Columbia University Press, 1997.

Index

About the Contributors

DENNIS ALTMAN is a Professor at La Trobe University, Australia. He is the author of nine books, including *Global Sex* (University of Chicago Press, 2000), *Power and Community: Organizational and Cultural Responses to AIDS* (Taylor and Francis, 1994), and *The Homosexualization of America: The Americanization of the Homosexual* (Beacon, 1983).

IAN BARNARD, a native of South Africa, received his doctorate from the department of literature at the University of California at San Diego. He has taught queer theory at Ohio State University and currently lectures at California State University at Chico. He has published in *Research in African Literatures, Genders, Radical Teacher,* and *Socialist Review*. His book *Queer Race: Cultural Interventions in the Racial Politics of Queer Theory* is forthcoming from New York University Press.

THOMAS D. BOELLSTORFF is a doctoral candidate in the department of Social and Cultural Anthropology at Stanford University. Since 1992 he has been conducting activism and research in Indonesia on gay/lesbian/transgender identity, as well as the impact of HIV/AIDS on these communities.

JAMES N. BROWN, currently an Honorary Associate in the Department of Cultural Studies, Division of Society, Culture, and Media, at Macquarie University, Sydney, Australia, has also taught at universities in Canada, USA, and New Zealand. He lives in London, Ontario, Canada.

ERICH DE WALD is in the doctoral program in American Studies at Cambridge University.

DAVID WILLIAM FOSTER is Regents' Professor of Spanish, Humanities, and Women's Studies at Arizona State University, Chair of the Department of Languages and Literatures, and nominee for the Modern Language Association executive council. He is the author of a great many books, including *Bodies and Biases: Sexualities in Hispanic Cultures and Literatures* (University of Minnesota Press, 1996) and *Sexual Textualities: Essays on Queer/ing Latin American Writing* (University of Texas Press, 1997).

CHRISTIAN GUNDERMANN's doctorate in German Studies is from Cornell University. His work has focused primarily on the intersections between race and sexuality in European gay writing and in Latin American discourses of decolonization. Among his publications are an essay on Gilles Deleuze in *diacritics*, and chapters forthcoming in *Legacies of Freud* (eds. Biddy Martin and Suzanne Stewart; Stanford University Press) and *Vagabondage: The Poetics and Politics of Movement* (ed. Jeffrey Timon; Berkeley Academic Press).

ELIZABETH GUZIK is in the doctoral program in English at the University of Southern California.

JOHN C. HAWLEY (editor) is Associate Professor of English at Santa Clara University. He has edited seven other books, including *Christian Encounters with the Other* (New York University Press, 1998), *Cross-Addressing: Resistance Literature and Cultural Borders* (State University of New York Press, 1996), and *Writing the Nation: Self and Country in Postcolonial Imagination* (Rodopi, 1996). The *Encyclopedia of Postcolonial Studies* is forthcoming from Greenwood Press.

LIANG-YA LIOU is Associate Professor of Foreign Languages and Literatures at National Taiwan University. She is the author of *yu-wang gun-yee-shih: ching-se shiao-shuo de jeng-ji yu mei-shue* (Engendering Dissident Desire: The Politics and Aesthetics of Erotic Fictions [Taipei: Meta Media, 1998]). Her forthcoming book, again written in Chinese, is on fin-de-siecle erotic fictions written in Chinese (Taipei: United Literature, 2002).

SONIA "GIGI" OTALVARO-HORMILLOSA is a performance artist from the Philippines. A graduate of Brown University, she received the 1998 Joslin Award and an award from the Brown Gay and Lesbian Alumni Association for outstanding service. She is currently an intern at LYRIC (Lavender Youth Recreation and Information Center, San Francisco).

PATRICIA M. SANT is an Honorary Associate in the Department of Cultural Studies, Macquarie University, Sydney, Australia. Recent publications include an edited collection (with James N. Brown), *Indigeneity: Constructions and Re/Presentations* (Nova Science Press, 1999).

BENZI ZHANG teaches in the English Department of the Chinese University of Hong Kong. Among his various articles is "Paradox of Originality" in *Studies in Short Fiction*.